The Rise and Decline of the
ENGLISH
WORKING
CLASSES
1918–1990
A Social History

The Rise and Decline of the

ENGLISH

WORKING

CLASSES

1918–1990

A Social History

Eric Hopkins

Weidenfeld & Nicolson
London

IN REMEMBRANCE OF
BARBARA JOAN HOPKINS 1919–86
YOU ALWAYS STAY

Contents

Contents

Preface

Some preliminary explanations might be helpful. In the first place, this is a book of social history, though it has been necessary from time to time to give an account of and comment on political events, especially those involving the Labour Party, set up originally to represent the working classes. Secondly, the title of the book refers to the English working classes. I have fixed on this wording because I am very ignorant of the domestic history of the Scots, the Welsh and the Northern Irish. It therefore seemed safer to stick to 'English' rather than 'British'. A.J.P.Taylor entitled his great work, *English History 1914–1945* (Oxford, 1965), justifying his use of the word 'English' in his Preface. If it was good enough for A.J.P.Taylor, it is assuredly good enough for me. Thirdly, why 'working classes' and not 'working class'? Largely because since industrialisation there have usually been important differences between skilled, semi-skilled and unskilled workers, so that the plural form 'classes' has always seemed more appropriate to me, as it did to many Victorians, who used both the plural and singular forms. I am not swayed by the fact that Marxist historians customarily use 'class', presumably to emphasise the economic homogeneity of the workers (as they see it), who have no property in the means of production, and only their labour to sell. This seems an absurdly old-fashioned and, indeed, misleading usage to me. A further consideration is that an earlier book of mine also used the expression 'English working classes' in its title, so that it appears not unreasonable to continue its use for this book.

Another oddity might be thought to lie in the word 'decline' in the title. Perhaps it would be as well to say here that its use is explained and discussed in the last chapter of the book, Chapter Eight. It is not suggested that the working classes somehow begin to disappear from sight by 1990, or that they all become born-again members of the middle class, dissociating themselves increasingly from their previous proletarian existence. More seriously, 'decline' is used here as a short-hand term for the weakening of the corporate image of the working classes, itself primarily the result of a combination of economic change and social change. The arguments for this view rest upon the changes discussed in Chapters Six and Seven, 'Darkening Horizons', which form virtually one long chapter, split for convenience into two. It should also be said here that Chapter Eight, the shortest, was the most difficult to write. It certainly brought home to me the problems of writing contemporary history. Among these problems, it is not so much the difficulty of selecting material and attempting to present it in a coherent and balanced form, as the uneasy and haunting feeling that in ten years' time it might all look very different. As one who is more used to writing about the eighteenth and nineteenth centuries, the work for this book has been an interesting and challenging experience. At least there has been no shortage of factual information, especially for the social trends of the past two decades, thanks to the government publications listed in the Select Bibliography.

Lastly, I would like to thank my colleagues in the Department of Economic and Social History in the University of Birmingham, headed by Professor J.R. Harris, and especially Mr Peter Cain, Dr Rick Garside and Dr Len Schwarz, for their comments on some of the ideas in this book. As always, they have listened patiently while I have gone on and on about some aspect of working-class history which has caught my fancy. The usual disclaimers apply – I am solely responsible for all errors of commission and omission, and all misconceptions and misapprehensions in the following chapters. Since I did all the typing and xeroxing myself, I cannot express thanks to our two excellent secretaries, Sue Kennedy and Diane Martin, in this respect, but like other members of the Department they have had to put up with my constant talking about the book, and so I thank them, too, for their patience and kindness.

Stourbridge   E.H.
August 1990

Prologue

The date 1918 is of great significance in England's national history, and indeed in world history, signalling as it does the end of one world war and the beginning of twenty years' uneasy peace before the outbreak of another world war. Commonly its importance is taken to be political, and it is not usually thought to signify any kind of turning point in social history. Yet, when viewed in perspective, the year 1918 marks not only the end of what at the time was called the Great War, but also the beginning of a period in which substantial improvement was made in the standard of living of the employed working classes, in the political power of ordinary men and women, in the quality of their health and their housing, and in the number and variety of their leisure pursuits. To understand the nature of these changes, it is necessary to review (albeit very briefly) the transformation of working-class life which had characterised the preceding century – a unique epoch in English history, and one which saw the growth of the world's first industrial nation.

During the first half of the nineteenth century, the working classes in England were rapidly becoming more industrialised and more urbanised as a greater and greater proportion of the economy was devoted to industry rather than to agriculture. This fundamental shift to manufacture and away from farming was not achieved without great social strains, as for example in the period of popular unrest after the Battle of Waterloo, 1815, in the struggle over the 1832 Reform Act, and in the critical years of Chartism in the 1840s. However, the governments of the day survived these rumblings of discontent, and for their part damped down the fires of incipient revolt by a succession of reforming measures, mostly adopted *ad hoc* and without any overall plan, regulating working hours in the textile factories, supporting the newly established church schools, reforming the Poor Law, and beginning public health reform. The reaction of the working classes to their changed industrial and urban environment was mostly defensive, and took the form partly of the setting up of trade unions, and partly (to a much greater extent) the establishment of friendly societies. The one sustained burst of political activity – Chartism – had shot its bolt by the mid-century.

The second half of the nineteenth century saw the working out of earlier developments. From the 1850s onwards, the typical Englishman and woman were industrial, not agricultural workers. Social reform continued, made inevitable by the growth of the new manufacturing society. Limited and slow progress was made in public health; working hours and conditions were increasingly regulated, and elementary education became first compulsory in 1880, and then free in 1891. Meanwhile, male workers in the towns secured the vote in 1867, and in the countryside in 1884. Trade unions grew at a faster rate than before, and the first working-class MPs (both miners) were elected in 1874. By 1900 working men could be found occupying positions as borough councillors or as members of school boards (locally elected bodies for running schools paid for from the rates), while in 1900 the Labour Representation Committee (later renamed the Labour Party) was established. Clearly, by 1900 the working classes (especially the male workers) were assuming new roles in society.

Who then were these newly emerging working classes? A hundred years previously in the early 1800s they were still known as the 'the lower orders', 'the masses' or even 'the mob', 'the rabble' or 'the swinish multitude', depending on the attitude of the observer. By 1900, all this was changed. The term 'working class' or 'working classes' seems to have come into popular use in the 1820s. (It is convenient to repeat here that the latter rather than the former expression is used throughout this book in view of the heterogeneity of work experience and of life style which has persisted to the present day.) By the end of the nineteenth century the working classes were becoming a respectable and potentially powerful sector of political society. In 1901 a good third of them were engaged in manufacturing industry, and if to this figure is added the number of those employed in mining and construction, the proportion rises to nearly a half (46 per cent). Trade and transport occupied another 22 per cent, other service industries a further 22 per cent. Agriculture, which had employed 25 per cent of the work force in 1831, employed only 9 per cent in 1901.

Of those who worked in industry, a substantial number were employed in factories, and for the most part the small domestic workshop had become a thing of the past. It would be wrong,

2

however, to suppose that most workers were employed in large, impersonal factories, attending to machines or working on assembly lines. In the first place, there was a wide variety of work-places, ranging from large establishments like shipyards, iron works and cotton mills to medium-sized workplaces like glass-houses, collieries, brickyards and ropewalks, down to smaller engineering shops, bakeries, tailoring shops and the like. Employ-ment on a machine such as an automatic spinning mule, or a power loom, or a turret lathe was confined to only a minority of workers. Secondly, it is often taken for granted that by the end of the nine-teenth century, most factories were of a considerable size. In fact, the replacement of the small domestic workshop by the factory does not mean that factories were necessarily much larger places. Even in the mid-1930s, 92 per cent of factories employed under 100, and 76.9 per cent employed twenty-five persons or under. It is worth remarking, too, that work discipline was not always most severe in the largest works. In practice, it varied from place to place, depending not only on the nature of the work process (work-ing on a loom was very different from working on a puddling furnace or making bricks in a brickyard), but also on the employers' attitudes, paternalistic or otherwise, and on the extent to which the work discipline had become accepted and internalised by the workers. There is plenty of evidence to show, for example, that in many textile mills the work force adjusted positively to the demands of mechanised industry, and developed something approaching a corporate identity and an associated works loyalty.

Thus the coming of the factory system did not turn all industrial workers into factory zombies chained for long hours to their machines. This is not to deny, of course that working conditions could sometimes be very harsh at the turn of the century, but the reality of the industrial work experience was too complex and various to be described simply in terms of long hours of what Marx called machino-facture. As for actual hours at work, the Factory and Workshops Acts of the nineteenth century limited hours for women and children, firstly in the textile industries, and later in other industries. Men's hours were not so restricted, but where men and women worked together, the limitation of women's hours affected the hours worked by men. Generally speaking, there was some reduction in the length of the working day during the second half of the nineteenth century, and by 1900 a fifty-four hour week and a ten- or a ten-and-a-half-hour day were common, with a half-day on Saturday, though trade union demands for an eight-hour day were growing (and achieved by miners by 1908). As for the working environment, some improvements in safety and the provision of amenities had been achieved by 1900, but the factory and workshops inspectorate was still too small to ensure that even the limited legislation of the time was properly enforced.

One changing aspect of life at work at the end of the nineteenth century was the extent to which machinery was replacing the skilled worker. Earlier on, in mid-Victorian times the amount of unskilled labour employed was certainly striking; possibly half the work force lacked any recognised form of skill – much of the work simply demanded hard physical labour. By the end of the century, a change had taken place. According to the census of 1911, skilled workmen constituted 28.7 per cent of the population, semi-skilled workers 34.3 per cent, and the unskilled only 9.6 per cent. The percentage of unskilled workers had clearly fallen sharply, but semi-skilled workers still outnumbered the skilled. Further, in some factories machine-minding had replaced the old skilled work processes, and 'deskilling' had occurred. However, even here, skilled workers were still essential for overall supervision, and the machine operators themselves needed a degree of skill, and accordingly were classed as semi-skilled. On the whole, the concern which was expressed at the end of the century about deskilling was confined to engineering, and in reality deskilling was not widespread. Machines were not everywhere replacing skilled men, though the introduction of machinery did require some adjustment in the need for the traditional type of craftsman.

In the social sphere, the skilled workman who had served his time – the aristocrat of labour – still remained at the top of the tree. He was in the most regular employment, earned the highest wages, enjoyed the highest standard of living and had the respect of his neighbours. He was likely to be a member of one of the older trade unions for skilled men, as opposed to the new unions for the unskilled created in the 1880s. John Burns described the 'old' unionists at the TUC meeting in 1890:

> Physically, the 'old' unionists were much bigger than the new ... A great number of them looked like respectable city gentlemen; wore good coats, large watch chains, and high hats ... Among the new delegates not a single one wore a tall hat. They looked workmen; they were workmen ...

However, all classes of workers, skilled and unskilled, who stayed in employment during the 1870s and 1880s benefited from the increase in real wages of the time, and even after 1900, when real wages fell, living standards were still markedly better than before. In the period 1860–1900 real wages rose by about 60 per cent. Yet even then the state of the unskilled worker, and of the intermittently employed, caused increasing concern at the turn of the century. Poverty was still an unpleasant reality among the working classes, especially in the industrial towns and cities.

In fact, there had been an awareness of poverty as a social problem throughout the nineteenth century, especially in the 1880s and 1890s. By that time it might possibly be assumed that the benefits of the new industrialisation would have made poverty of far less consequence than before. Indeed, it was in order to refute claims that a quarter of London's population was living in poverty that Charles Booth undertook his massive survey, *Life and Labour of the People in London* (1889–93). His conclusion was that 30.7 per cent were living in poverty, while 8.4 per cent (354,444 persons in all) were living in *abject* poverty. The size of this last group was confirmed by William Booth, the founder of the Salvation Army, and in his *In Darkest England and the Way Out* (1890) he estimated that about a tenth of the entire population (the Submerged Tenth, numbering about three million) was living in direst poverty. Further confirmation was provided by Benjamin Seebohm Rowntree's survey in York (published in 1901), where 27.84 per cent were in poverty, of whom 9.91 per cent were in extreme or primary poverty. Rowntree also pointed out that labourers experienced three distinct cycles of poverty throughout their lives. In his words:

A labourer is thus in poverty, and therefore underfed –
(a) in childhood – when his constitution is being built up.
(b) in early middle life – when he should be in his prime.
(c) in old age.
The accompanying diagram may serve to illustrate this –

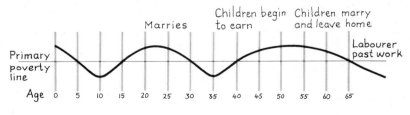

It should be noted that women are in poverty during the greater part of the period when they are bearing children.

Rowntree also calculated that over half of the York working classes (51.96 per cent) in primary poverty were poor because although they were in regular work, their wages were too low. Another 22.16 per cent of those in primary poverty had large families (more than four children), while a further 15.63 per cent were suffering from the death of the chief wage-earner. Other causes of primary poverty were illness or old age, irregularity of employment, and unemployment.

Against these hazards of working-class life, the skilled worker had some defences – a well-paid, steady job, and usually membership of a friendly society which could provide sickness or out-of-work benefits in time of need. For the unskilled man it was a different story, and it was this man and his family who might be forced to go to the Poor Law authorities. Outdoor relief was available for the genuine applicant, but it was small in amount and usually in return for a task of work within the workhouse yard. Although the poor law system had been improved in the second half of the nineteenth century, the workhouse itself was still feared and thought degrading, so its occupants were largely the old, the sick and the very young, who had nowhere else to go, and had entered the House as a last resort.

Thus the working classes about 1900 present a very varied picture, with at one end of the social spectrum the skilled workers, and at the other a formidable mass of workers living in extreme poverty. It was the existence of the second group which caused so much concern and controversy at the time, especially when Sir Frederick Maurice claimed that 60 per cent of the recruits for the Boer War (1899–1902) were unfit for military service (the figure was afterwards reduced to 34 per cent failing to meet the required standard of height, weight and eyesight – still a striking enough proportion). This concern led firstly to the appointment of a Royal Commission on the Poor Laws in 1905, and then later to an impressive string of Liberal social reforms just before the First World War broke out in 1914, of a kind many historians have considered as paving the way for the Welfare State. Local authorities were permitted to provide school meals, school medical inspection was introduced, the law relating to children was codified, old-age pensions were begun, working conditions were further reformed, labour exchanges set up, and trade union rights extended. The most important act of all, the National Insurance Act of 1911, compulsorily insured all workers against ill-health, thus beginning a limited kind of national health service, and at the same time the act introduced an insurance scheme against unemployment for two and a quarter million workers most subject to unemployment.

These remarkable reforms represent the high-water mark of social legislation before 1914, and indeed provide the starting point for much of the social reform of the inter-war period. They are remarkable not only for their extent and impact, but also for the fact that they were passed by Liberal governments committed to the cause of individual liberty and to laissez-faire attitudes. The Liberals were not socialists, and on the whole were opposed to state intervention and collectivism. Nevertheless, they were prepared to take state action in order to help the weakest to help themselves. Churchill, then President of the Board of Trade, talked of 'spreading a net over the abyss' to help the very poorest, and also of the old-age pension as 'a lifebelt'. At the same time, the Liberals stressed the importance of the insurance principle in the 1911 Act as a means of allowing self-help to assert itself, while benefits were kept deliberately low to encourage savings. Whatever interpretation is placed on this New Liberalism, and whether it was really a departure from traditional liberalism or not, the fact is that state intervention had been employed on a greater scale than ever before to help the working classes when times were hard. Valuable precedents had been set for the years ahead.

For the immediate future, however, the programme of social legislation had to be suspended during wartime. The contribution made to winning the war, both at home and on the battle front, by the working classes was enormous. About three-quarters of a million men from Britain (9 per cent of all men under forty-five) were killed, and 1.6 million wounded. Two and a half million men volunteered for the army and navy before conscription was imposed in March 1916. The cheerful spirit of the men on the Western Front, fighting in the most appalling conditions, was remarkable; only after the war did bitterness emerge at what was thought to be the indifference of the generals to the mass slaughter of the great setpiece battles in France. Lloyd George's description of the generals is famous – 'epauleted egoism, impervious to criticism'. Siegfried Sassoon, who served with distinction on the Western Front, put the same point a little differently:

Good morning, good morning! the General said
When we met him last week on our way to the line.
Now the soldiers he smiled at are most of 'em dead,
And we're cursing his staff for incompetent swine.
'He's a cheery old card,' grunted Harry to Jack
As they slogged up to Arras with rifle and pack.

But he did for them both with his plan of attack.

On the home front, the great emphasis was on war production, of course, and especially on the making of munitions. The pre-war militancy of the trade unions had caused fears of a general strike because of the number of national strikes in 1912 and 1913, and also because of the spread of syndicalist ideas which preached the importance of the general strike as a political weapon for the working classes. This militancy soon disappeared when war came, and wholehearted support was given to the prosecution of the war. Strikes were forbidden in 1915, though they still occurred occasionally, as on 'Red Clydeside' in March 1916. In fact, the trade unions agreed to forgo the right to strike (disputes were to be referred to arbitration), and they also agreed to dilution (that is, the breaking down of skilled operations into less skilled or unskilled work processes which could be carried out by unskilled labour, in particular by women); but they actually acquired increased importance in the eyes of the government, which needed the maximum co-operation if the war was to be won.

Since there was an increasing shortage of labour as men went into the army, unemployment fell, and trade union membership rose, from 4.145 million in 1914 to a peak of 8.347 million in 1920, when the post-war boom came to an end. At one point, the unions were actually given the right of deciding who should be exempted from war service because of the importance of his work on war production. Another striking example of the increased influence of the trade unions is that Arthur Henderson, secretary of the Labour Party (financed by the trade unions), joined the government in 1915 as President of the Board of Education. Two other Labour MPs were given minor government posts. In 1916, Henderson was promoted to the inner cabinet, and John Hodges, of the steel workers, became Minister of Labour. George Barnes, of the engineers, became Minister of Pensions. These appointments indicate the improved position of the trade unions, rather than the Labour Party, whose MPs numbered only thirty-six in 1914.

However, the Labour Party increased its support from the electorate during the war period, although initially it was somewhat weakened by the resignation of its leader, Ramsay MacDonald, who opposed the war on political grounds, as did another leading figure, Philip Snowden. Then in 1917 came the two Russian Revolutions, which increased popular interest in social reform in this country. Early in the next year the Labour Party published its own Statement of War Aims (before President Wilson's Fourteen Points), and followed this by issuing a new constitution of the Party, including the famous Clause Four:

> To secure for the producers by hand or by brain the full fruits of their industry, and the most equitable distribution thereof that may be possible, upon the basis of the common ownership of the means of production and the best obtainable system of popular administration and control of each industry or service.

Later in 1918 a new programme of reform entitled *Labour and the New Social Order* contained further references to socialist measures such as the need for a national minimum living standard, democratic control of industry and so on. All this does not mean that the Labour Party had turned markedly to the left. The major influence in the Labour movement as a whole was the trade unions (whose financial support made the Labour Party possible) and not the Labour Party itself; and the trade unions were hardly socialist in their thinking, though on the whole supporting state intervention and collectivism. The unions stood for class consciousness and class loyalty, whatever middle-class intellectuals such as the Webbs (who had framed Clause Four) thought the aims of the Party should be. So, in spite of the new constitution and reform programme, the Labour Party in 1918 was still more of a 'labour' party than a 'socialist' party; and probably most of the two million Labour voters in the 1918 general election voted for a party which stood for the working classes rather than one aiming directly at socialism. At all events, the Party increased its number of MPs from thirty-six to fifty-seven, of whom twenty-five were members of the Miners Federation of Great Britain.

To turn once more to social conditions on the Home Front: money wages kept pace with the rise in prices, and expenditure on Poor Law actually fell. The call-up of men for the services gave greater opportunities to women to find employment, sometimes in what had hitherto been regarded as men's occupations, such as those of railway porter and bus conductor. Many women – nearly a million – became munition workers, earning much more than domestic servants, whose numbers declined by about a quarter. The war certainly gave a greater economic freedom to working-class women than before, together with a certain measure of increased social freedom; but this must be kept in perspective, for the end of the war saw the return of men to their civilian jobs, and many women lost employment as a result. The one concrete gain by women as a consequence of the war was the vote for women of thirty and above, together with the removal of all barriers against women occupying public posts because of their sex. Thus in 1919 the first woman MP, Lady Astor, took her seat in the House. The same 1918 Act enfranchising women also widened the male franchise, which had hitherto been restricted to about two-thirds of adult males, that is, males of twenty-one and over. All adult males were now given the vote.

Understandably enough, little progress was made otherwise during the war in the sphere of social reform. Housing in particular was neglected, and the housing shortage rose to 600,000 by 1918 – hence Lloyd George's promise of 'homes fit for heroes' after the war. The school population benefited by Fisher's Education Act of 1918, which fixed the school-leaving age at fourteen without any of the previous exceptions; but plans for day-continuation education up to sixteen and then eighteen were later abandoned. A new Ministry of Health was set up, and even a Ministry for Reconstruction, but the latter was soon closed down in June 1919.

The major problem in beginning any chronological survey of the fortunes of any social class or classes is to supply a helpful perspective. What needs to be said to supply the necessary background to what is to come? Two things should by now be evident, and they deserve emphasis: the first is that by 1918 the working classes in this country had come a long way since the beginning of the previous century, both politically and socially. All men now had the vote, and all women of thirty or over – something virtually unthinkable to all but advanced and radical thinkers in 1800. At the place of work, conditions had improved greatly, and the trade union movement gave working people both industrial power and political influence through the Labour Party. In the social domain, the standard of living, which had improved at the end of the previous century, had been maintained during the Great War, and was to improve further in the immediate post-war years. Housing was still bad, but the standard of public health was rising, and a better educational system was promised. The social position of women had begun to improve, and a first and major step taken towards votes for women. In all these ways, enormous progress had been made in improving the social position of the working classes.

The second thing which should be apparent is that in 1918 the working classes had a reasonable expectation of further political and social progress. Their own political party, barely twenty years old, had emerged from the war with confidence, and with four times more votes in 1918 than had been secured pre-war. Socialism was in the air: the Russian Revolutions in 1917 had seen to that. The pre-war social reforms showed what might be done by even a Liberal government which in theory was opposed to state intervention. Once the necessary adjustment had been made to the great losses of life during the war, there seemed no reason why the quality of working-class life should not be improved still further. As Winston Churchill put it in a pre-war election address with reference to social reform: 'Humanity will not be cast down. We are going on – swinging bravely forward along the grand high road – and already behind the distant mountains is the promise of the sun.' What in fact did happen will be discussed in the following chapters. It may be remarked that few in 1918 could have realised how changing economic conditions in the next twenty years were to hit some sections of the working classes very hard, yet benefit other sections, indeed the majority, to a marked degree. Most working men and women must have thought simply of getting back to pre-war conditions, back to normal. In fact, there could be no real going back, and the working-class social experience between the wars proved to be surprisingly complex and varied.

Lastly, the popular image of the working classes was still of a very traditional kind. Their great characteristic was that overwhelmingly they were manual workers, some highly skilled earning good wages, others less skilled but not badly off, while at the bottom of the social pyramid were the unskilled, the *lumpenproletariat*, many of them the denizens of the inner-city slums. The worker himself was still recognisable in his working clothes with cloth cap and muffler, readily identifiable today in a thousand photographs of mass meetings outside the factory gates, or crowding the terraces at football matches (though his Sunday best might run to a suit from Montague Burton or the Fifty Shilling Tailors) – still inclined to make way respectfully for a gent or toff, still voting in large numbers for the Conservative or Liberal Parties rather than the new Labour Party. The next two decades, let alone the next half-century, had remarkable changes in store for them.

Chapter *1*

Between the Wars

Economic Conditions

Few working people in 1918 would have been aware of the effect the war had had on the national economy. That it had been extraordinarily costly was well known, of course, and it is not surprising that a demand arose that Germany should pay 'the whole cost of the war' – or, as one politician put it, Germany should be squeezed financially 'till the pips squeaked'; but what was not fully realised was that the war had greatly accelerated the pre-war decline internationally of the British economy. In the second half of the previous century, Britain's economic supremacy in the world had been built upon the great staple industries of textiles, iron and steel, coalmining, shipbuilding and engineering. Already by 1914 that supremacy was being challenged, in particular by the new industrial powers of the USA and Germany. At that time the staple industries employed about a quarter of the total work force in Britain, and produced three-quarters of the vital export trade. During the war, valuable overseas export markets were lost to the USA and Japan, industry concentrated on war production, capital equipment was run down, old trading connections were lost for good. Between the wars, the textile industry, especially cotton, suffered grievously from competition from Japan, India, the USA and Italy; iron and steel production dropped in the face of more efficient production in both Europe and the USA; coal production was heavily reduced, partly because the industry was old and inefficient as compared with its rivals, and partly because of reduced demand both abroad and at home. Oil was replacing coal as fuel in ships, and depression in the staple industries naturally resulted in a decreased demand for coal. The most striking reduction in production perhaps was in shipbuilding. In 1920, a record two million tons were built, mostly to replace the heavy losses of shipping during the war. In 1933, a year of severe depression, only 133,000 tons were launched. Though this figure was improved upon subsequently, Britain's share of world tonnage fell from 39.2 per cent in 1913 to 26.5 per cent in 1937.

A description of Britain's economy between the wars which concentrates exclusively on her traditional industries cannot avoid being gloomy, and the results for the working people in those industries are necessarily sombre. Fortunately, this is not the whole picture. Even before the First World War, newer industries were beginning to emerge and achieve national importance. They include motor manufacture, the electrical industry, chemicals, aircraft, rubber, food processing, rayon and films. All these industries grew between the wars, supplying the home market rather than overseas customers. Further, they utilised semi-skilled labour rather than the traditional skilled labour of the staple industries (often female labour was employed), and much use was made of electrical power rather than steam power. Hence, the new industries were not located on the coalfields, but anywhere labour and electrical supplies were on hand and communications were good. In particular, they developed in the Midlands, in London and the home counties, and in the south-east. As a result, the industrial map of Britain between the wars presents a curiously chequered appearance: on the one hand, the areas where the staple industries had grown in the previous century – Lancashire and Yorkshire, South Wales, the north-east coast, the north-west and Clydeside – all suffered depression. On the other hand, there were the prosperous areas where the new industries predominated – the Midlands, the London area and the south-east. It should be mentioned also that there was one older industry which flourished between the wars, especially in these latter areas – the building industry. So working-class life of the time yielded a variety of experiences dependent on where it was lived, in areas of depression or in the new industrial areas. For a minority of workers, of course, it was lived in the countryside, where conditions remained depressed in the 1920s, but with some improvement after government intervention in the 1930s.

So far a somewhat static picture has been presented. It should now be helpful if we consider the main periods of economic change between the wars. Immediately after the war there was a short-lived boom which collapsed by the end of 1920, and was followed by depression. This lifted somewhat from the mid-twenties on-wards, but then in 1929 came the Wall Street crash in America, and the results of this were felt worldwide. Between 1929 and 1932 a very severe depression set in again, the worst of the inter-war period. It led to the collapse and resignation of the second Labour government in 1931, and the formation of a National (coalition) government. From 1933 conditions began to improve, and recovery was quickened from 1936 by the new rearmament programme, though there was another minor recession in 1938 before the outbreak of war in September 1939.

By now it should be quite clear that the two major determinants of a worker's mode of life between the wars were the kind of industry, old or 'new', he or she was engaged in, and then the general state of the economy at the time, whether prosperous or depressed. Though it is true that the staple industries were in a parlous condition, it would be wrong to give the impression that the economy *as a whole* was failing. In fact, industrial growth rates between the wars were very similar to those before the war, and compared favourably with Britain's European rivals – only Germany, Norway and Sweden grew faster than Britain in the years 1929–38. Moreover, productivity increased over four times faster between 1920 and 1938 than it had done between 1870 and 1913; and industrial production went up by 62 per cent over the inter-war period. So there were some encouraging signs of economic growth. The most unsatisfactory feature was the fall in exports. They fell by 1.2 per cent between the wars, in contrast to a 2.7 per cent rise in the pre-war period 1870 to 1913. This in itself shows the severity of the decline of the staple industries, and in practice spelt unemployment for never less than a million workers throughout the entire period between the wars.

The Employed: Working Conditions

Although unemployment was such a marked and ugly feature of working-class life between the wars, the majority of working people at any one time, even in the worst years of depression, were in work. Moreover, it seems that whatever the sufferings of their less fortunate brethren, those who stayed in work enjoyed improved working conditions, and a rise in real wages. To take working hours first: although the pre-war agitation for an eight-hour day had been suspended during the war, in 1918 it was resumed, with impressive results. Whereas previously the fifty-four hour week was common, in 1919 there was a reduction to forty-eight hours in many industries; in this year alone, hours were reduced by 40.6 million hours per week, affecting 6.3 million workers in all. In subsequent years, some minor variations took place, and of course both overtime and short-time working were common, but the overall trend was downward, and even in the 1930s some reductions were still taking place. For example, in 1936 there was a reduction of 804,500 hours weekly, and in 1937 one of 953,000 hours. In this year, the Factory Act ended the legal maximum sixty-hour week (fifty-five and a half hours in textiles), and fixed forty-eight hours as a new maximum for all women and young persons, with a daily maximum of nine hours. During the 1930s there was also a noticeable spread of the five-day week. *The Enquiry into Average Earnings and Hours of Labour* (October 1935) contains some interesting information regarding working hours. The position in motor engineering, for example, is set out in Table 1.1. Obviously, there was considerable variation, but hours were shorter on the whole in the larger firms.

Table 1.1   Working Hours in the Motor Industry, 1935

Normal working hours	Firms with +10 workers (% of total)	Firms with -10 workers (% of total)
-44	4.8	2.6
44	4.4	6.1
$44\frac{1}{4}$–$46\frac{3}{4}$	7.3	7.0
47	76.6	27.4
$47\frac{1}{4}$–$47\frac{3}{4}$	1.0	4.3
48	1.7	19.4
48+	4.2	33.2
(Total number of firms)	(158,167)	(2,783)

Source: *Labour Gazette*, 1937.

As for holidays, in the early 1920s the minimum number of days off work were the six days a year made obligatory by the Bank Holiday Acts, but these were often extended by a day or so, and a week's holiday without pay was usual in the summer. By 1937 about four million workers were entitled under collective agreements to holidays with pay, while the Holidays with Pay Act of 1938 brought in about eleven million workers by June 1939, which covered about half of the manual workers in the country.

On the whole, it seems there was a decided reduction in the working week between the wars with a corresponding increase in leisure time, but a good deal of variation can be seen from year to year, and in some years there might be a positive increase in hours in some industries. For example, in 1926 (the year is significant) there was a substantial increase of 932,000 in the numbers whose hours had increased in the year. Between 1933 and 1937, however, every year saw a net reduction in weekly hours. A further variation was provided by seasonal fluctuations. Thus in the Midlands motor industry it was customary to work longer hours after the autumn Motor Show than in the summer. However, overtime was limited by the 1937 Act to six hours a week (100 hours maximum in the year), and no overtime was permitted under the age of sixteen.

What of conditions on the shop floor? Safety appears to have improved overall, with a reduction in the number of fatal accidents. The mortal accident rate, which was about nineteen per 100,000 employed in the period 1901–7, dropped to an average of eleven to twelve per 100,000 in 1928–34. Factory inspectors encouraged safety precautions and the appointment of safety supervisors. Much depended on the kind of machinery employed, and the attitudes of the management. Power presses, for example, were notoriously dangerous, while foundry work was usually hard and exhausting. At Austin's in Longbridge, Birmingham, a campaign to reduce the number of accidents started in April 1929 and achieved a reduction of 41 per cent in the accident rate in less than three years. The larger firms could afford ambulance rooms or first-aid rooms, or even a nurse. Cadbury's at Bournville were famous for their caring attitude to their workers (the Cadburys were and still are well-known Quakers), and in the 1930s they employed three fully qualified dentists, a dental mechanic and five dental nurses; up to the age of sixteen, toothbrushes and tooth powder were provided free (all very appropriate in a chocolate factory). They also had a medical department, with a doctor and three nurses. This was highly exceptional, of course. Other firms could be relatively indifferent to safety rules, and smaller firms were not always equipped even with a first-aid box.

As for other amenities, the provision of water closets and

adequate heating was already compulsory in 1918, and the law was tightened up by the Factory Act of 1937, which introduced further regulations relating to washing facilities, accommodation for clothing, seating and drinking water. It was the bigger firms again which provided canteens and rest rooms. These were sometimes organised on a voluntary basis. The Lady Inspector, Miss Schofield, described one such mess room in 1920 which she said was very popular 'as having the atmosphere of cheer in it'.

> A gas cooker and a tea urn are available, and crockery and cutlery are provided. A woman caretaker prepares the room and clears away after the girls have left. A piano is apparently a great attraction, and there is a fire in winter. Each worker pays a small sum per week for use of the accommodation.

One novel amenity to be found in some workplaces as early as 1930 was 'Music While You Work', the playing of radio programmes or records over the loudspeaker system which was to become very popular during the Second World War.

It remains to say something of the changing nature of work processes themselves. As was remarked earlier, it is too readily assumed that factories became larger and larger everywhere in the early twentieth century, and that more and more workers worked on assembly lines, conveyor belts and large automatic machines in extensive workplaces. This is not without some degree of truth, of course. Factories did get larger between the wars. Thus the number of factories employing 501–1000 in 1933 was 800; in 1936 the number had increased to 1,016. Larger factories with over a thousand workers grew in numbers from 335 in 1933 to 519 in 1936. So there is no dispute about this; but at the same time many factories in 1937 remained remarkably small (see Table 1.2). It should be noted that the word 'factory' was now applied to any workplace using power – that is, this analysis of factories must have included many small workshops. It is evident that in 1937 there was still an overwhelming majority of smaller workplaces. Large factories with some degree of automation did exist, but they did not constitute the typical workplace. Small factories with not more than twenty-five workers were much more typical, and constituted more than three-quarters of all factories.

Whether or not discipline tightened up generally between the wars is hard to say, but it seems unlikely that there was much

Table 1.2 Size of Factories, 1937

Size of factory	Percentage of total
1–25	76.9
26–50	8.9
51–100	6.2
101–250	5.1
251–500	1.8
501–1,000	0.7
1,000+	0.4

Source: Report of the Chief Inspector of Factories and Workshops, 1937.

appreciable change, simply because there was no widespread change-over to mass production methods in large-scale factories. Admittedly there was a good deal of talk among managers and directors about so-called 'scientific management', much of it with reference to time-and-motion practices in the USA, where it was to be satirised by Charlie Chaplin in the famous factory sequence in *Modern Times*. The best-known systems of scientific management, Taylorism and the Bedeaux system (both named after their inventors) were imported from America between the wars, but made only limited progress, partly because of their (at times) theoretical nature, and partly because of the understandable hostility of the shop floor (though the trade unions were not uniformly opposed to the Bedeaux system). Taylorism, the earlier system, was not unknown here even in 1914, and mass production methods were encouraged by the need for large-scale production of munitions during the war; but it was not until the 1930s that Bedeauxism made any noticeable progress. It spread mostly in the newer industries of food processing, light engineering and chemicals, and was also found in a few more traditional industries such as iron and steel, textiles and hosiery. By 1939 there were about 250 firms utilising the system. Its very limited adoption gives little indication of any general movement throughout industry to strengthen work discipline; so although, naturally, attention was paid to the idea of greater efficiency, in practice it seems that the positive gains of working people in the form of shorter hours and safer and more congenial surroundings at work were not offset by increasing stress caused by a harsher work discipline.

The Employed: The Standard of Living

Improved working conditions and a shorter working day – most workers in 1939 were working an hour less a day than in 1914 – did not in themselves mean that their standard of living was rising. The most important factor here was what was happening to real wages. There seems general agreement that money wages rose during the First World War, and continued to rise in the post-war boom until they were two and a half to three times their pre-war level. After 1921 they fell, but then there was little change till the early 1930s. The serious depression at that time caused a further minor fall till 1934, when there was a slow rise to 1938. At that point they were still twice the pre-war figure. There was some variation between industries, of course, with lower wages being paid in the staple industries, and lower wages for women generally, but, overall, money wage levels changed little between the wars.

Prices, on the other hand, moved sharply downwards between 1920 and 1934, when they rose again slowly to 1938. In more detail, retail prices peaked in 1920 at an index figure of 157.6, falling rapidly to 111.4 in 1925, then to 93.4 in 1931, and to the lowest inter-war figure of 89.2 in 1934. The moderate rise which followed reached 98.7 in 1938. In all, retail prices fell by more than a third between 1920 and 1938. The result of these price changes was that real wages fell very slightly after 1921, picked up in 1927, and improved markedly from 1930 onwards, with a slight decline after 1936 (in summary form, 1921, 94.1; 1927, 95.8; 1930, 100; 1935, 108.3; 1938, 107.7). Hence, by 1938 real wages were 30 per cent higher than in 1913. These figures naturally cover wide variations in pay – car workers, printers and skilled workers generally might earn over £4.00 a week in the 1930s, while agricultural workers and labourers earned less than £2.00; women's and young persons' earnings were the lowest of all. Nevertheless, the general improvement in real wages, especially in the 1930s, is unmistakable.

What this means in practical terms is quite striking. More money was available for spending for the average family in work. Of the extra spending money, it has been calculated that a quarter went on more nutritious food, and 45 per cent on clothing, rent, fuel and light, household equipment, newspapers, tobacco and transport. The remainder was spent on strictly non-essential items such as holidays and entertainment, and on consumer goods such as radios and vacuum cleaners. In real terms, consumer spending

per head increased from £75.38 per year in the period 1910–14 to
£92.76 a year in 1933–8. This is an increase of 23 per cent. It
should also be remembered that the decline in the size of the family
which began before the First World War continued after the war,
and resulted in a larger share of the family income being available
for each member. All in all, the rise in real wages and the reduction
of the working day, taken together, meant a significant rise in the
standard of living for the employed between the wars. It has been
argued that these two beneficial changes alone brought an improvement in the standard of living of up to 50 per cent. However, the
standard of living does not depend exclusively on real wages and
working conditions. The home environment must also be taken
into account, and to this aspect we may now turn.

Housing and the Home

Earlier on it was noted that there was a considerable housing
shortage in 1918. Further, much of the existing housing stock was
in a bad condition, especially in the older parts of industrial cities.
Birmingham had by no means the worst housing in the country, yet
in the central slums there were about 200,000 people housed in
43,366 back-to-backs; 42,020 houses had no separate water supply,
sinks or drains, while 58,028 had no separate water closets. Lloyd
George's government was pledged to provide 'homes for heroes',
and Addison's Housing and Town Planning Act of 1919 made clear
the responsibility of local government bodies for building new
housing, at the same time providing housing subsidies for both
local authorities and private builders. Under this Act, some
213,000 houses were built, though they were built to surprisingly
high standards and were very expensive; the government paid £800
for houses costing only £300 a year later. Chamberlain's Housing
Act of 1923 gave a further subsidy to private builders, which led to
the building of another 438,000 houses. Another Act in the following year, passed by the first Labour government and known as
Wheatley's Act, increased the subsidy to local authorities for
building houses at controlled rents. This Act resulted in the building of another 520,000 council houses. In the 1930s private building was encouraged again by the reduced cost of building materials
and by low interest rates, so that a positive building boom resulted,
particularly in the more prosperous Midlands, the London area
and the south-east.

In one sense, this actually ended the physical shortage of houses, though many of the urban slums were in a frightful condition. George Orwell gave some examples in his *Road to Wigan Pier* (1937) in Wigan itself:

1. House in Wallgate quarter. Blind back type. One up, one down. Living room measures 12ft by 10ft, room upstairs the same. Alcove under stairs measuring 5ft by 5ft and serving as larder, scullery, and coal-hole. Windows will open. Distance to lavatory, 50 yards. Rent 4s 9d, rates 2s 6d, total 7s 3d.
2. Another near by. Measurements as above, but no alcove under stairs, merely a recess two feet containing the sink – no room for larder, etc. Rent 3s 2d, rates 2s, total 5s 2d.
3. House in Scholes quarter. Condemned house. One up, one down. Rooms 15ft × 15ft. Sink and copper in living room, coal-hole under stairs. Floor subsiding. No window will open. House decently dry. Landlord good. Rent 3s 8d, rates 2s 6d, total 6s 2d.

Another house in Sheffield he described as follows:

House in Thomas Street. Back-to-back, two up, one down [that is, a three-storey house with one room on each storey]. Cellar below. Living room 14ft by 10ft, and rooms above corresponding. Sink in living room. Top floor has no door but gives on open stairs. Walls in living room slightly damp, walls in top rooms coming to pieces and oozing damp on all sides. House is so dark that light has to be kept burning all day. Electricity estimated at 6d per day (probably an exaggeration) ... Rent 6s 6d rates included.

A family of six (parents and four children) lived in this house, and the father suffered from tuberculosis.

Hence, in addition to providing new accommodation, local authorities had also to demolish much decrepit and overcrowded housing. The 1930 Housing Act gave subsidies for this purpose, and in 1933 the government planned to demolish more than a quarter of a million houses, rehousing more than a million people. The Overcrowding Survey 1936 showed how bad overcrowding still was in many urban slums. In Jarrow, 17.5 per cent of families were overcrowded as compared with only 1.0 per cent in Oxford. In Scotland, 22.6 per cent of working-class houses were overcrowded; in England, 3.8 per cent. The problem of the slums was far from being solved by 1939, but nevertheless the figures for new building by then are impressive. Local authorities built 1.1 million houses in the inter-war period, and private builders built 400,000 homes with government subsidies, and 2.5 million houses without subsidy. Thus approximately 4 million houses were built, and large numbers of working-class people found themselves in new houses rented either from the council or from private owners.

What was life like on the new council estates? They were not all built to the same pattern, and designs of houses varied, but many of the new tenants for the first time in their lives enjoyed roomy accommodation, their own water supply with hot-water provision, and their own internal water closet. The most favoured design was the semi-detached or short terraced house, with or without a parlour on the ground floor, but with a bathroom and usually three bedrooms above. Gardens were provided, front and rear. Such housing was positively luxurious compared with the insanitary slums of the inner cities. Most estates were well planned, with grass verges and trees, and the size of some of the largest estates rivalled that of small towns. Council estates provided a new kind of working-class environment between the wars, and one which developed its own ethos depending on the particular area and its social mix.

Undoubtedly council estates were an enormous improvement in simple physical terms on slum property, but they were by no means the complete answer to problems of working-class housing. The most widespread complaint was that the rents were too high for the poorest class of tenant; and indeed it was deliberate policy on the part of some councils to keep rents at a level which only the skilled or semi-skilled could afford, so that the first generation of council tenants should set a good tone. The result was that the poorest, living in the worst slums, who needed rehousing most, were left where they were. Only later on would councils rehouse the unemployed and provide rent subsidies when required. Other complaints were that there were increased travelling costs to work (since new estates were usually on the outskirts and not centrally placed); that prices were higher in council-estate shops than in the central shopping area; that amenities such as public houses, churches, clinics, libraries, baths and clubs were far too few; that family relationships were affected by young marrieds moving from the family home to an outlying estate (the classic case is that of the

London County Council (LCC) rehousing Bethnal Green tenants miles away in Dagenham in Essex); and it was even complained that more furniture was required in the larger premises, and that as children's appetites were greater in the fresher air of the estates, it cost more to feed them. Undoubtedly the higher rents charged were a serious problem, but for the majority of the many thousands who moved into new council housing, their new surroundings denoted a striking improvement in their standard of living. Nor must it be forgotten that many workers rented new private housing rather than municipal accommodation. In more prosperous areas such as Birmingham, a small minority of well paid workers bought their new homes. It was calculated that in this city in 1939 one-third of the population of one million were living in houses built since 1918 – a considerable achievement.

As for amenities provided in the new houses, by far the greatest advance was probably the provision of electricity rather than gas, so that as the National Electricity Grid was built in the early 1930s, electric light and, to a lesser extent, the use of electric cookers and electric fires became widespread. Electric kettles, irons, vacuum cleaners and refrigerators also came on to the market, but were usually restricted to middle-class households. Radios were to be found everywhere, often in the poorest households, and run from the mains rather than on the earlier batteries and accumulators. The amount and quantity of furnishing would depend on the household income, but the customary floor covering was linoleum (the era of cheap wall-to-wall carpeting was yet to come), though carpets and rugs were to be found, especially where the house possessed a parlour, which would be reserved for visitors and Sunday use. Furniture was of the conventional kind, mostly purchased through hire-purchase agreements (known as 'the never-never'). Smaller items might be obtained from door-to-door salesmen, who collected weekly or monthly payments ('tallymen'), or ordered through mail catalogues. Kitchens still had shallow earthenware sinks with wooden draining boards, gas coppers were used for boiling clothes, bathrooms had cast-iron, unenclosed baths, brass taps, and often a water closet (which occasionally might still be in the yard) with a high-level cistern, and a chain for pulling. The parlour (if there was one – some designs did not have one) was undoubtedly the best room, with ornaments on the mantelpiece over the fireplace, pictures on the wall (though with rather less clutter and fewer knicknacks than in the typical Victorian room), and if the household was sufficiently affluent, a gramophone or piano, also bought by hire-purchase. Such were the homes in which millions of more fortunate working-class children grew up in the 1930s – a very marked contrast to the squalid conditions in the older slums described by Orwell.

The Health of the Working Classes

If real wages increased between the wars, and hours of work were shorter, it is to be expected that the general health of the nation would improve. Moreover, any improvement in welfare services would contribute towards this improvement. In fact, although there were no major extensions of welfare services, both death rates and infant mortality rates were reduced between the wars. The death rate averaged 13.9 in the pre-war years of 1911–14; for the years 1935–8, it averaged 11.9. Infant mortality rates were also reduced from 105 in 1910 to 56 in 1940. Deaths were noticeably reduced among children from tuberculosis, measles, diarrhoea and bronchitis. However, there was a good deal of regional and even local variation in these figures, for example, in the prosperous south-east the infant mortality rate in 1935 was only forty-seven, but in Wales it was sixty-three, in Northumberland and Durham seventy-six, and in Scotland seventy-seven. So, although the general trend of improvement was satisfactory enough, there was still some disquiet at the extent of ill-health among the poorest families. We shall return to this subject a little later in this chapter.

The health services between the wars were still in a rudimentary state. Insurance against sickness was compulsory for all workers earning less than £160 per annum under the National Insurance Act of 1911 but the scheme did not cover the dependants of the insured, and sickness benefits when away from work were still lower than unemployment rates. Further, the range of benefits was limited, and hospital treatment was not free unless provided in poor law infirmaries. Treatment in municipal hospitals or voluntarily run hospitals still had to be paid for. The health service was run not by the Ministry of Health, but by approved societies, in practice mostly insurance societies. As a system, it suffered from administrative weaknesses and duplication of effort, and the Royal Commission on National Health Insurance 1926 recommended that the system be reformed; the Minority Report even recommended that the administration of the system be removed from the societies altogether. In 1929, the Local Government Act allowed local authorities to take over the poor law infirmaries, and to run them as municipal hospitals. Not many did so, and in 1939 about half of all public hospital services were still provided by the poor law infirmaries. By that year, it would be fair to say that there was something resembling a national health service for the working classes, but it was still very limited in scope (it might or might not include dental treatment, depending on the society concerned), and although treatment by general practitioners was free for those covered by the scheme, as we have seen, hospital treatment might have to be paid for.

There were two other major social services affecting the general health of the nation. The unemployment insurance scheme underwent considerable major changes between the wars, and will be dealt with separately later in this chapter. The other large-scale social service was the old-age pension scheme. Introduced first in 1908 on a non-contributory basis, this originally paid five shillings a week to old people of seventy and over, subject to a means test. In 1919 the payment was raised to ten shillings, and in 1925 a further important extension under the Widows, Orphans, and Old Age Contributory Pensions Act merged the scheme with the health insurance scheme. Contributions now had to be paid for a pension beginning at the lower age of sixty-five, but there was to be no means test, and the former non-contributory scheme took over at the age of seventy. A widow's and children's benefit was also incorporated into the scheme. By 1937 about twenty million people were covered by the 1925 Act.

On the whole, social services advanced significantly between the wars, and the welfare and general health of the working classes benefited as a result. Certainly government spending on services rose from £101 million in 1913 to £596 million in 1938, with a per-capita increase from £2.2 million in 1913 to £12.5 million in 1938. When price increases are taken into account, this meant that expenditure had increased by over three times between 1913 and 1938. But improvement was made in a piecemeal fashion, with no overall planning. Much was left to local government initiatives. In some places free milk and child welfare clinics were available and social workers provided advice, in others they were totally absent. Free meals for poor children were served in schools, but sometimes only after a good deal of enquiry into family means. Private charities still operated to help the really poor with gifts of clothing, free boots for children, and so on. Indeed, as will be seen shortly, there was much concern in the 1930s not only at the extent of unemployment and the condition of the unemployed, but at the continuance of real poverty in the most depressed areas of the country.

Education

Before dealing with these weighty problems, a word is necessary on the subject of a welfare service of another kind – the state educational service. Fisher's Education Act of 1918 promised some improvement in the schools, but as was noted in the Prologue, its plans for day-continuation schools fell victim to the government economy cuts in the early 1920s. No other major education Act was passed in the inter-war period. The school-leaving age remained at fourteen, and secondary education for working-class boys and girls was very limited. Apart from the small minority who obtained free places in the secondary schools set up by county authorities under the 1902 Act, the vast majority of children stayed in the same buildings after the age of eleven, in a so-called senior department or school. What was wanted was a separate system of secondary education, preferably in separate buildings. The Labour Party made its own views clear in 1922 in a pamphlet entitled *Secondary Education for All*, which demanded that all working-class children should have a free secondary education to the age of fifteen, and later to sixteen.

In 1926 the Hadow Committee issued a report which echoed these views. It suggested that the term 'elementary education' should be discarded, and that in future education up to eleven should be termed 'primary education', and the next stage from eleven onwards 'secondary education'. In addition to the county secondary schools, there should be new secondary schools known as modern schools, with a curriculum suitable for less academic pupils, but still including some science and a foreign language. These schools were to have a status equivalent to the existing county schools, which were to be renamed county grammar schools: 'It is not an inferior species, and it ought not to be hampered by conditions of accommodation and equipment inferior to those of the schools now described as secondary.' The school-leaving age should also be raised to fifteen.

The times were against the Hadow Report. Many local

Table 1.3 Secondary School Population, 1913–37

Year	No. of secondary schools	No. of pupils in secondary schools
1913	1,027	187,647
1921	1,249	362,025
1937	1,397	484,676

Source: S.J.Curtis, *History of Education in Great Britain* (7th edn, 1967).

authorities lacked the resources to build new schools or even divide up existing schools, especially when government grants were reduced following the financial crisis of 1931. In that year, teachers' salaries were cut, and parents whose children had won free places in secondary schools had to face a means test. The school-leaving age was not put up to fifteen until 1936, and even then was not to come into force until 1 September 1939 (when its operation was promptly postponed, as war was so near). Still, some limited progress was made between the wars. In 1920, only 33 per cent of pupils in county secondary schools had free places; by 1931, the proportion had risen to 47 per cent. In 1931, about 25 per cent of older children were in separate secondary schools or departments; in 1938 the figure was 64 per cent. There was a distinct rise in the secondary school population, as Table 1.3 shows. So although progress was slow, the principle of separate secondary education (previously thought of as somewhat unnecessary for ordinary working-class children) had been established. More clever working-class children were enabled to go to grammar school, and then on to university, though overall the numbers were small. Education beyond the school-leaving age was still a difficult and costly business, and many academically able children left school as soon as possible at fourteen in order to get a job and earn their keep. It was not until the Education Act of 1944 that a further attempt was made to improve secondary education for the working classes.

Unemployment

The dimensions of the unemployment problem between the wars are well known. At no time from 1920 onwards were there less than two million registered as unemployed, and a peak of nearly three million was reached in 1932–3. These figures represented 23 per cent of all those insured, but did not include agricultural workers, or domestic servants, or the self-employed; the true total in September 1932 has been estimated as 3.75 million. The staple industries were worst hit, of course. In 1932, the percentages unemployed in these industries were:

Coal mining	33.9	Shipbuilding	62.2
Woollen and worsted	20.7	Pig-iron making	43.5
Cotton	28.5		

It follows that unemployment was concentrated heavily in certain parts of the country – the north-east, Lancashire and Yorkshire, and South Wales – and the most striking and commonly quoted examples are to be found in the mining villages in Durham. In 1932 in Tow Law, for instance, 80 per cent of the men were out of work, and nearly 100 per cent of the men in Shildon. But it would be wrong to suppose that in more prosperous areas like the West Midlands unemployment was never of any real consequence. This is not so at all, especially in the worst years of depression. Thus in 1931 normally prosperous Birmingham had 17.7 per cent unemployed, while Dudley (one of the fifteen towns in the Black Country to the west) had a figure of 38.8 per cent, and another four nearby towns were over 30 per cent. A further seven Black Country towns were all over 27 per cent. Thus, even in this normally thriving area of new industry, times could be bad in particular years (by way of contrast, in 1937, a prosperous year, Birmingham's rate was down to 4.3 per cent, which in Beveridge's terms represented full employment, and the Dudley figure was 9.3 per cent).

Not all the unemployed were out of work indefinitely, and the host of the unemployed was made up of different categories of workers. In 1931, unskilled workers were the largest group, 30.5 per cent of them being out of work; among the skilled and semi-skilled, only 14.4 per cent were out of work, and only 5–8 per cent of white-collar workers. Older men were the least likely to gain re-employment; in 1936, more than a third of all unemployed were aged forty-five to sixty-five. The young, on the other hand, might be given jobs straight from school, only to lose them when they became entitled to adult wages. Although skilled men had a better chance of keeping their jobs, once out of work some of them remained unemployed because they refused to take unskilled work. Lastly, during the whole period there was a mounting number of long-term unemployed who had been out of work for more than a year. They constituted 25 per cent of all the unemployed in August 1939. In some mining villages the period of unemployment was far longer than a year. In the north-east in 1938, 71 per cent of the men had been unemployed for more than *five* years; in the Rhondda in South Wales in 1938, the comparable figure was 45 per cent. A report in 1938 drew a striking contrast between Deptford in south-east London and the Rhondda valley. In Deptford, the long-term unemployed were 6 per cent of the unemployed, but 63 per cent in the Rhondda. Further, the report went on:

> Among every 1,000 workers, four in Deptford, but 280 in Rhondda have failed to get a job for at least a year . . . The difference between a prosperous and a depressed area is thus not in the neighbourhood of 1:7, but 1:70. In a depressed community, there are 70 long-unemployed men, whereas in a prosperous community there is one.

The story of what the government did to combat the problem of unemployment is somewhat complicated, and is concerned more with attempts to extend the unemployment insurance scheme which existed in 1918 than with any efforts to revive the staple industries. The 1918 scheme was very limited and initially applied to only 2.25 million workers in trades subject to seasonal unemployment. In 1919 the government introduced so-called out-of-work donations – non-contributory grants intended to tide over ex-servicemen and former war workers till they had found new jobs. The 1920 Unemployment Act extended the scheme to most workers earning less than £250 a year, but, as depression spread, many workers used up their entitlement under the scheme without finding work, and were faced with having to go to the poor law guardians. To avoid this, they were permitted to go on drawing benefits, in theory financed from future contributions ('uncovenanted benefit', after 1924 called 'extended benefit'). Anyone not entitled to assistance under the scheme in the first place was still obliged to seek outdoor relief under the poor law. In 1924 the first Labour government raised the basic rate of benefit from fifteen shillings to eighteen shillings a week, while in 1925 the Blanesburgh Committee was appointed to report on the whole insurance scheme. It was clear that the scheme had never been intended to cope with heavy and sustained unemployment, and it was creaking badly under the financial strain. The Committee reported in 1927, recommending that standard and extended benefit be merged, and given to anyone with thirty weeks' contributions to his credit. Other workers without these contributions were allowed to draw 'transitional benefit'. The Unemployment Act of 1928 put these recommendations into effect.

The position at the end of the 1920s was that the original insurance scheme had been greatly extended, and the pre-war idea of financing unemployment benefits from unemployment contributions was increasingly lost sight of as the Insurance Fund plunged more and more deeply into debt – £28 million in 1928. By this time, the unemployed obtaining relief fell into three categories:

(1) those given relief based on insurance contributions;
(2) those who had exhausted their benefit under the scheme, but were given 'transitional relief', financed by the Treasury;
(3) those who were not insured at all, and had to seek relief from the poor law guardians.

In 1929, the poor law system, which was under great financial pressure, was reformed when the Boards of Guardians (responsible both for the workhouses and for outdoor relief) were done away with, and their powers transferred to special committees of the county councils, the Public Assistance Committees, or PACs. The PACs now became the last resort of all those who had exhausted benefit under the insurance scheme.

The 1930s opened with the second Labour government making it easier to obtain transitional benefit by doing away with the requirement that all applicants should be 'genuinely seeking work' (the phrase lingers on today); but in the financial crisis of the following year 1931, the cabinet split over the proposal to cut benefit by 10 per cent, and the government resigned. The coalition National government which replaced it reduced the dole from the 1928 level of seventeen shillings to 15s 3d, restricted benefit to twenty-six weeks only, and transferred 'transitional benefit' to the PACs, subject to a means test. From then on, any unemployed person out of work for more than six months was rigorously examined by the new poor law authorities in order to assess his family income, including savings, pensions and all forms of occasional earnings. The means test caused enormous resentment, not only because of its prying nature, but also because it forced fathers to become dependent on contributions from children who were in work. Naturally enough, some children left home rather than be forced to supplement the family income in this way. The means test was not new in itself – it had formerly been applied to old-age pensions – but as a way of reducing entitlement to benefit it was much disliked by those who had to submit to it, and it became one of the most humiliating memories of life on the dole in the 1930s.

At long last, after repeated efforts by governments since 1919 to extend and adapt the original scheme, the Unemployment Act of 1934 placed relief on a new and more efficient basis. Part I of the Act reorganised the insurance scheme, restoring the 1931 cuts, and bringing in groups of workers hitherto excluded from the scheme such as agricultural workers. The new scheme was to be run by a statutory committee, and was intended to meet the needs of workers normally in work. Part II faced the problem of long-term unemployment by setting up a new Unemployment Assistance Board on a national basis. This Board took over from the PACs about 800,000 persons on transitional payments, together with a further 200,000 actually on poor relief. The costs of the Board were to come directly from the Treasury, that is, were centrally not locally funded. The means test was to continue, though in a modified form. It was not completely abandoned till 1941.

Part II was clearly a complete departure from the old idea of a scheme which was self-financing through the insurance principle. Such a scheme had clearly proved quite inadequate as a means of dealing with long-term, massive unemployment which far exceeded the 4 per cent of the insured which was originally intended. The new scheme worked reasonably well, though at first there was some confusion because UAB rates were sometimes lower than the rates paid by the PACs, which varied from one local authority to another. For a time, applicants could claim whichever rate was the higher; but by 1937 uniform rates had been fixed, and the new Act was operating satisfactorily. The whole story of the relief of the unemployed since 1918 had been one of repeated government efforts to modify an inherently unsuitable scheme, but to do so as cheaply as possible. This may be thought admirable from the point of view of the taxpayer, some of whom thought the unemployed were a lazy lot who could find work if they really tried;

but it was very hard on the unemployed man or woman, genuinely out of work through no fault of their own.

The other way of relieving unemployment was job creation, of course, but not very much was done by the government in this respect. Belief in laissez-faire was still strong in 1918, and it was not until 1931 that free trade was abandoned and tariff reform at last put into effect. Even then, governments had little faith in public work schemes, and it seems that rather more was done in the 1920s than in the 1930s to provide jobs. The Unemployment Grants Committee gave grants to local authorities for public works, but the amounts given were limited to £69.5 million in the period December 1920 to January 1932. Only 60,000 were employed under such schemes in 1931. These grants were suspended between 1931 and 1932 as a consequence of government economy cuts. When the worst of the depression was over, the Special Areas (Development and Improvement) Act 1934 gave financial aid to the distressed areas, now renamed more tactfully 'special areas'. Later on, the Special Areas (Amendment) Act 1937 allowed firms setting up in special areas to be excused rates, rents and taxes; but the help given under these Acts was very limited. By 1938, only £8.5 million had been spent, and about 50,000 jobs created by 1939. Efforts were also made to transfer labour from the depressed areas to more prosperous parts, and training centres were also set up. Between 1928 and 1937 some 190,000 were helped to transfer, and voluntary unaided migration was much greater. It is estimated that over a million people of working age moved into the south-east between the wars, and there was an additional movement into the Midlands. It is surprising that even more did not move from the special areas in search of work, but it must be remembered that there were strong psychological barriers, especially for married men, against moving from an area in which a worker had lived all his life, where he had accommodation of a sort, and where he was a known and respected workman.

Whether the government could have done more to stimulate the economy at the time remains an open question. Certainly the Liberal Party advocated large-scale spending on public works in their policy statement 'We can conquer unemployment' (1929), but unemployment on the scale of the early 1930s was unprecedented, and so was the idea of massive government spending to reduce it. It is true that the greatest economist of the time, John Maynard Keynes, argued that the government should stimulate the economy by spending its way out of the slump, but his general theory was not published till 1936, and dealt with cyclical rather than structural unemployment; in any case many of the traditionally minded thought that the proper role of government was to save rather than to spend more of the taxpayers' money. At all events, the unemployed could not expect much in direct government aid. By and large, there seemed little that they could do except wait for better times, and in the meantime sweat it out.

Life on the Dole

What life was like on the dole is an enormous subject. There is no shortage of evidence in the form of numerous enquiries into conditions in particular towns or areas, together with some striking literary evidence, such as Walter Greenwood's *Love on the Dole* (1933), Ellen Wilkinson's *The Town that was Murdered* (1939), J.B.Priestley's *English Journey* (1934), and George Orwell's *The Road to Wigan Pier* (1937). Some of this writing had a strong ideological bias, though this in itself does not invalidate its descriptive force. Orwell was an honest reporter, and did not fabricate evidence, though at times he finds it difficult to restrain his indignation at the degrading nature of unemployment, and at the capitalist society which permitted it; nor can he resist the odd reference to the 'fat-bellied bourgeoisie'. Not much evidence is available directly from the working classes themselves, so it is often necessary to rely on middle-class writers recording their observations. Orwell and Priestley excel in describing the physical environment – cotton towns with silent mills, chimneys without smoke, and men loitering about in the streets; shipyard towns with yards shut and deserted; mining villages with the winding gear stilled, and no one at work. Priestley has a memorable and much quoted passaged describing Jarrow:

> One out of two shops appeared to be permanently closed.
> Wherever we went, there were men hanging about, not
> scores of them but hundreds and thousands of them. The
> whole town looked as if it had entered a perpetual penniless
> Black Sabbath. The men wore the drawn masks of prisoners
> of war.

Priestley gives us an equally graphic description of Stockton-on-Tees:

34

Stockton has shipyards which have been closed for years, so
that the grass is growing in them ... It has big marine
engineering shops that are now empty shells of brick ...
And it has a large number of citizens, excellent skilled
workmen, who have been unemployed not merely this year
and last year, but for 7 and 8 years ... The real town is
finished. It is like a theatre that is kept open merely for the
sale of drinks in the bars and chocolates in the corridors.

The contrast here between the depressed areas and the scene in
London and the home counties is remarkable. Just west of London, near the Chiswick flyover, a new industrial estate was built in
the thirties on the Great West Road. The factories were set in
spacious grounds with green lawns and trees, built in the contemporary style of flat-roofed, cream-washed ferro-concrete, and
sometimes floodlit or outlined in neon lighting at night. Here indeed was another England, the England of the new industry,
smart, modern and prosperous.

The major effect of unemployment on family life is obvious
enough – a reduction of income, and a life spent at or near subsistence level. The rates of unemployment pay were kept deliberately
low, of course, to discourage scroungers, and this made life hard
for the great majority who were out of work through no fault of
their own. It is estimated that three out of every ten households of
the long-term unemployed were below the poverty line, and even
when the worst years of depression were over, a large section of the
unemployed were still living in poverty (the extent of poverty
nationally will be considered in the next section). However, it must
be remembered that many of the unemployed would have been in
poverty (especially the unskilled) even when in work. Some were
positively better off on the dole. For example, in South Wales it was
calculated that one-third of the single men, and nearly half the
married men, were better off on the dole than in their last job. This
certainly says little for their basic standard of living when
employed. The actual effect of unemployment on any one family
would depend, of course, on a variety of things – how many in the
family remained in work, whether odd part-time jobs were available (and undisclosed to the authorities), and above all, on the
housewife's ability to prepare cheap and nourishing meals, and
generally to make do and mend.

The effect of such a low standard of living on health is easy to guess, but difficult to assess statistically. Although the relatively poor diet must have taken effect, many poor districts had always had bad health records. Jarrow, for example, had a high rate of tuberculosis during the depression, but the rate had always been high, even in days of full employment. Psychological illness due to feelings of depression was certainly common among the out-of-work. In 1932, an average of two unemployed men committed suicide for every day in the year. In the period 1921–31, suicides among men under twenty-five years of age rose by 60 per cent (though some of these might have taken their own lives even if they had been at work). No direct link has been found between unemployment and crime, though juvenile crime statistics went up in the 1930s (this might have been due to better detection). As for alcoholism, the per-capita consumption of alcohol fell inter-war; it was too expensive for the out-of-work, it is said, and other forms of entertainment were available. Gambling continued on a minor scale as before, since a mild flutter on the horses did something to break the monotony.

How then did the unemployed pass the time? A good deal of voluntary work took place to provide recreational activities. Clubs for the out-of-work were established by the YMCA and by the Salvation Army. The National Council of Social Services organised a nationwide network of clubs. There were about 400 of these in 1935, with a membership of a quarter of a million. Priestley described a club of this sort which he visited in 1933 in Blackburn. It was in an elementary school which had recently been condemned:

> It was a dismal hole in a dark back street. In the first room, some youngish men were at work. One or two were cobbling boots, chiefly soling and heeling, for which they pay – in order to cover the bare cost of the leather – a shilling for men's, ninepence for women's, and sixpence for children's boots. The other men were making things out of wood. They were mostly things for their homes, such as cupboards, bookcases, coal-boxes, and little desks for children ... They were also making toys for Christmas ...

Some towns were adopted by more prosperous parts of the country, for example, Jarrow by Surrey.

Those who didn't go to the clubs passed the time between reporting to the labour exchange in a variety of ways. In summer, they might go for walks, go cycling, dig the garden or allotment, or simply gossip in the street. In winter, there was the problem of keeping warm. They could stay in bed, or go out to the library, or visit cheap cafés or milk bars. The more studious might attend Workers' Educational Association (WEA) or Extra-Mural courses. Then there was the weekly visit to the cinema, and sometimes to the local football match, while at home there was the radio to listen to. In one way or another, time passed by. Individual reactions varied from bitter resentment to indifference and sheer apathy. There were few violent demonstrations against unemployment. Marches by the unemployed were organised by the National Un-employed Workers Movement, led by the communist Wal Hannington (on the whole, the Communist Party was more active than the far larger Labour Party in this respect). The most famous march of the unemployed was that of the Jarrow workers to London. However, relatively few joined either the Communist Party or the fascist Blackshirts, founded in 1932 by Sir Oswald Mosley, who had resigned from the Labour Party. It is remarkable that so few chose political action as a form of protest. Orwell thought that this was because of the availability of cheap luxuries which made life more bearable:

> Of course, the post-war development of cheap luxuries has been a very fortunate thing for our rulers. It is quite likely that fish and chips, art-silk stockings, tinned salmon, cutprice chocolate (five two-ounce bars for sixpence), the movies, the radio, strong tea, and the football pools have between them averted revolution.

Orwell went on to say that some thought that this was an astute manoeuvre by the governing classes to hold the unemployed down, but he personally didn't think the governing class had that much intelligence. His own analysis of the reason why the revolution failed to take place is scarcely profound, but still has a certain easy plausibility.

Lastly, whatever the miseries of the individual unemployed man or woman, the mainstay of many families was the housewife and mother. It was she whose work had to go on as before, often performing minor miracles on a severely reduced family income, keeping the family fed and the house respectable. No one actually starved to death on the dole, but the margins were very narrow. Life became an endless round of cooking meals, shopping, housework and darning and sewing (clothes often had to be patched).

Millions of women kept their families going in this way, and for years on end. Among their number are the unsung heroines of the years of depression in this country between the wars: they should all have had campaign medals.

The Extent of Poverty

As was noted in the Prologue, the subject of poverty was first investigated statistically in late Victorian times when Charles Booth's immense survey of the London poor showed that nearly a third of the population had an income insufficient to maintain a minimum, tolerable standard of life. Moreover, 8.4 per cent were in a state of abject poverty (primary poverty). Similar figures were found for York in Rowntree's survey of York in 1899. Between the wars it is obvious that many workers enjoyed a rising standard of living when they occupied steady jobs, while at the other extreme those who suffered long spells of unemployment lived very much on the minimum necessary to sustain health. Indeed, in the 1930s there were allegations that the dole was too low to avoid actual malnutrition. The question is, how much real poverty was there? Was it increasing or decreasing between the wars?

A further survey made by Rowntree in York in 1936 provides an interesting contrast to the 1899 figures. The 1936 report adopts a more generous poverty line than in 1899, including a higher dietary requirement, together with items for beer, tobacco, a wireless and newspapers. The results are shown in Table 1.4. It is clear that in York things had improved greatly for the average worker. According to Rowntree, '... we should probably not be very far wrong if we put the standard of living available to the workers in

Table 1.4   Poverty in York, 1899 and 1936

	1936	1899
Below poverty line	17.7	27.8 (percentage of York population)
Primary poverty	3.9	9.9 (percentage of York population)
Primary poverty (of the working classes)	6.8	15.8

Source: B. Seebohm Rowntree, *Poverty and Progress: A Second Social Survey of York* (1941).

1936 at about 30 per cent higher than it was in 1899'. Rowntree
went on to analyse the reasons for 17.7 per cent still being under
the poverty line. The biggest single cause was that, although the
head of the family was in regular work, his wages were too low
(32.8 per cent); the second major cause was that the head of the
family was out of work (28.6 per cent); and the third biggest cause
was old age (14.7 per cent). Rowntree then repeated the argument
put forward in the earlier report, that working-class people were
subject to recurrent bouts of poverty throughout their lives ('the
poverty cycle'). Almost half of them were born into poverty (the
coming of the family bringing financial strain), but they would
become better off once they had left school and become wage-
earners. They would experience poverty again when they married
and started a family, but their standard of life would improve once
the children earned a wage, then finally become poor again when
retired in old age.

York was not a typically depressed or especially prosperous city,
but studies in other towns, sometimes with different poverty lines,
seemed to show that the York figures were fairly typical. In Bristol,
for instance, in 1937 only 10.7 per cent of working-class families
were 'poverty-stricken'. In Merseyside for the years 1928–32, the
equivalent figure was 16 per cent, but when adjusted to Rowntree's
minimum standards, the figure shot up to 30 per cent. In London,
in 1928, only 9.1 per cent were 'in poverty'. All the local surveys
appeared to agree that unemployment and inadequate wages were
the major causes of poverty – about a third of it due to unemployment and inadequate benefit, another third due to low wages, a
sixth to old age, and the remaining sixth to sickness and other
minor causes.

More recently, further local studies of the statistics have shown
how they can be misleading in that averages can conceal quite high
figures in particular districts. For example, the London average of
9.1 per cent in poverty does not reveal that in 1928 the figure for
Poplar was 24 per cent, and for Bethnal Green 17.8 per cent. It has
been suggested that some officials were embarrassed by local health
statistics, such as high infant-mortality figures, because critics
could use them to show that the dole was apparently not enough to
maintain adequate standards of health. The figures were therefore
manipulated to hide this fact. It has also been argued that, as it was
freely admitted that rates of benefit were generally lower than the
lowest wages, then nutritional standards must have fallen among

some of the unemployed at least. This seems logical, but it has already been pointed out that some families were better off on the dole than earning very low wages. There is also the additional point to be considered that unemployment benefit included allowances for dependants, however small, while ordinary wages did not. What appears undeniable is that the fortunate majority did enjoy an improvement in real wages; but it may be that the extent of deprivation among the really poor has been underestimated in the past.

One way of assessing the extent of poverty, of course, is to concentrate on diet, and on how far the family income permits the purchase of the minimum amount of food necessary for good health. Argument here naturally centres on what really constitutes such a minimum diet. Sir John Boyd Orr's investigation of this in 1936, *Food, Health, and Income*, caused a sensation: he argued that one-half or more of the entire nation was undernourished. His findings were severely criticised in that his sample was very small, his standard of need was questionable, and he made no allowance for regional variations. He himself admitted that the consumption of food per head between the wars had actually increased, except for flour, and he later dropped his claim from one half to a third. A similar study to that of Boyd Orr's in 1937 suggested a figure of a fifth undernourished, rather than a third.

Local studies do not do much to qualify Boyd Orr's figures any further, though the Birmingham Schools Medical Officer reported in 1937 that cases of malnutrition were nearly five times more numerous in the central slums in Birmingham than on the new council estates on the outskirts of the city. A survey of nutrition and the family on a very large Birmingham housing estate in 1939 aimed to compare the minimum spending on food necessary (using the BMA minimum diet scale of 1933) with housekeeping money available for food after necessary deductions for rent, light, clothing and so on. A table (reproduced below as Table 1.5) was then drawn up to show what proportion of the families surveyed were on or below the minimum standard of sufficiency. This estate housed relatively well-paid workers in a prosperous region; only 7.7 per cent in Birmingham were unemployed at the time. It shows that of the families with two children, nearly half were on or below the minimum standard, while nearly all the largest families were on or below this standard. It is possible, of course, to criticise the detail here, and especially the construction of the minimum

Table 1.5   Families on or below the Minimum Standard on the Kingstanding Council Estate, Birmingham, 1938

	%
Families with one child under 14	13
two children under 14	45
three children under 14	65
four children under 14	85
five children under 14	96
six or more children under 14	96

Source: M.S. Souter, E.H. Wilkins and P. Sargant Florence, *Nutrition and the Family: Report on a New Housing Estate* (1939).

standard, but it still seems clear that the larger the family, the more inadequate wage-levels became. In other words, the case for family allowances was made again by the report. The authors commented that new housing in itself was not the answer to bad living accommodation; larger families needed additional help in the form of some scheme of allowances or additional social services.

Although it is obviously impossible to estimate precisely the extent of poverty between the wars, two things seem tolerably certain: the first is that it had decreased since before the Great War. The second is that it had by no means disappeared, even though the idea of what constituted poverty had changed (as it has changed today, and presumably will go on changing). It was to be found particularly in areas dominated by the old staple industries, and it was caused mainly by unemployment, by low wages (especially when the family was large), and to a lesser extent by old age. For the majority of working people, however, the standard of living was rising, especially in the 1930s. This was due to the rise in real wages, cheap food from abroad, shorter working hours, smaller families and improvements in productivity. Moreover, since the average rate of unemployment in the period 1921–39 was 14 per cent, then in theory an average 86 per cent of working people were in work, and enjoying a better standard of living. Obviously this 86 per cent requires substantial adjustment in a number of ways – for example, not all workers were on the employment register throughout; but it is safe to say that well over half of the workers were better off. Professor Burnett puts it cautiously, 'The proportion of the very poor fell between the wars, and that of the moderately prosperous increased.' Professor Aldcroft is rather more emphatic, 'No one can seriously doubt that the working classes on the eve of the Second World War were better fed, better clothed, and better housed than their parents had been a generation earlier.'

The Labour Movement

In the Prologue it was pointed out that by 1918 the working classes had acquired their own political party, and at the same time had increased their industrial power during the First World War through the trade union movement. Further, the extension of the vote in 1918 to all adult men, and to women of thirty or over, constituted an important increase in political power. This does not imply, of course, that the working classes as a whole had suddenly become politically minded. A substantial proportion, perhaps up to a third, were traditionally minded, and voted Conservative and not Labour between the wars. Some found political events simply boring, and preferred the football and racing results. Again, although trade union membership sailed up to eight million by 1920, this still left well over half the working population outside the unions. So, although the outlook for the Labour movement seemed promising in 1918 (and indeed threatening, from the governing classes' point of view), a realistic appraisal of future possibilities might expect some progress after 1918, but no immediate success. In the event, the trade union movement was to wilt under the impact of the depression in the staple industries, and of the General Strike in 1926; while of the two minority Labour governments formed between the wars, the second (1929–31) collapsed ignominiously in the financial crisis of 1931.

To take the trade unions first: with the return of peace, the unions regained the rights which had been surrendered during the war, in particular the right to strike; and the 1919 Industrial Courts Act set up an industrial court for the voluntary settlement of industrial disputes. The first two years of peace were years of prosperity which saw a number of serious strikes including strikes by the police in Liverpool and in London, and a national rail strike lasting a week in September 1919. A national coal strike was threatened in the same year when the miners demanded a 30 per cent pay rise, a six-hour day and the nationalisation of the mines. The mines were still under government control as they had been during the war, but the Prime Minister, Lloyd George, acted swiftly by appointing a coal industry commission, on which Labour was well represented by two economists favourable to their cause, plus the socialist economic historian R. H. Tawney. The major issue, of course, was nationalisation. Of the four final reports of the Sankey Commission, issued in June 1919 two recommended nationalisation and two opposed it. Although seven in all out of the thirteen members of the Commission supported national ownership, Lloyd George took no further action since his Conservative-dominated coalition government would not have accepted it. All the miners got was the Mines Act of 1919, which conceded the seven-hour day, together with an acceptance of the principle of nationalisation of royalties. The Act did little to bring peace to the mining industry, where there was a long history of hostility between the employers and the men.

In 1920 there was more industrial strife, first in the form of the *Jolly George* incident, when London dockers refused to load munitions on a ship intended for the Poles, at that time fighting the armies of the newly formed socialist Soviet Union; and later the pre-war Triple Alliance was revived, and the railwaymen and other transport workers came out on strike in support of the miners, who were striking for increased pay. The government was forced to capitulate and order a wages increase. Another trade union victory came when the dockers, led by a Transport Workers Federation official, Ernest Bevin, won their case against the employers in the new Industrial Court.

The year 1921 saw the end of the post-war boom, and also the ebb-tide of union militancy. Total membership, which had been 8.3 million in 1920, was reduced to 6.6 million in 1921, and although days lost in striking peaked in 1921 at 85.87 million, the 1922 figure was only 19.85 million days. In 1921 the miners were again in the news when they rejected wage cuts by the mineowners, to whom the government had just returned the mines. Once more the Triple Alliance came into action, but this time the railwaymen, led by Jimmy Thomas, withdrew at the last moment on Friday, 15 April (Black Friday), on the grounds that there was still room for negotiation. The miners were forced to go on strike alone. After two months, they had to return to work, having gained nothing. Thereafter the Triple Alliance was referred to mockingly as the

'Cripple Alliance'. The miners felt betrayed by the railwaymen, and Thomas was nicknamed by his opponents 'Traitor' Thomas. It should be noted, however, that one useful development in trade union history in the early 1920s was the amalgamation of several unions in the interests of gaining greater strength. Thus the Amalgamated Engineering Union was formed in 1920, and also the Transport and General Workers Union in 1921 (with Ernest Bevin as secretary), and the Union of General and Municipal Workers in 1924. Also in 1921 the Trades Union Congress replaced its old Parliamentary Committee by a new and more powerful General Council.

In 1925 trouble erupted again in the mining industry. This time it arose from the government's decision to go back to the gold standard, which had been temporarily abandoned during the war. Going back at an over-valued figure for the pound made coal exports dearer than before, and the owners had only one answer when profits dropped – a cut in wages. The new General Council of the TUC thereupon called a meeting of the unions of the railwaymen, other transport workers and the seamen (all involved in the transport of coal), who agreed to stop all movement of coal if and when the miners went on strike. The government was faced with an apparent revival of the Triple Alliance, and even the possibility of something like a General Strike. The Prime Minister, Stanley Baldwin, hastily appointed a commission of enquiry, to be led by Sir Herbert Samuel, and gave a temporary grant to the employers so as to avoid the threatened cut in wages. His actions pleased the unions, who promptly named the day 'Red Friday'. Though Baldwin was a genuine believer in conciliation, nevertheless he set about preparing in secret in case there was a General Strike. England and Wales were divided into ten regions, each with a cabinet minister in charge, local committees were appointed and volunteers enrolled. A special body, the Organisation for the Maintenance of Supplies, was set up, with government support. The TUC, on the other hand, made very few preparations; the secretary of the Miners Federation, the excitable and dedicated communist A. J. Cook, declared that his mother-in-law for some time past had been buying an extra tin of salmon when she went shopping, to which Jimmy Thomas retorted, 'My God! A British revolution based on a tin of salmon!' More seriously, Cook made it plain that the miners would stand firm whatever the outcome of the Samuel Commission:

I don't care a hang for any government, or army or navy.
They can come along with their bayonets. Bayonets don't cut
coal. We have already beaten not only the employers, but the
strongest government of modern times.

These were brave and defiant words, but they bore little relation to
reality.

The Samuel Commission's report, published in March 1926,
pleased neither side. It recommended that the government subsidy
be withdrawn, the industry reorganised and wages cut, though on a
national not district basis. There should be no alteration in the
length of the working day. In fact, the owners wanted the restora-
tion of the eight-hour day, and district agreements on pay. For
their part, the miners rejected both wage cuts and the longer day –
as Cook put it, 'Not a penny off the pay, not a minute on the day'.
Negotiations took place between the government, the mineowners, the Industrial Committee of the General Council of the
TUC, and the miners, but without result. At the end of April,
things moved swiftly to a climax.

On 30 April, the owners declared a lock-out, and the government thereupon declared a state of emergency. The General
Council took charge on behalf of the miners, and in the intensified
negotiations of the next two days, agreement seemed at least possible when on 2 May Baldwin abruptly broke off talks with the
General Council. His reasons were twofold: he claimed that notices
had already been sent out by the unions for a General Strike, and
also that certain 'overt acts' had occurred, including an inter-
ference with the freedom of the press – a reference to the *Daily Mail*
printers refusing to print a leader claiming that a General Strike
was revolutionary in nature. The General Council leaders were
taken aback: these did not seem substantial reasons for ending
negotiations completely. They retired for discussion, disavowed
the action of the *Daily Mail* printers, then went back to Downing
Street. They found the conference room in darkness, and were told
that Baldwin had gone to bed. To employ Baldwin's last words to
them, it was the end. The General Strike began the next day, 3 May
1926 and lasted nine days.

The immediate cause of the General Strike is clear. Baldwin had
decided that negotiations had gone on long enough, and that the
matter must be put to the test. It has been argued that he was
exhausted by the long negotiations, and finally yielded to the

demands of the more pugnacious members of the cabinet such as Birkenhead and Churchill, who were willing to take on the miners. On the other hand, some biographers have suggested that, even if he had continued negotiations, the miners were completely intransigent, and would never have given way. But there are more profound reasons for the strike than this, of course. The fact is that the coal industry was old-fashioned and inefficient, yet the owners were not prepared to do anything to bring it up to date, and (as we have seen) had only one remedy for loss of profits, and that was wage cuts. Hence the continued strife in the industry. The owners must certainly take some blame for what happened. The editor of the *Observer*, G. L. Garvin, wrote on 25 April: 'The owners have been tactless and irritating to the last degree. No responsible body of men has ever seemed more lacking in the human touch . . .'Lord Birkenhead, himself no great admirer of the miners, wrote:

> it would be possible to say without exaggeration that the miners' leaders were the stupidest men in England if we had not had frequent occasion to meet the owners.

Nor were the leaders of the General Council and of the miners without blemish. The miners in particular were determined not to yield an inch either. Unfortunately, too, for their public image, they allowed what they regarded as basically an industrial dispute to be represented by the government as a constitutional crisis, and a direct challenge to parliamentary democracy.

In a narrow legal sense, the government were actually quite right in maintaining this. Clearly a General Strike – something without precedent in the country – was an attempt to coerce the government and the employers into accepting the unions' demands, so that on the issue in question the TUC and not parliament would be the final arbiter. The General Strike had always been the weapon advocated by the syndicalists for overthrowing the capitalist system and establishing worker control. Naturally the TUC did not see the strike in this light, preferring to call it a 'National Strike' rather than a 'General Strike' but the government chose to conjure up the bogey of a socialist threat to the constitution, posing the challenge of an alternative government representing merely the unions rather than the nation. The strike, according to Baldwin, was 'a gross travesty of every democratic principle'. The unions had no very effective answer to this kind of propaganda. For years, the idea of a General Strike had haunted the imagination of left-wing thinkers.

Suddenly, it had become an uncomfortable reality for the far from revolutionary TUC, and they had desperately to grapple with the consequences.

In fact, considering their almost complete lack of preparation, the trade union organisation worked very well through a system of local committees. Not all unions were called out, only certain key unions in iron and steel, gas and electricity, building, printing, the press and transport. The government's advance preparations ensured that essential supplies were kept moving. They were assisted by a mass of largely middle-class volunteers who drove trains, buses, trams and lorries. A government attempt to use the British Broadcasting Company for its own purposes was successfully resisted by its director, John Reith. The government published its own official newsheet, the *British Gazette*. It was edited by Winston Churchill. Baldwin regarded this as one of his masterstrokes, since appointing Churchill to this post effectively absorbed the energies of one of the most belligerent members of the cabinet. Baldwin was concerned at all costs to keep the temperature down. It is customary to praise British *sang-froid* and lack of violence during the strike, quoting as evidence the football matches played between strikers and the police; by contrast, general strikes on the continent were usually much more violent. As a matter of fact, the strike was relatively peaceful, but some violence did take place against strike-breakers, and against the police and volunteer drivers. There were 3,149 prosecutions for breaches of the peace and for incitement to sedition in England and Wales, and some signs of an increase in violence towards the end of the strike.

Meanwhile, it was quite clear that the government would not give way to either the TUC or the miners, maintaining throughout that the strike was 'a challenge to parliament, and the road to anarchy and ruin'. In these circumstances the TUC was forced to look for a way out. By 11 May Sir Herbert Samuel had had talks with the TUC leaders, and a Memorandum was drawn up, outlining possible terms for a settlement. This Memorandum was formally accepted by the General Council, who ignored the objections of the miners and sent a deputation to the Prime Minister, informing him that the strike was to be called off forthwith. In fact, the strike was still solid, and many strikers were taken aback to find that their leaders had given in.

Once a return to work was made on 13 May, many workers found that they had been dismissed in their absence, and Baldwin had to warn employers against victimisation. The miners still stayed out, considering themselves betrayed by the TUC. Baldwin made one further abortive attempt to settle the wages dispute, but after its failure he left the miners to their fate. By the end of the year, their strike was broken, and they were forced to return on the owners' terms – reduced wages on a district basis, and the eight-hour day (the government had already suspended the seven-hour day). In spite of the government's warning, some miners' leaders were victimised, and never worked on the coalfields again. In 1927 the Trades Disputes and Trade Union Act was passed. It banned sympathetic strikes, forbade civil servants to join trade unions or bodies connected with the TUC, redefined the law relating to picketing so as to make legal picketing more difficult, and replaced 'contracting-out' by 'contracting-in' (that is, instead of part of a union member's subscription going automatically into the union's political fund unless he specifically objected, or 'contracted-out', in future none of it would go for political purposes unless he specifically said so, or 'contracted-in'). This had the effect of reducing Labour Party income from the political levy by a quarter. The Labour movement considered the Act a spiteful act of revenge, and it was repealed in 1946 by the third Labour government.

The General Strike was never intended by the TUC to be a bid for political power. It aroused some class feeling at the time – class loyalty on the part of the working classes, who supported the miners wholeheartedly during the strike; and class antagonism on the part of the many middle-class volunteers, some of whom thought that the constitution really was in danger, and the workers were getting above themselves and becoming too bolshie (a word in common use at the time). But no permanent damage was inflicted on the trade union movement. Membership fell from the high figure of 8.3 million to 5.2 million in 1926, and it dropped further to 4.9 million in 1927. A low was reached at 4.4 million in 1933 after the worst years of depression of 1931 and 1932, but then membership increased as economic conditions improved until it reached 6.3 million in 1939. After the upheaval of 1926, industrial relations became more peaceful, and over the period 1927–39 the average annual loss of working days was only just over three million – much lower than the comparable figure for 1919–25, which was twenty-eight million days. The reason for this may be the obvious one, namely a simple disinclination to go on strike after the failure of the General Strike, but it is also significant that there were far fewer national strikes involving large numbers than local strikes after 1926. The trade unions themselves adopted moderate policies in the 1930s which owed much to the guidance of Ernest Bevin, secretary of the biggest union, the Transport and General Workers Union, and of Walter Citrine, secretary of the TUC (much abominated on the left as a right-wing reactionary: 'Latrine must Go'; 'Down with Citrine, down the drain, And don't forget to pull the chain . . .'). By 1939, the union movement could congratulate itself on having survived the worst of the depression years, and still having the substantial support of the working classes, though they continued to resent the restrictions placed on it by the 1927 Act.

As for the political offspring of the unions, the Labour Party, it profited to a remarkable degree from the splitting and decline of the Liberal Party in the early 1920s. This was undoubtedly a major factor in Labour's solving the problems facing any third party in a basically two-party system. The party won fourteen by-elections between 1918 and 1922, and in the general election of 1922 Labour secured 142 seats, which was 26 seats more than the Liberals. The Parliamentary Labour Party now became the official opposition party in the Commons, only sixteen years after its formation in 1906 – an extraordinary achievement. Moreover, there were now far more non-union MPs on the Labour benches – about half the total – so that opponents could no longer claim that the Labour Party was simply a trade union pressure group. Certainly, it was becoming much more of a national party. In 1923 the Conservative Prime Minister, Stanley Baldwin, called an election, having unexpectedly declared in favour of modifying free trade and introducing some form of tariff reform. In the ensuing general election in December 1923 the Conservative Party was divided over the issue, while both the Liberals and the Labour Party still supported free trade. The Conservatives lost 88 seats, their numbers dropping to 258, while the Labour Party increased to 191, and the Liberals to 158. Baldwin then resigned, and as Labour was the bigger of the two opposition parties, and as Asquith, the Liberal leader, was prepared to support Labour in office, the Labour Party formed its first government in January 1924. It was an astonishing development. Its leader, Ramsay MacDonald, had failed to secure a seat in the 1918 election, due mainly to his opposition to the war, but had regained a place in the Commons in 1922. He was now

Prime Minister. No wonder J.R.Clynes, Lord Privy Seal, wrote later in his *Memoirs*:

> as we stood waiting for His Majesty, amid the gold and crimson of the Palace, I could not help marvelling at the strange turn of Fortune's wheel, which had brought MacDonald, the starveling clerk, Thomas the engine-driver, Henderson the foundry labourer, and Clynes, the millhand, to this pinnacle ...

It was indeed a remarkable business.

Since this is not a political history, the history of this government (and of other Labour governments as well) will not be examined in detail. It was hampered throughout, of course, by being a minority government, so that it could not afford to antagonise the Liberals if it wished to maintain a majority in the House; but in any case it was a government of moderates. Its greatest success was probably in foreign policy, where MacDonald took the post of Foreign Secretary as well as being premier. He chaired the London Conference of 1924 which revised the arrangements for German reparations in new proposals known as the Dawes Plan. He also extended diplomatic recognition to the Soviet Union, and proposed treaties which included financial assistance to the new socialist state. In home affairs, the most important reform was Wheatley's Housing Act (mentioned earlier on), while MacDonald was careful to keep the trade unions at a distance, even threatening to use troops when a docks strike broke out in January 1924. In financial matters, the Chancellor of the Exchequer, Philip Snowden, adopted ultra-conservative policies, abolishing the wartime McKenna import duties in favour of free trade.

The ministry lasted only nine months, and the end came when the Liberals, who had disliked MacDonald's overtures to Soviet Russia, sided with the Conservatives to outvote the government over a minor matter, the 'Campbell Case'. This case for sedition against a communist, J.R.Campbell, had been broken off for lack of evidence, but favouritism was alleged in the matter by the Opposition, who defeated the government in a vote of confidence. The general election which followed is remembered mainly for the most famous (or notorious) of all election scares – the Zinoviev Letter. This was supposed to be a secret letter from Zinoviev, President of the Third Communist International in Moscow, to the British Communist Party (formed 1920), containing instructions on how to spread communist ideas in Britain, especially in the armed forces and industry. Copies were obtained by the Foreign Office, and by the *Daily Mail*, who published it just before polling day. MacDonald gave instructions that its authenticity should be investigated, but otherwise does not seem to have taken it very seriously. How far it was really genuine, and how far a forgery intended to scare voters into voting Conservative, it is still difficult to say. Admittedly Labour lost seats (a drop from 191 to 151), but they actually increased their share of the popular vote from 30.7 per cent to 33.3 per cent. The Liberals suffered more severely, dropping from 158 to 42. The Conservatives did much better, increasing their numbers to 419. Baldwin thereupon resumed office as Prime Minister again. It was an honourable defeat for Labour.

Although the first Labour government did not achieve a great deal, historically it is of great importance in that it showed the electorate that Labour leaders, nearly all of working-class origin, were perfectly capable of ruling the country; and indeed of governing in the national interest, and not merely as the agents of the trade unions. Moreover, from now on it was clear that Labour had replaced the Liberals as one of the two great political parties. The moderation of their policies when in office showed that the electorate need not expect any great socialist reforms from a Labour government – the implementation of Clause Four was certainly not high on their agenda. So it might be expected that it would not be long before the voters would give Labour another chance to govern. Within five years, Labour were in office again.

In 1929 Labour won 288 seats in the general election, the Conservatives 260, and the Liberals 59. The Labour Party again formed a government under Ramsay MacDonald, with Snowden at the Exchequer and Arthur Henderson at the Foreign Office. It ended in complete disaster. The Wall Street crash in 1929 began a world depression which sent unemployment up to 2.5 million by the end of 1930. Jimmy Thomas, who as Lord Privy Seal was put in charge of the problem, proved utterly ineffective. The one member of the government with positive ideas on economic reform, Sir Oswald Mosley, resigned when his views were not accepted. In August 1931 the May Committee Report predicted a large government deficit, and recommended the traditional remedies of cuts in government spending and increased taxation. Its predictions were probably alarmist, but a run on gold began. The cabinet drew up a programme of economy cuts and increased taxes, at the same time seeking loans from abroad; but the New York bankers would lend only if the government cut expenditure drastically, including a 10 per cent cut in the dole. On this rock the cabinet foundered – eleven being for the cut, and nine against. MacDonald was convinced that there was no alternative to balancing the budget, cutting the dole and staying on the gold standard – a very conservative policy. He therefore handed in the resignation of his government to the King.

This was bad enough – the Labour government had manifestly proved unequal to the task of solving a financial crisis – but further blows to Labour pride were to follow. MacDonald was persuaded by the King, Baldwin and Samuel to stay on as Prime Minister of a National (that is, coalition) government which would put through the necessary reforms. As MacDonald noted laconically in his diary:

> – 10: King, Bal: Sam: Decided only Nat. Govt wd do to meet the crisis & on urgent request of all, I consented to continue as PM under safeguards written on a sheet which I have given to Ishbel [his daughter].
> – 12: Cabinet: Consternation when I reported . . .

Only three members of the original cabinet were prepared to continue in office – Snowden, Thomas and Sankey. They were joined by Baldwin and Samuel. The National government passed the cuts (including the cut in the dole), and in September went off the gold standard – the very thing which MacDonald had earlier refused to do, although urged to do so by J.M. Keynes, the economist. All the cuts were opposed by the Labour Party and the TUC. In October, a general election was held in which the so-called National government stood for election; the Labour Party refused to support it. The National government won the election with an overwhelming victory, gaining 556 seats. Labour seats dropped from 288 to 46 – a crushing defeat. Subsequently the three Labour members of the government either resigned or retired, and the Liberal members withdrew after the 1932 tariff reforms. Ramsay MacDonald was left as Prime Minister of a virtually Conservative government till his retirement in 1935. The débâcle was complete.

Traditionally, and indeed to the present day, Ramsay Mac-Donald has been regarded in Labour circles as the villain of the piece who was responsible not only for the collapse in 1931, but also for clinging to office, deserting his party and becoming a

Conservative in all but name. Attlee afterwards described his actions in 1931 as 'the greatest political betrayal in our annals'. At the time it was said that MacDonald had deliberately contrived the resignation of his government so as to bring about the creation of the National government. Sidney Webb wrote to a correspondent in September 1931:

> But we have reason to believe that JRM has had the idea of a 'National Govt' in his mind for some months at least. Underlying everything, there is the fact that he has come to dislike almost every section of the Labour Party, for one or other reason.

Webb's views were probably quite mistaken, but no doubt he was conveying them (to a rank-and-file party member) honestly enough. Certainly MacDonald's liking for mixing with the upper ranks of society also told against him. According to Snowden's memoirs, when Snowden remarked to him that he would find himself popular in strange quarters, MacDonald is said to have replied, 'gleefully rubbing his hands, "Yes, tomorrow every Duchess in London will be wanting to kiss me!"'

Yet much of this is besides the point. MacDonald genuinely believed he was putting the interests of his country before party, and that when the dust had settled he would be able to rejoin the party which had expelled him. He does not seem to have anticipated the general election, the continuance of the National government, and a further spell in office. As for his colleagues, at the time he thought they had deserted him, not the other way round. In his diary on 1 September he wrote:

> The desertion of colleagues and the flight of the Lab. Govt having grievous effect ... what a destruction of all we have done. Had the Govt done its duty there would have been little interruption in that work. They ran away & left everything unprotected.

However, he must share responsibility for the cabinet split in 1931, and he certainly and disastrously failed to take the party into his confidence. A further point is that he seems to have misunderstood the best way of tackling the economic crisis; but here (as one of his biographers has said), his economics were at fault, not his motives. To continue calling him a traitor to his party (and to the working classes) seems unjust, but such a judgement is a deeply ingrained element in Labour Party mythology, together with a belief that the crisis itself was cooked up by capitalist opponents of the government, a so-called 'bankers' ramp'. Undoubtedly MacDonald's services to the Labour Party and the Labour movement up to 1931 were great, yet his name is still execrated among the party faithful.

Another general election was held in 1935. Baldwin succeeded MacDonald as Prime Minister in that year, and the Conservatives won the election very comfortably, though Labour managed to recover their electoral strength by an increase in their number of seats from 46 to a much more respectable 154. Their new party leader was the quiet, essentially middle-class C.R. Attlee, MP for Limehouse, who had been educated at Haileybury and Oxford University. There was no further change in Labour's strength in the House of Commons before war came in 1939. So a good recovery had been made from the disaster of 1931, and seen in perspective the Labour Party had made great strides since 1918, replacing the Liberals as one of the two great political parties, drawing support from the middle classes as well as the working classes, and offering policies of moderate social reform to the electorate as a whole. At last the working classes had a well-established political party to represent them in parliament – though, as noted earlier, a substantial proportion remained politically faithful to the Conservative and Liberal parties.

Leisure Interests

For the majority of the working classes, leisure activities between the wars became more numerous and more varied as working hours were shortened, and real wages went up. Moreover, two major technological advances brought an enormous increase in off-duty pleasure: the advent of broadcasting, and the coming of the talking picture. Wireless had been used in a rudimentary way during the war as a means of communication, and in 1922 the British Broadcasting Company, a commercial venture, had been set up. In December 1926 the British Broadcasting Corporation, a new form of public utility, was established by royal charter, with the aim of providing not only entertainment but educative programmes as well. This meant that some of the programmes were very dull from the working-class point of view (or, rather, from the point of view of most of the working classes), but by the 1930s there were programmes of dance music (even an official BBC dance orchestra led

by Henry Hall), comedy shows, variety and music-hall programmes, sports commentaries and regular news bulletins in the
evening. A unique form of home entertainment came into existence; by 1939 the number of radio licences had risen to nearly nine
million. The earliest wirelesses were primitive affairs, which
required much tuning in, separate batteries and accumulators, and
earphones. By the thirties, they had built-in speakers, were plug-
ged into the mains, and often had cabinets made of the first widely
used plastic, bakelite. Although the first television transmissions
were made in 1936, the audience for them was tiny until the 1950s.

The second great technological advance came in 1927 with the
coming of the talkies. The cinema was already popular well before
this, but Al Jolson in the *Jazz Singer*, the first successful talking
picture, increased its appeal enormously. By the 1930s a vast new
entertainment industry had been created, centred on Hollywood,
where nearly all the films were made and the stars lived; the British
film industry was puny by comparison. A vast output of American
films flooded Britain – musicals (such as the classic Fred Astaire–
Ginger Rogers films), comedies, westerns, dramas, gangster and
prison films, Walt Disney cartoons. They were usually accompanied by a weekly newsreel – the Pathé Gazette, or the
Gaumont–British News. Great chains of new cinemas were
erected – the Odeon, ABC and Gaumont cinemas, which provided
programmes consisting of a major film, a supporting film, a newsreel, and sometimes advertisements and popular organ music, all
for less than a shilling in the cheapest seats, and all in warm and
comfortable surroundings (other older cinemas, often less
civilised, were called flea-pits). Faced with this, the music hall and
variety theatres suffered a rapid decline. Cinema attendances
reached extraordinary levels, and included Sunday opening in the
1930s (some cinemas even opened on Christmas Day); by 1937,
about twenty million went to the cinema weekly, and about a
quarter of these patrons went more than once a week (most cinemas
changed their programmes mid-week). Thus the working classes
saw a remarkable variety of American films, mostly depicting a way
of life entirely alien to their own. There were plenty of middle-class
critics who thought that the working classes would somehow be
corrupted by what they saw, but there is little or no evidence to
substantiate such fears. The weekly trip to the cinema was simply a
cheap and agreeable outing, enjoyed greatly by those who went
there (including courting couples, of course, even though they

sometimes saw rather less of the films than other patrons).

Other innovations include the cheap family motor car, though motor cars were confined mostly to the middle classes. Popular models included the tiny Baby Austin, the rather larger Morris Oxford and Morris Cowley, and the Ford Popular, which sold at about £100. Working people could not usually afford either to purchase or run cars, but some had motorcycles, and also motorcycle combinations (that is, with side-cars). The wider use of the motor cycle led to a new form of spectator sport, dirt-track or speedway racing, much patronised by the working classes. So was another form of outdoor, urban entertainment, greyhound racing on permanent, floodlit tracks, first introduced in 1926.

To turn to other, more traditional forms of leisure activity outside the home: the public house retained its popularity, and larger, more luxurious public houses were built in urban areas, often with an eye on middle-class custom. The ordinary working-class pub was still the meeting place for working men's clubs and friendly societies, for games of dominoes, shove ha'penny, darts and (to a decreasing degree) skittles. Drunkenness decreased between the wars, and the consumption of beer actually fell, as did the number of licences issued. The wartime restrictions on opening hours were continued in peacetime, and contributed perhaps to the decrease in drunkenness. One other outdoor activity which retained and in fact increased its popularity was attending professional football matches. Leading footballers began to acquire a national popularity, though still paid little more than skilled workmen. Amateur football and cricket still had many participants, of course. Cycling was very popular, too, with local clubs organising speed trials in the early morning before traffic became troublesome. Rambling and country walking (hiking) attracted many younger people, and the Youth Hostel Association (the YHA) was founded in 1930. The railways continued to run day excursions, but now had to face the competition of trips organised by charabanc or motor-coach firms. For workers in the great conurbations, a Saturday or Sunday trip to a local park or beauty spot on the motor omnibuses which were beginning to replace trams could be a cheap and agreeable afternoon out. Some (but a diminishing number) still made their principal Sunday excursion to church or chapel.

Finally, the home remained the centre for simple relaxation, with the radio being the most important additional form of amusement. The piano was not yet entirely displaced, and sheet music of popular songs still sold well (and were kept in the piano stool). Everywhere, men and women smoked; more cigarettes, but less pipe tobacco. Beer was drunk at home, from bottles, not cans. Cards were played. Outside in the street, betting slips were passed, but betting shops were illegal. A new form of betting, on the football pools, came in, with ten million customers by 1938. In 1937 there was a special mail train from Liverpool to Birmingham each week carrying 235,000 football coupons for the Birmingham area. Newspaper reading increased, the Labour *Daily Herald* having a circulation of two million. The *Daily Mirror* became a tabloid in 1934, though the popular press was less sensational than at the present day. At home, racing pigeons or whippets were still kept out at the back, and often a scrap of garden was maintained – more would be available for a council house, of course. Saturday night was still the great night out, at the pub, cinema or club, or, for the younger folk, at the dance hall. Traditional patterns of leisure thus continued, though the radio and the cinema helped to make for a greater element of professional, mass entertainment and perhaps for a greater uniformity in the enjoyment of leisure than before the Great War.

Between the Wars: Some Conclusions

Twenty years is not a long period, even in the twentieth century, to identify significant and permanent changes in the lives of the working classes of England, but it seems undeniable that important changes did take place between the wars. Although millions suffered the dreariness of life on the dole, and although many on the left argued that the whole capitalist system, which was the root cause of unemployment, was about to crack up, just as Marx had predicted, in fact for those in work, capitalism provided a higher standard of living. Critics like Orwell either ignored manifestations of increased consumer spending or brushed them aside, as we have seen, as cheap luxuries which kept the masses quiet but had no other significance. For Orwell, there was a stark choice between socialism and fascism, and unless more people accepted socialism, fascism would triumph:

> Socialism, at least in this island, does not smell any longer of revolution and the overthrow of tyrants; it smells of crankishness, machine worship, and the stupid cult of

Russia. Unless you can remove that smell, and very rapidly, Fascism may win.

In fact, fascism did not win in this island, and the majority of the working classes between the wars enjoyed a more leisured and a more civilised mode of existence, especially in the 1930s, whatever was happening in political life. As a whole, and with the exceptions already noted, the working classes were experiencing increasing prosperity when war came again in September 1939.

Chapter 2

The Second World War

A People's War

All modern wars are People's Wars, in the sense that wars are no longer fought between professional armies meeting each other in pitched battles, the names of which are later enshrined in the textbooks – one thinks, for example, of the great eighteenth-century battles such as Marlborough's Blenheim, Ramillies, Oudenarde and Malplaquet. Today's wars involve conscript armies and all those unfortunate civilians who get in the way of the fighting, or have their houses and possessions destroyed by one side or the other, whether it is in, say, Vietnam or Afghanistan. Yet some eminent historians, and in particular A. J. P. Taylor, have described the British participation in the Second World War as a 'People's War'. The term seems to have been used first in left-wing periodicals in the dark days of 1940, but after the war was widely used by historians writing about this period. If this is an appropriate description, then it must be assumed that the war had special characteristics which distinguish it from other wars; and indeed the Second World War does form a very important episode in the history of the working classes. It is not simply a matter of the extent of casualties – they were far fewer in the second war than in the first war, and in fact were extremely limited for the first three years. In what ways then can the use of the term 'People's War' be justified?

The answer lies in a number of unique features of the Second World War. In the first place, conscription for men applied from the very beginning – conscription had actually been imposed some months before war was declared in September 1939. Women were also conscripted from 1941 onwards – single women between nineteen and twenty-four, and later, from eighteen and a half to fifty – though they were given the choice between serving in the women's services, in civil defence, or in essential civilian jobs. By the end of the war, nearly half a million women were serving in the women's forces (the ATS, WAAF and WRNS), while five million men were in the men's forces. So, for the first time in the country's history, both men and women were called up for military service. Secondly, after the disaster of Dunkirk (which the nation contrived to treat almost as a victory, perhaps because the army was extricated almost intact, and the casualties were relatively light), national unity increased with the realisation that only the British remained to fight Germany. An extraordinary mood, almost of elation, seemed to grip the nation. Thirdly, this mood was intensified after the Battle of Britain and the bombing of London and other cities, when it became apparent that the German daylight attack had been beaten off, and that the night bombing raids were also failing to force the nation into submission. In the phraseology of the time, London could take it, and so could the provincial cities. When Hitler prophesied that he would wring Britain's neck like the neck of a chicken, Churchill remarked, 'Some neck, some chicken . . .' For these reasons alone, the war seemed to involve everyone, and the mood of national unity and comradeship was strengthened as a result. As for actual opposition to the war, it was very limited. Over the six years, 2,900 conscientious objectors were given complete exemption, and 40,000 conditional exemption. By summer 1940, only 0.5 per cent of those registering for service were COs. Some prosecutions were also undertaken for spreading alarm and despondency, but these were very few and far between.

In contrast to what happened during the first war, there was none of the feeling that fighting was going on in appalling conditions overseas, while those at home in England went on relatively comfortably with their lives, some of them actually making fat profits from munitions. In fact, in the Second World War there was more action on the home front after Dunkirk than abroad for at least a year; in the first three years of war, more women and children were killed than soldiers. The civilian population was really in the front line at this time, and were to suffer further attacks from the air even after D-Day on 6 June 1944. It should also be said that from 1942 onwards following the publication of the Beveridge Report, there was continual discussion of what reforms were necessary after the war. This discussion was positively encouraged by the Army Bureau of Current Affairs, which issued valuable newsheets relating both to military developments and to reform proposals such as the Beveridge Report itself; there were even compulsory weekly discussions among the troops. Forces newspapers were published in the different theatres of war, for example, *SEAC*, for the South-East Asia Command. Towards the end of the war, Brains Trusts and Forces Parliaments kept discussion going on post-war reforms (the Cairo Forces Parliament is a famous example). In all these ways, ordinary people were made to feel that they were not being ignored, and that the winning of the war would not mean a return to the dole queue, but to a better life all round. This belief was also encouraged by the presence of leading Labour politicians in the wartime coalition government – Clement Attlee was deputy Prime Minister, Ernest Bevin was Minister of Labour and Herbert Morrison was Home Secretary, all of whom acquired valuable experience of office, and enhanced their image in the public eye.

For all these reasons, the idea that the Second World War was a People's War has substance. Of course, class distinction did not vanish overnight, especially in the services, where it was deeply entrenched in the hierarchy of ranks. Most officers spoke with recognisably middle-class accents; George Orwell, the Old Etonian, wrote defensively before the war about his own accent, and of the need for the middle classes to join forces with the working classes: 'and probably when we get there it will not be so dreadful as we feared, for after all, we have nothing to lose but our aitches'. A very different kind of writer, Evelyn Waugh, was also well aware of differences in speech between the classes. He antagonised his men on parade by mocking their accents and their inarticulacy (he was a brave but very poor officer). His post-war trilogy of novels about the war made it clear that the life of an officer in a traditional regiment was still worlds apart from the lives of the rank and file. Nevertheless, at home in Britain the universal belief in the need to defeat the Nazis formed a strong unifying bond, together with the comradeship forged during the air raids and at work, and the equality of sacrifice enforced by rationing and restrictions and shortages of all kinds. This applied especially in the critical period 1940–1, the

'Finest Hour', as Taylor has called it. Mysteriously and unexpectedly, for a time the British of all classes talked to each other and became a united people; and so it was indeed a 'People's War'.

Military Service

Military service in the Second World War was different from service in the previous war, which was so heavily concentrated on trench warfare in France. At first, there was very little fighting. The great defensive fortifications of the Maginot and Siegfried Lines seemed to rule out any major advance by either side, in spite of the cheery optimism of the popular song of the time:

> We're going to hang out the washing on the Siegfried Line
> Have you any dirty washing, mother dear?

When the Germans attacked through Holland and Belgium in May 1940, it was soon over with the French and British armies. The British Expeditionary Force was evacuated from Dunkirk, having suffered casualties during May and June of 68,111 – a serious loss, but not much more than the total casualties of the first day of the Battle of the Somme in 1916. Thereafter British troops were not to enter France again in force until D-Day in 1944. Meanwhile they were in action from 1941 onwards in North Africa against the Italians and then the Germans, and then again against the Japanese in Burma. There was also continuous fighting at sea to keep open lines of communication and supply, especially across the Atlantic (the Battle of the Atlantic); and after the Battle of Britain in September 1940 there was an ever increasing bomber offensive against Germany. This was in remarkable contrast to the policy adopted before the fall of France, when the RAF dropped propaganda leaflets on Germany, not bombs. Taylor has it that the Secretary for Air, Sir Kingsley Wood, was horrified by the suggestion that German forests should be set on fire: 'Are you aware that it is private property? Why, you will be asking me to bomb Essen next.' In the course of time, Essen was duly bombed, many times. The war experience of the working classes in the services was gained therefore in a number of different theatres of war, and thus was intensely varied, with the RAF playing a far greater part than in the First World War.

It would be impossible, of course, to sum up those experiences in a few sentences. In the army, there was of necessity much training and bullshit ('If it moves, salute it; if it doesn't, paint it') before fighting began again in Africa, Italy and Burma. In Africa, the predominant memory of many is of heat, flies, sand and tank battles of unprecedented dimensions. In Burma, there was again the heat, the jungle and a peculiarly ferocious and cruel enemy. At sea, the war meant the constant danger of attack from the air or from German U-boats, especially on the notorious convoys to Murmansk. War in the air brought its own hazards of destruction by enemy aircraft or anti-aircraft fire, or of limping home sometimes mortally wounded. The casualty rate of bomber aircrew was extraordinarily high, at least as high as that of officers in the trenches in the Great War, when life expectation was limited to a few weeks. For those on active service in all branches of the forces, ways of getting killed were infinitely various: one could be shot, blown up, drowned, roasted alive in tank or aircraft, or starved or beaten to death as a prisoner of war of the Japanese (those imprisoned by the Germans stood a rather better chance of survival). These horrors are still vivid memories of ex-servicemen alive today. Yet, even in the services, many were lucky enough to escape actual combat, and may even be said to have had 'a good war': office workers and administrative staff, technicians and skilled workers, even ground crew on air force stations in this country (understandably, aircrews sometimes tended to regard ground staff as mere civilians). In these many different ways, experiences in the six years of the Second World War form an imperishable part of the social history of the working classes. The names of those who were killed are to be found on war memorials up and down the country, and on the gravestones of the war cemeteries in France and further afield. About 300,000 were killed in the armed forces, together with 35,000 in the merchant navy.

Air Raids and the Blitz

Before 1939 it was anticipated that in any future war the casualties resulting from air raids would be very heavy. The general public was aware of the destruction wrought by bombing in the Spanish Civil War, especially at Guernica, and the air-raid scenes in the film version of H. G. Wells' *Shape of Things to Come* contributed to the fear of aerial attack. The government itself grossly overestimated the number of hospital beds necessary to accommodate air-raid victims – the official figure was from one million to three million beds, with 600,000 dead and 1.2 million injured in the first sixty days – and this helps to explain why a massive evacuation scheme was prepared well before the war. As a consequence, about a million and a half children, together with mothers under five, were moved principally from the cities to safer areas, usually in the countryside. An additional two million evacuated themselves unofficially when war was declared. The expected air raids did not materialise. A million soon returned home in the early months of the war, but moved out again when raids began in the summer of 1940. Later on in the war as the scale of attack diminished, increasing numbers went home once more. The impression made on middle-class families by some of the evacuees from the worst city slums was quite shattering. Some of these children were dirty and verminous, wet their beds, and defecated and urinated in the corners of rooms. These habits provoked much middle-class comment. However, the vast majority of children were better behaved than this, and most working-class children went to working-class families where settling in was not too difficult. How far the children benefited on balance from their change of environment is difficult to say. No doubt some found separation from their parents traumatic, others adapted themselves quite quickly. In any case, only a minority spent any length of time away from home. The effect of evacuation and of air raids on the education of the children who stayed behind will be considered later in this chapter.

Large-scale raids began on London in September following the defeat of the German daylight raids in the Battle of Britain. Raids took place every night from 7 September to 2 November 1940. Up to 13 November, about 200 tons of bombs were dropped every night by about 160 bombers, together with 182 cannisters of incendiaries, each containing approximately seventy-two fire-bombs. Some nights were worse than others, for example, on 15 October when the moon was full, 410 bombers dropped 538 tons, killing 400 and starting 900 fires in London. This was the London Blitz ('Blitz' being short for *Blitzkreig*, or 'lightning war'). At the end of the year on Sunday, 29 December 1940, a great fire-bomb attack on the City of London started 1,500 fires, wiped out much of the Cripplegate area of London Wall, and cleared the ground for the post-war architectural horrors of the Barbican. The raid ended about midnight with a substantial part of the City of London well alight. Not many lived in the area save caretakers, and considering the size of the conflagration the mortality figures were relatively limited, 163 were killed. Meanwhile in November other cities were attacked, such as Coventry, which on 14 November was subjected to ten hours of bombing, with 554 deaths and 865 seriously injured. Ports were attacked next, including Merseyside, Bristol, Southampton, Portsmouth and Plymouth. The raids eased during January and February 1941, but were stepped up again with the coming of spring. London had its worst attack on 10 May 1941 when 1,436 were killed and 1,792 seriously injured. Some relief came when in June 1941 Hitler invaded Russia, and the Blitz came to an end for the time being.

Undoubtedly London took the most severe battering during the height of the Blitz, and the East End (where the docks were situated) was hit far harder than the West End. The East End is still a largely working-class area (apart from middle-class yuppie intrusion into new housing in the docks area), and the workers suffered far worse than the inhabitants of the West End, most of whom could afford to evacuate themselves into the country. The East Enders had first to undergo the ordeal of a prolonged daylight raid on the docks on 7 September 1940 which cost 430 civilian lives. Within the next two months or so, four out of ten houses in Stepney were damaged or destroyed. When a small bomb fell on Buckingham Palace, it was positively welcomed by the King, George VI, who said that he could now look the East Enders in the face. But other cities also suffered serious raids. Coventry and the ports have just been mentioned. Raids began on Birmingham in August 1940, and there were four major raids – on 19 November, about 400 killed; 22 November, 113 killed; 11 December, 263 killed; and on 9 April 1941 there were 1,121 killed. So although London understandably figures large in accounts of the Blitz, other cities took their share of the bombing as well.

How did the urban working classes respond to all this? At the time, everyone had his own bomb story; often they were of extraordinary adventures, many macabre in nature, but some humorous enough. In fact, the story of the Blitz is the story of co-operative effort, of high courage and sometimes heroic self-sacrifice by men and women of many different groups – air-raid wardens, bomb-disposal units, heavy rescue squads, firemen, policemen and ambulancemen. In addition, there were many volunteer workers, mostly in the Civil Defence service, together with fire watchers, Home Guard units, the Women's Voluntary Service and the Salvation Army. It is this co-operation by ordinary folk which really justifies the term a 'People's War'. Panic was rare, and though lack of sleep and continuous tension took their toll, psychological breakdown was also uncommon. In Birmingham, the Child Guidance Clinic Report for 1940 noted that the strain of war had not caused any noticeable increase in neurosis and maladjustment, but that greater excitability and aggressive behaviour had been noticed following air raids, together with diminished powers of memory and concentration as measured by mental tests. This was only to be expected. Nationally, the suicide rate fell, and the figures for drunkenness were reduced by more than half between 1939 and 1942. Some looting occurred during and after raids, but not on an extensive scale.

As for actual protection against bombing, in the course of time many local authorities provided shelters in parks and other public places, but during night-time raids most people simply stayed in their own homes, on the ground floor or under the stairs or, if there was a garden, in the metal Anderson shelter, dug well in, and covered with earth or sandbags (such shelters were extremely cold and damp in the winter-time). House windows were covered in sticky tape as a precaution against flying glass, which was always a major hazard; glaziers plied a roaring trade during the Blitz. By midsummer 1941 an indoor shelter (the Morrison) became available: it resembled a steel table with a heavy top and lattice-work sides, and would comfortably accommodate a mattress and bedclothes inside. In central London, seventy-nine Underground stations were open all night for shelter, and by the end of September 1940 177,000 people were sleeping in them, fascinating the sculptor Henry Moore, who made many drawings of their shrouded forms. Not all stations were deep enough to be bomb-proof. In October 1940 four stations suffered hits in three nights. In January 1941 the Bank Station received a direct hit, and 111 were killed – the worst incident of its kind in the war.

Sometimes, after what Churchill called the 'banshee wailing' of the sirens had sounded the alert, there could be long periods of strained boredom when nothing seemed to be happening locally, until at last the all-clear sounded. More often, even before the sound of approaching aircraft could be heard, there would begin the stupendous racket of nearby anti-aircraft fire, then the whine and explosion of bombs, and the clatter of shell fragments from above. Incendiaries glowed with a peculiarly vivid white light, roads ran with water from smashed hydrants and leaking firehoses, and were frequently blocked by falling masonry. Glass crunched underfoot, and the air was full of the acrid smell of burning. Then there was the digging out of the dead and injured. Grotesque and even comic happenings abounded, such as in north London, where the lady of the house was taking a bath when the house was hit by a bomb, reducing much of it to rubble, but leaving the bath suspended on high by its water pipes with the lady still in it ... By June 1941 when Hitler attacked Russia, more than two million houses had been damaged, 60 per cent of these being in London. By the end of the war, the total had risen to 3.75 million, while only one in ten houses in central London had not been damaged. The number of deaths from bombing in 1940 and 1941 was 43,000; the final total for the war came to 60,000, nearly half of these deaths being in London. In addition, about 86,000 were seriously injured, and 151,000 had minor injuries.

However, the war against Russia did not mean that the Germans abandoned the Blitz completely. In January 1944, raids recommenced, and London was again hit, together with Hull, Bristol and South Wales. D-Day in June 1944 brought the hope that bomber raids would be discontinued, but meanwhile home radar stations had been given warning of a new pilotless flying bomb shortly to be launched by the Germans. Precisely a week after D-Day, the first flying bomb (the V1) exploded in England. The amount of fuel carried limited their range to London and the home counties, and it was the south and east London boroughs which suffered most, Croydon most of all; 142 flying bombs fell on this borough, destroying over 1,000 houses. Another mass evacuation took place from London, nearly a million and a half going by the end of August. Meanwhile, every effort was made to destroy the bombs (nicknamed 'doodle-bugs' by the long-suffering Londoners) at the coast before they penetrated inland. AA guns were moved to the Channel, the latest and fastest aircraft were used to attack the bombs in mid-air, and the balloon barrage round London was greatly strengthened. Gradually, the new threat was mastered. By August, eight out of ten were being destroyed. Duncan Sandys, in charge of operations against the V1, declared on 7 September that 'The Battle of London is now over, except possibly for a last few shots'.

In fact, this rather underestimated the number of shots still available – a further seventy-nine V1s were launched on London in the following seven months – and the day after Duncan Sandys' statement, the first V2 fell on London. This was a large rocket which weighed fourteen tons; by November, six rockets a day were landing on London, a total of 518 in all. These were a far more serious threat than the V1s because it was impossible to intercept them, and they caused tremendous damage. Four rockets alone landing in Croydon damaged 2,000 houses. They travelled faster than sound, so unlike the V1, they gave no warning of their descent. Doodle-bugs were appropriately named: their engines gave out a droning note, and when the sound stopped, the bomb fell and it was time to take cover. V2s, on the other hand, approached silently, then exploded on impact with an enormous crash. They killed 2,724 and badly injured more than 6,000. The only way of stopping them was to capture the launching sites, and this was not achieved till the spring of 1945. The last V2 fell on Orpington on 27 March 1945.

There is no doubt that the four years or so of the Blitz constitute a unique episode not only in the history of the working classes, but in that of the nation as a whole. Few if any historians have attempted any major revision of accepted interpretations of this period, although perhaps it should be pointed out that the Germans also remained remarkably steadfast under sustained allied bombing, some of which – for example, the bombing of Dresden at the end of the war – reached heights of horror never experienced here. Nevertheless, a people had been put to the test, and had not been found wanting. There were, of course, grumbles about the inadequacy of ARP (Air-Raid Precautions), especially in the early days. The British always grumble. All the same, the unity which had been achieved among all classes during the Blitz contributed greatly to the general determination to create a better society after the war.

Life at Work

Meanwhile, war production was as essential as it had been during the First World War. Hours lengthened in the factories, especially after Dunkirk, and great emphasis was placed on aircraft production. A new Ministry for Aircraft Production was headed by the dynamic newspaper proprietor Lord Beaverbrook. Bombing naturally interrupted production, but to a lesser extent than was feared. Dummy factories were sometimes obligingly erected for the Germans to bomb. Women's employment increased considerably, especially on munitions (7,000 employed in 1939; 260,000 in October 1944), but also in engineering and vehicle building (the proportion of women employed went up from 9 per cent to 34 per cent), and in commerce as well (33 per cent to 62 per cent). Little progress was made towards equal pay. In metal work and engineering, women's pay was only half that of the men in January 1944. Feminism and women's lib had yet to be invented.

The control and direction of labour was also inevitable in the light of the experiences of the First World War. The Emergency Powers (Defence) Act of 1940 provided for the issue of a special regulation, Defence Regulation 58A, which gave wide powers of control to the Minister of Labour, Ernest Bevin. Under Order 1305, strikes and lock-outs were made illegal, while wage disputes were to go to a National Arbitration Tribunal, which had issued 816 adjudications by the end of the war. The Restriction on Engagement Order of 1940 permitted the engagement of labour only through an approved trade union or a labour exchange. Lastly, the Essential Work (General Provisions) Order, March 1941, controlled the employment of skilled labour. Once in a specified skilled job, the worker was not permitted to leave it, though his wages and working conditions were subject to government regulation. Through these major instruments of control, the worker's freedom to work where he wished was fettered. In theory, at least, he was subject to more regimentation and restrictions than his opposite number in Germany. He was obliged always to carry his Identity Card, of course. There does not seem to have been much complaint about these regulations and restrictions, which were accepted as part of the price which had to be paid for winning the war.

The government also tried to maintain good relations in industry in the interests of maximum production. At the top there were Regional Boards of Industry established in 1941, together with a Ministry of Production; and in 1942 a National Production Advisory Council. Lower down there were Joint Production Committees on which workers were represented – about 3.5 million were so represented by 1945. Wages were still left to free negotiation, but here and there they were so low that the government had to intervene. Thus in 1940 the Central Agricultural Wages Board was set up to fix minimum wages for male farm workers, and in 1943 the Catering Wages Commission was established under the Catering Wages Act of that year. In 1945 the existing trades boards were converted into wages boards with wider powers. Welfare provisions improved in factories with the appointment of welfare officers where more than 250 workers were employed. More factory doctors and nurses were appointed (in 1939, there were 35 whole-time and 70 part-time factory doctors, increasing by 1944 to 181 whole-time and 890 part-time; factory nurses were 1,500 strong in 1939, and 8,000 by 1943). Entertainment was provided in the midday dinner hour, the shows being broadcast in 'Workers' Play-time', and special half-hour programmes of popular music were broadcast twice a day with the title 'Music While You Work'.

For some time after Dunkirk, there was little need to enforce work discipline: the problem was rather to stop workers from overworking and collapsing from exhaustion. Unemployment dropped to remarkably low levels. In June 1943 the highest number of registered unemployed was 112,000. Later on, though il-legal, strikes became more frequent – in 1943, there were 1,783 (1.8 million days lost), and in 1944, 2,194 (3.7 million working days lost). But the trouble was largely in the mining industry (miners were exempt from military service and there was a labour shortage) where half the national number of working days were lost in 1943, and two-thirds in 1944. Most of the difficulties in the mining indus-try arose over low piece-rates which were not adjusted by the owners as prices rose. Strikes did not usually last long – in the engineering and associated industries, 90 per cent of all strikes in 1943 and 1944 lasted for less than a week. Prosecutions for striking were possible in theory, of course, but throughout the entire war, there were only seventy-one prosecutions in Scotland, and thirty-eight in England and Wales. In 1944 there were only three pro-secutions in all in England and Wales, and fines of £5 were usual rather than the maximum of £25. All in all, labour relations seem to have been good, with less of the ill-feeling which arose towards the end of the previous war. Odd incidents still occurred, of course: in Coventry, a worker was dismissed for refusing to call the manager 'Mr'. The incident led to a bitter strike. Service technicians were sent on detachment from the RAF to help repair radio equipment in the EMI Works at Hayes, Middlesex; the trade unions raised no objections, and the young airmen were welcomed enthusiastically by the female workers. As in the First World War, trade union membership rose as unemployment was reduced to vanishing point: in 1938 membership was 6.05 million, rising to 8.07 million in 1944. It fell to 7.87 million in 1945, but rose again to 8.8 million in 1946. The co-operation of the unions was essential if maximum production was to be achieved, and they were represented on the Regional Boards for Industry, on the National Production Advisory Council, and on the joint production committees. As noted earlier, they also profited from having Labour Party leaders in senior ministerial posts, while the foremost trade unionist of the time, Ernest Bevin, was Minister for Labour.

Day-to-Day Living

The working classes as a whole were probably too busy to take much notice of what was happening to the standard of living, but their day-to-day observation told them that the working day had become longer, and that the shops were growing emptier. Rationing of essential foods began in 1940, and other foodstuffs and clothing went on the ration in the next year (on 'points', which were more flexible than 'coupons'). Petrol was also restricted to essential users, which affected the middle classes rather than the working classes. By mid-1941, personal consumption was down by 14 per cent on pre-war spending, and less was being spent on everything except beer, tobacco, the cinema and public transport. One major wartime social problem was the plight of those rendered homeless by bombing. It was estimated that for every civilian killed, thirty-five were made homeless.

Yet a leaner, fitter Britain seemed to have been the result of all the shortages. Certainly health statistics appear to bear this out. Infant mortality figures declined from fifty-six per 1,000 live births in England in 1936–8 to forty-five in 1944–6. The government provided cheap milk for younger children and expectant mothers, who were also supplied with orange juice, cod-liver oil, vitamins and an extra egg ration. At work, factory workers could have a hot midday meal in the canteen. The government encouraged people to grow their own vegetables (the slogan was 'Dig for Victory'), and supplied recipes for cheap and nourishing meals. There was a maximum charge of five shillings on all meals in public restaurants. Local authorities themselves opened 'British Restaurants', cheap eating places with the emphasis on plain but wholesome meals. Personal consumption probably levelled out at about the pre-war, skilled-artisan level, which meant a distinct rise in consumption for unskilled workers. Medical care also improved with the further development of blood transfusion, penicillin and the sulphonamide drugs, and improvements in plastic surgery.

As for the cost of living, there was a rise of about 50 per cent by 1944, and money wages rose less than this, but nevertheless, real wages rose very considerably, by over 81 per cent. This was because of longer and more regular hours, and in particular because of overtime worked, week-end work and more piecework. The figures tell their own story, as can be seen from Table 2.1 below. It should be noted that the cost-of-living figures are an adjustment to the official figures, which substantially underestimated the true rise in the cost of living. An important consideration here is that rents were frozen from 1939 onwards. Women's wage rates rose more than men's, but, as noted earlier, were often only half the men's rate.

Table 2.1   Wages and the Cost of Living, 1935–45

Year	Wage rates (September 1938 = 100)	Cost of living (1938 = 100)	Weekly earnings (October 1938 = 100)
1939	104	102.5	–
1940	113–14	120	130
1941	122	135	142
1942	131–2	143	160
1943	136–7	146	176
1944	143–4	150	181.5
1945	150–1	–	180.5

Source: Sidney Pollard, *The Development of the British Economy, 1914–1980* (3rd edn, 1983).

The weekend still remained the most important part of the week for relaxation, and both professional cricket and football continued. Rather remarkably, the attendance at Lord's in 1943 was less than a third below its peacetime figure in 1939. Professional football suffered particularly from having players called up for military service. The most striking illustration of this was a match played between Brighton & Hove Albion and Norwich City. Brighton fielded a side consisting of five Brighton players, two Norwich reserves and four soldiers who volunteered from the crowd. Norwich won 18–0. Greyhound racing continued, while amateur football and cricket were still played, of course. Service sides were powerfully augmented by professionals who had been called up. Outside the home, the cinema remained the most popular form of entertainment, and most army and air force camps had their own cinemas. Attendances rose to new heights; weekly attendances were between twenty-five and thirty millions. Three-quarters of the entire adult population went regularly to the cinema. However, the pub continued to be the working man's club, though it had to struggle with shortages of beer, weaker brews and a changing clientele, often including Polish, American and Dominions servicemen. The Americans in particular had to adjust themselves to strange new social customs. At first, they were popularly thought of as being 'over-paid, over-sexed and over here', but both sides made allowances, and eventually a number of US servicemen returned home with GI brides. American troops were certainly popular with children, who badgered them for chocolate and chewing gum – 'Got any gum, chum?' A new local social centre was provided by the Civil Defence Centre where air-raid wardens and firewatchers would meet, drink tea and play darts or cards between raids.

At home, the radio remained the supreme form of entertainment, supplying regular news bulletins, sometimes including eyewitness accounts from the main theatres of war, and even a famous BBC report made direct from a bombing raid over Germany. The radio also provided talks and discussions, the best-known discussion programme being the *Brains Trust*, dating from January 1941, in which a panel of experts answered listeners' questions. There was also a number of comedy shows, the most famous being *ITMA* ('It's That Man Again'), the man in question being Tommy Handley, a brisk and cheerful Liverpudlian comedian, assisted by a variety of weird and comic characters, such as Funf (a mysterious, Germanic character), the bibulous Colonel Chinstrap ('I don't mind if I do'), the Diver ('Don't forget the diver, sir'), Mrs Mopp, the cleaner ('Can I do yer now, sir'), and the lugubrious Mona Lot ('It's being so cheerful that keeps me going . . .'). There were other comedy programmes such as *Hi Gang* and *Variety Bandbox*, but *ITMA* reigned supreme until Handley's untimely death in 1945. A. J. P. Taylor has remarked that Handley deserved but did not receive a place in Westminster Abbey.

Popular dance music with its catchy tunes and simple lyrics continued to be the ordinary man's and woman's music on the radio, much of it still imported from America, and one American swing band in particular became a great favourite – Glen Miller and his orchestra. Record-request programmes such as *Forces Favourites* were very popular, and one British singer of sentimental ballads was in great demand throughout the war – Vera Lynn. Her two great hits were 'The White Cliffs of Dover' and 'We'll Meet Again'. In the latter, she spoke for many parted by the war:

> We'll meet again
> Don't know where, don't know when
> But I know we'll meet again
> Some sunny day . . .
>
> Keep smiling through
> Just as you always do
> Till the dark clouds roll away . . .

In a well-known passage in a pre-war play, Noël Coward has one of his characters comment on the 'potency of cheap music'. Vera Lynn expressed the feelings of millions of ordinary men and women in the simple lyrics of these songs.

The government was not unaware of the need to encourage an interest in the fine arts, and CEMA (Council for Education in Music and the Arts) arranged concerts of classical music and exhibitions of the visual arts. Tours by the Old Vic and by opera and ballet companies such as the Sadlers Wells Ballet Company and the Marie Rambert Ballet were also sponsored. Lunch-time chamber music concerts were held in the National Gallery, even during the Blitz. Much of this had only a limited appeal to working-class audiences, but some were attracted to new artistic experiences hitherto thought beyond them. For those who wanted something lighter, there were still the survivors of the variety stage such as Robb Wilton (traditional northern comedian), 'Hutch' (ballad singer), Clapham and Dwyer (comedians) and Max Miller (comedian, specialising in smutty material). Dance halls were still extremely popular, usually very crowded and very hot, once the black-outs were up. For the services themselves, the government set up a new organisation providing light entertainment – Entertainments National Service Association, usually known as ENSA. These initials were also said to stand for 'Every Night Something Awful'. In fact, ENSA did sterling work not only in garrison theatres at home and abroad, but also in hospitals and convalescent homes for the forces.

All in all, daily life on the home front was often monotonous and drab, especially after the euphoria of 1940–1 had faded away, the Russians and Americans had come into the war, but victory still seemed far off. The promised Second Front in France was not opened till June 1944. Even when the Germans were at last driven back in Europe, and a limited degree of street lighting was permitted after so many years of black-out, Londoners found themselves assailed by V1s and V2s. In these circumstances, some form of relaxation and entertainment was essential. Above all else, the radio and the cinema provided what was wanted, together with a host of stage performers of many different kinds. After the war, a new form of popular entertainment was to become established, with momentous consequences for the whole of show business – television; but during the Second World War, its time was yet to come.

Schooling in Wartime

For most of the working classes, schooling before 1944 still meant an elementary education between the ages of five and fourteen, often in the same building throughout, passing from Infants to Juniors and then on to the Senior Department. Only a minority had places in a separate secondary school. All classes of schools were severely disrupted by evacuation in the early months of the war. City schools were mostly closed completely at first, but were reopened in stages on a basis of voluntary attendance as the expected bombing failed to materialise. Meanwhile, shelters were hurriedly erected in playgrounds, and the schools themselves sometimes had rooms taken over for use as First-Aid Posts, Air-Raid Warden Posts, and even for the billeting of soldiers. Away from home, evacuated children had to adapt themselves to new and strange surroundings in the reception areas. In fact, increasing numbers returned home by the end of 1939 – 344,900 of the 764,000 originally evacuated. In the cities, there was a great deal of uncertainty as to future plans. Many authorities continued to implement plans for Home Teaching – the teaching of small groups of children in the home, in church halls and elsewhere, the idea being to avoid bringing children together in large numbers. Early in 1940, the government at last began to enquire into the national situation. A nationwide survey in January showed that of the 1,493,967 elementary-school children, only 47 per cent were attending school. Another 24 per cent were in Home Teaching classes, and 27.9 per cent were not being taught at all. Another survey in March disclosed that the number of children receiving full-time elementary education varied from place to place. In Birmingham the figure was 74.5 per cent, but in Liverpool only 24.4 per cent, and in Manchester 23.6 per cent. The government thereupon made it known that all attendance might be made compulsory from the beginning of April 1940. Thus, after seven months of war, the government at last attempted to get back to normal and enforce attendance.

Unfortunately, within a few months, bombing attacks began, and a further evacuation of children took place. Many city parents chose to keep their children with them, however, so that for the next year or so, most school children shared the perils of the raids with their parents. The effects of the bombing varied from place to place, of course, but damage to schools was often extensive. To take Birmingham as an example: following the heavy raid of 22 November 1940, the local Inspector, a Mr F.T. Arnold, wrote to his superiors at the Board of Education (safely ensconced in Bournemouth) to tell them that 75 per cent of the schools had been closed, mainly because of the failure of the water supply over two-thirds of the city. 'About 40 schools have received heavy damage, most of them direct hits. About another 100 have received minor damage.' Arnold seems to have been exhausted by the strain of the bombing. He concluded gloomily: 'To sum up: the educational machine as it was functioning up to Nov. 20th has been smashed beyond repair. An emergency machine will have to be created.'

Thus, in the period of heaviest bombing, the school system was under great pressure. So were the children, who nightly suffered loss of sleep from the raids. This applied equally to teachers. In addition to their daily duties, they were also required to do their share of fire-watching; they often volunteered for the Home Guard as well. Moreover, as teachers were called up, a serious shortage of teachers developed. Classes naturally grew larger. H.M.I. Arnold in Birmingham was very concerned at this. Writing in September 1941 he gave figures for shortages in the area, and went on to declare:

All this proves my assertion up to the hilt that shortage of staff is doing more damage to education than all Goering's bombs, and is far and away the most serious problem confronting us.

Later in the same letter, he spoke pessimistically of the effects of the raids on the cities:

> evacuated children have probably lost the blessings of Hadowisation [that is, separate secondary schools] but have gained a wealth of new and stimulating experiences ... but for the children who remain in the cities, it is all loss. Their environment is even more hellish than it was in peacetime.

Again it must be remarked that Arnold was probably feeling the strain of what was happening all around him, but during the worst of the bombing it must have been hard to keep going, let alone maintain anything like pre-war standards. Attendances fell off seriously, and for a time there was a good deal of simple truancy. The chairman of Birmingham Education Committee asserted in February 1941 that some 40 per cent of the city's children were playing truant.

From the summer of 1941 onwards, the raids were less intense, and some improvements in schooling could be seen. Attendances returned to something like normal, and there was a vast expansion of nursery education in order to free mothers for war-work. Further, the provision of milk and meals increased dramatically. As early as February 1942, 80 per cent were receiving school milk daily in one-third-pint bottles. By this time, meals were being taken by most children, and the meals service had been transformed from providing mostly for the needy into catering for the majority of children as a standard practice. As for academic standards, there was a distinct rise in the numbers taking both the Schools Certificate and the Higher Schools Certificate (though this applied only to secondary schools, of course). In September 1944, the official evacuation scheme was ended – just at the time when the launching of the V1s and the V2s caused a further evacuation from London and the south-east. Birmingham became a reception area for 6,000 children from the areas under attack.

Altogether it appears that the school system settled down to a more normal kind of existence between 1941 and 1945. But appearances can be deceptive. Within this period, the shortage of teachers continued, and grew worse. In 1941, the Ministry of Labour proposed to call up all male teachers without exemption (the age of reservation had been thirty), and only strong protests from the Board of Education changed this to reservation at the age of thirty-five, with a further 10 per cent of key elementary teachers reserved. This still meant a loss to the forces of the very experienced 30–35 age group. Class sizes continued to increase. In the summer of 1944, Birmingham had 279 classes with more than fifty children in them, as compared with 72 such classes in 1938 (the recommended size of class in elementary schools was forty). Liverpool had 496 classes of over fifty (293 in 1938), and Sheffield 406 (2 in 1938). So increasing numbers of children were taught in over-sized classes, by more and more elderly teachers, some of whom had come out of retirement. Books and paper were in increasingly short supply by the end of the war – many textbooks were out of print. The curriculum itself was not much affected, though young PE staff were hard to find, and playing fields were sometimes occupied by the military or used for vegetable growing. Medical and dental services also suffered a decline as the call-up was intensified.

When all these adverse influences are taken together, it appears that it was highly unlikely that anything like pre-war standards could be maintained in the ordinary elementary school. It is true that it is sometimes claimed that the evacuated children benefited from their new experiences (see Arnold's remark above), and this may be true, even though they must have been disadvantaged by staffing problems, and by the shortage of books, paper and equipment, like everyone else; and in any case, they were in a small minority by 1944. Again, the increase in nursery schools, improvements in milk and meal services, and, above all, the 1944 Education Act are often represented as great gains resulting from the war. This is also true enough, but scarcely outweighs the day-to-day experiences of those children subject to deteriorating standards, especially in the first three years of war. Army tests in 1946 of men who had spent their last three years at school in 1939–42 showed an all-round drop in academic standards, and a serious increase in the numbers who were educationally backward and retarded. In London, which had suffered particularly badly from air raids, the average retardation was up to a year. It is too often forgotten that if a child was so unfortunate as to start school for the first time in September 1939, he would spend two-thirds of his school career under wartime conditions. Indeed, he might not have attended school at all for the first six or seven months. All in all, in the long run the working classes may have gained considerable educational advantages from the Second World War, but during the period of the war itself the average boy or girl probably experienced a decline in educational standards.

Planning the Future

The Second World War witnessed a good deal of planning for post-war social reform, and one major reform, the 1944 Education Act, was passed even before the war had ended. Until recently, most historians attributed this planning to the growth of social solidarity after 1940. This social unity was thought to be an expression of the national mood after Dunkirk, a natural consequence of the need to work together on the basis of fair shares for all, as seen in practice in the rationing system. Further, the evacuation of the children and the bombing of working-class homes had helped to reveal how much poverty and social deprivation still existed. Then again, so much control had come to be exercised by the government over so many aspects of life that it seemed both natural and inevitable that the state should provide more comprehensive social services. Add to this the general determination that pre-war unemployment should not be permitted again, and it becomes clear that there were powerful forces favourable to social reform from 1940 onwards.

However, detailed research over the past few years has sought to qualify these views. It has been suggested, for example, that although there is no doubt that some kind of consensus existed for a certain degree of social reform, both politicians and civil servants were much less enthusiastic about the famous Beveridge Report than has been assumed. Some considered its proposals an inconvenient luxury best left until after peace had returned, and both Conservative and Labour politicians were at first reluctant to make binding commitments to extensive social reform. Another interpretation is that the major force for change was less the impact of Dunkirk than the revival of political and industrial conflict towards the end of the war, and the government's need to damp this conflict down. These revisionist views deserve attention, but the Beveridge Report was published as early as December 1942, and (as we shall see a little later) it proved enormously popular at the time, when the end of the war was still two and a half years in the future. So, although it is clearly possible to oversimplify the causes of the many reform proposals made during the war, there can be no doubt of the very strong movement for reform among many politicians and certainly among the general public from mid-1940 onwards. On the left, as one might expect, there were vehement demands for a better deal for the ordinary man and woman. The popular writer Cassandra (William Connors) of the *Daily Mirror* provides a good example of reformist rhetoric in dedicating his pamphlet, *The English at War* (1941), to:

> the Common People who fight, who slave, who drown, who are burnt, who are mutilated, who are entombed and who bear the fierce unremitting yoke of pain and tears ...

In spring 1942 Churchill actually wanted to close down the *Daily Mirror*, which had become the favourite newspaper of the working man, because of its persistent attacks on the government; but he was persuaded to confine himself to a solemn warning. Thus there is no lack of evidence to show vigorous public demand both for the active prosecution of the war and for social reform.

The results of this pressure for social change seem to be that while Churchill characteristically concentrated on the military side of the war, reformers of both the main parties, together with experts in economic matters such as J.M. Keynes, and experts in the social services such as William Beveridge, began to plan for the future. Keynesian thinking influenced the budget in 1942, and in December 1942 the first manpower budget was drawn up. In education, the Board of Education issued plans for reform known as the Green Book. In health, the Medical Planning Commission in May 1942 recommended that a national health service should be set up. The Uthwatt Report in September 1942 made proposals for post-war town planning. The Labour Party produced its own plans for reform in 1942 entitled *The Old World and the New*. At the end of 1942 the most influential report of all, on the social services and their reform, was published as the Beveridge Report.

This was by no means a revolutionary report, and was based on Beveridge's deep knowledge of the social services, dating back to the pre-First World War Liberal reforms. It began by praising the existing social services, which it claimed were excellent in many ways, but goes on to point out their principal deficiencies – the health and unemployment schemes provided different rates of benefit, and both were too limited, for example, in supplying maternity and funeral benefits. The workmen's compensation scheme (for injury at work) was also too restricted. Another deficiency was that the administration of the schemes was too complicated. Beveridge then went on to list the problems which faced working people in their day-to-day life – the five Giants (as he called them) of Want, Disease, Ignorance, Squalor and Illness. Of these, Want could be abolished by a system of social insurance or social security. Social security was then succinctly defined as:

> the securing of an income to take the place of earnings when they are interrupted by unemployment, sickness or accident, to provide for retirement through age, to provide against loss of support by the death of another person, and to meet exceptional expenditure, such as those connected with birth, death, and marriage.

The inter-war surveys had shown that three-quarters to five-sixths of Want was due to the interruption or loss of earnings; the remaining quarter to a sixth was due to the family being too large for the household income. Two things were necessary therefore to get rid of Want – better social insurance, and family allowances. Another major recommendation in the report was that the Plan should cover all classes, and all ages, and that all should contribute. A full range of benefits should be made available, covering all eventualities – unemployment, disability, sickness, old age, birth and death; and there should be family allowances. In this way, security would be achieved from the cradle to the grave. Finally, a special Ministry of Social Security should be set up to run the whole scheme.

The Beveridge Report was very much of its time. It built upon existing social services, it preserved the old Liberal idea of insurance (so that in theory the individual was only drawing on what he had paid in, and not getting a straight state hand-out), and its keynote was the wartime belief in universality – all must participate, and share and share alike. Another aspect which is characteristic of the time is the use of the word 'plan' – planning was popular in 1942, especially as Russia with its Five Year Plans had now joined in the war. The report proved enormously popular, for it was in effect a blueprint for a welfare state, a phrase which came into common use in the 1940s. 635,000 copies of the report were sold, and a public opinion poll returned 86 per cent in favour of adopting it. Understandably, the government expressed support for it in principle, but in private there were doubts about its sheer cost, and its practicability, especially among older Conservatives such as the Prime Minister. Equally expectedly, the Labour Party as a whole supported it strongly, but individual members had reservations. Fearing possible wage reductions, Ernest Bevin was against both children's allowances and the changes in workmen's compensation. So there was some disagreement on detail. The government thought it unwise to try to put the Plan into effect during wartime, and Churchill talked about a Four Year Plan to be implemented when peace returned. All the same, the report stimulated further discussion of social reform. In 1943 a Ministry of Reconstruction was set up, and in 1944 a number of government White Papers were issued on matters contained in the Beveridge Report (Beveridge called it 'the White Paper Chase'). In February 1944 a White Paper proposed the setting up of a national health service, and in May 1944 a White Paper on employment policy firmly committed the government to the maintenance of a high and stable level of employment after the war, at the same time making clear that Keynesian ideas of government action to achieve this were accepted. In September, there was another White Paper, this time on social insurance, which adopted the main principles of the Beveridge Report. Beveridge himself returned to the fray in November with a book on full employment (an objective rather taken for granted in his report) entitled *Full Employment in a Free Society*.

While all these proposals were being discussed, one major reform took place in education. The Green Book was followed by a White Paper in July 1943, and then by the 1944 Education Act. This important Act was piloted through the Commons by the Conservative R. A. Butler, President of the Board of Education, and it was based partly on the Hadow Report of 1926, with its call for secondary education for all, and partly on the Norwood Report (1943). This wartime report, on the curriculum and examinations, divided children of secondary age into three groups – the academic, the technically minded and the remaining majority, for whom the Hadow Report had already suggested the establishment of so-called modern schools (modern in that they would not work on the traditional grammar school curriculum centred on Latin grammar). Bearing these principles in mind, the Education Act (the 'Butler Act') brought about a great reorganisation and expansion of state-provided education.

In the first place, the Act divided educational provision into three stages, primary, secondary and further education, and made local authorities responsible for all three. County colleges were to be set up to expand the third stage (a feature of the 1918 Act, never implemented), giving part-time education to the age of eighteen. All education provided in local authority schools was to become free, and this included the grammar schools. The school-leaving age was to be raised to fifteen (this should have happened in 1939, but the war had prevented it). Church schools and some other older foundations were to have further financial help, being divided into voluntarily aided schools (the governors met half the cost of repairs and alterations, but appointed their own staff), and controlled schools (where the local authorities took full charge of buildings, and had a greater control of staff). Religious Education became the one compulsory subject, and there was to be a daily act of corporate worship. Local education authorities were reorganised, 169 out of 315 in England and Wales being abolished. The old Board of Education became the Ministry of Education, and the former President acquired the new title of Minister.

For the working classes, the 1944 Act seemed to offer a more democratic system of education in that there was to be secondary education for all up to fifteen, and state grammar schools, like other secondary schools, were to be completely free. Moreover, new secondary modern schools were to be built to give as good an education (but of a different kind) as that traditionally given in the grammar schools. All three types of secondary school were to have 'parity of esteem' (one of the educational cant phrases of the time). Since many parents, given a free choice, would wish their children to go to the well-established grammar school, local authorities had to devise selection procedures at eleven (the age of entry to secondary schooling), so that children could be directed to the school most appropriate for their academic ability – hence the origins of the 11+ exam, which usually included an intelligence test. The intention here was that bright working-class children, whose academic attainments might be low, could nevertheless show their innate ability and gain a grammar school place.

The intentions behind the 1944 Act were good, and it did have some notable successes to its credit: undoubtedly more working-class children gained a free grammar school education, some excellent new secondary modern schools were built, and more children stayed on till fifteen and beyond. Indeed, some middle-class parents were affronted at no longer being able to purchase education for their offspring in state-run grammar schools, and therefore sent them to the new category of direct grant schools, where a proportion of the places still had to be paid for (alternatively, they could simply send them to the long-established public schools which remained untouched by the Act). The real problem with the 1944 Act was that it worked on the assumption that children could be divided conveniently into three simple categories at the age of eleven (of which the grammar school contingent constituted roughly only a fifth), so that all that was necessary was a simple sorting-out test at that age. Unfortunately, the 11+ prognostic tests proved unreliable (there was another transfer test at 13+, but it was not widely used). Those children who qualified for grammar school were later able to take the new O and A Level General Certificate of Education exams, and had the opportunity of going on to university. Those who went to the secondary modern school were not entered for such exams (only later was the rather different Certificate of Secondary Education introduced) so that the secondary modern school child was too often regarded as a grammar school 'failure'. Indeed, his or her school was often housed in inferior buildings with less qualified teachers. In these circumstances, the idea of 'parity of esteem', as envisaged in the Hadow Report, was doomed to failure. It was simply too idealistic. It is not surprising that in the 1950s and 1960s opposition grew to the 11+ exams, and to the whole idea of reserving the traditional kind of academic education to a limited number of children selected at the age of eleven. The idea of the comprehensive school began to spread.

It is convenient at this point to mention one other reform, passed by Churchill's caretaker government in June 1945. This was the Family Allowances Act. By this time, the case for doing something to help the larger family living on low wages had become irresistible. Curiously enough, not everyone agreed that family allowances were the best way of tackling this problem. Some in the Labour Party thought the better approach was to fix minimum wages, family allowances being regarded as a cheap way of relieving want without getting to the root of the matter. At all events, the measure was passed, and gave a grant of five shillings per week for every child after the first. The allowance was to be paid direct to the mother, and not the father. The housing situation also received attention early in 1945 when it was proposed to build 300,000 new houses during the first two years of peace. £150 million was also allocated for the provision of prefabricated houses, to provide emergency accommodation, and to have a life of some twenty years. In the event, many were in use for much longer than this.

The End of the War

The war against Germany ended in May 1945, but the war against Japan continued, and at first it appeared that it would be a long-drawn-out affair, necessitating an invasion of the Japanese mainland. When the war in Europe ended, Labour withdrew from the coalition government, and Churchill formed a temporary caretaker government until a general election could be held, the first since 1935. Both the major parties, Conservative and Labour, promised social reform after the war – full employment, a national health service, social security – though Labour was more enthusiastic in its support for the Beveridge Plan. Labour also promised a certain degree of nationalisation, for example, of the Bank of England, iron and steel, the railways, the coalmining industry – none of it very revolutionary in nature, and acceptable enough to many voters at the time, used as they were to wartime government controls. The Conservatives were hampered by their pre-war association with industrial depression and unemployment, and also with the failure of their pre-war policy of appeasement of Hitler. No doubt the service vote went against the Conservative Party, though it is wrong to suppose that it was this that defeated it at the polls; more than half of the serving men and women failed to vote. In fact, the Conservatives were not overwhelmed in the popular vote, though they lost the election heavily in terms of seats contested. Labour gained a great victory here with 393 seats as compared with 213 for the Conservatives, and 12 seats for the Liberals. The third Labour

Table 2.2   The General Election, July 1945

Party	Votes cast	Percentage of vote	Number of seats
Conservative	9,988,306	39.8	213
Labour	11,995,152	47.8	393
Liberal	2,248,226	9.0	12
Communist	102,780	0.4	2
Common Wealth	110,634	0.4	1
Others	640,880	2.0	19

government was then formed, led by Clement Attlee, with a clear majority over all other parties. Within a few weeks, Japan had surrendered, following the dropping of two atom bombs. The new Labour government had now to win the peace, after six years of war.

The Rise of the Working Classes

What had been achieved by the working classes as a result of these six years? Obviously enough, victory against the evil Nazi tyranny, but was there anything else? Churchill had promised the nation only 'blood, toil, tears and sweat', and this certainly had been the lot of many. A substantial proportion of the third of a million British deaths during the war came from the working classes, ordinary men and women, who on the whole simply did as they were told, and suffered, and died. Most of the fighting was done by the unglamorous infantry – the PBI, or Poor Bloody Infantry. The better-educated went into the Royal Air Force either as aircrew or on the technical side as so-called tradesmen; only a minority in the RAF had no particular qualifications and were assigned to dogs-body jobs as GDs, General Duties, without a trade to their name. All this, right or wrong, fair or unfair, was accepted cheerfully enough by most of the working classes. They took it for granted, in the words of the refrain of a popular canteen song, 'She Was Poor, But She Was Honest':

> It's the same, the whole world over
> It's the poor what gets the blame
> It's the rich what gets the pickings
> Ain't it all a bleedin' shame?

Yet something odd had happened after Dunkirk to the working classes. The war had shaken up the old class relationships. There was an increasing realisation of the real need for further social reform, and the nation as a whole accepted this. Writing in the early 1960s, A. J. P. Taylor observed that in the Second World War the British people came of age in what was a People's War. He concluded in a memorable passage:

Imperial greatness was on the way out; the welfare state was on the way in. The British Empire declined; the condition of the people improved. Few now sang 'Land of Hope and

Glory'. Few even sang 'England Arise'. England had arisen all the same.

In more prosaic terms, the working classes had undoubtedly risen, both politically and in economic terms. Their representatives in the House of Commons were now in a position to exercise supreme power in the state. A bloodless revolution seemed to have been achieved. A Conservative MP, surveying the ranks of new Labour MPs in the House of Commons, is supposed to have exclaimed, 'Good gracious, they look just like our constituents!' This was an apt enough observation. Those same Labour MPs sang 'The Red Flag' (those who knew the words) in the debating chamber. The words had been written for another, more sanguinary kind of revolution, and its dreary tune is very different from the brisk march intended originally by the author of the lyric. Doubly inappropriate then, 'The Red Flag', gave little indication of the intentions of the new government. The fact that Churchill was cheered loudly by Labour MPs as well as by the Opposition benches on his first entry into the new House supplied a better prediction of the class co-operation rather than class conflict which was to follow. Yet there is no doubt that not only England, but the English working classes, had risen.

Chapter 3

The Coming of the Welfare State 1945–1951

Politics and the Economy

After such a sweeping victory in the general election of 1945, it would appear at first sight that the new Labour government had a supreme opportunity to bring about a socialist revolution in Britain. Indeed, Labour's election manifesto stated clearly that its ultimate aim was to establish a socialist commonwealth in the country, and there were some at the time who thought that a new age of liberty, equality and fraternity was about to begin. The majority of supporters, however, were more realistic about the possibilities of transforming society. Two major obstacles lay in the path of would-be radical reformers: the nature and outlook of the Labour Party, and the state of the post-war economy. As for the first, the Labour Party was not in its origins set up to promote socialism in any narrow or doctrinaire sense, but rather to represent the interests of Labour in the widest way possible. Over the years, the word 'socialist' has been bandied about by supporter and opponent alike without any clear meaning being attached to it. As noted in the Prologue, when Clause Four was included in the Labour Party constitution in 1918, it satisfied the intellectual needs of middle-class members of the Party, but scarcely represented the thinking of rank-and-file trade unionists. The Labour Party was certainly not a Marxist party; it did not envisage a taking over of the whole economy so that the means of production, distribution and exchange could come completely under government control and be devoted to the production of goods for use rather than for profit (and if it had put this forward as an aim in the manifesto, it seems very unlikely that it would have been elected with such a large majority). Instead, its approach was essentially low-key and pragmatic, building on past experience in two Labour governments, and also on very active recent participation in the wartime coalition. For the most part, the new Labour government was led by solid, middle-class figures (in fact, four ministers were members of the House of Lords). Only three of the senior ministers had strong left-wing backgrounds – Aneurin Bevan (Minister of Health), Emanuel Shinwell (Minister of Fuel and Power), and Sir Stafford Cripps (President of the Board of Trade). Nationalisation was only a small and relatively insignificant part of the manifesto programme, and virtually no preparations had been made for it prior to the election. The Red Flag did not fly over 10 Downing Street in 1945, whatever the vocal efforts of the new Labour Members in the House of Commons.

The second barrier to really wide-ranging reform of society was the state of the economy in 1945. It was in a parlous condition. Exports had been reduced by about two-thirds since 1939, and merchant shipping was also down by 28 per cent. Such had been the concentration on the war effort, invisible income from abroad, always a strong and important element in the economy, had been halved. As Keynes said, 'We threw good housekeeping to the winds. But we saved ourselves, and helped to save the world.' Capital equipment in many cases was worn out by the war, and large-scale investment in industry had become vital. The standard of living had fallen overall since 1939. Unless the economy could be revived as a matter of urgency, especially in the field of exports, the government was facing disaster – a crisis far deeper and less transitory than in 1931. To make matters rather worse, when the war ended against Japan, the United States abruptly terminated the Lend–Lease arrangements begun in 1941. In these circumstances, it was essential that the economy be restored if even the limited reforms set out in the Labour manifesto were to be achieved. In theory, perhaps, it might have been possible for the Labour government to have embarked on a more drastic reform programme, relying on their electoral support and the reformist mood of the times to see them through. In practice, this kind of political adventuring was hardly in their nature. They took what seemed the obvious economic remedies, and in the event, they achieved some success.

Economic Events

Events in the economic field during the lifetime of the Labour government provide the necessary background to the social changes of the period. As in 1931, the government turned to America for financial help, but fortunately with happier results than on that occasion. The urgent need was for a large-scale loan to get the wheels turning. The Americans were asked for a loan of $6,400 million; they drove a hard bargain, and responded with a loan of $3,750 million, interest payable at 2 per cent, repayments to start in 1951. Sterling was to be made freely convertible – a serious inconvenience to Britain – and imperial preferences were to be abandoned. At the same time, Canada also provided a loan of $1,250 million, generous enough in the circumstances.

With the economic pump primed in this way, a good start was made on the road to recovery, and an impressive list of social reforms was also initiated in 1946. The government's declared economic policy at this stage was clear enough: their aim was a managed economy, the main features being the maintenance of full employment, high taxation, cheap money (that is, low rates of interest), and an export drive (one of the slogans of the time was 'Export or Die'). As part of this programme, the nationalisation of certain key industries as promised in the manifesto was carried out, since in theory this would give control of 'the commanding heights of the economy' (one of the fashionable expressions of the time). In practice, this control did not amount to very much. The Bank of England Act 1946 nationalised the Bank of England, but as it was already under close government control little change was to be seen. The same applies to the Cable and Wireless Act 1946, nationalising long-distance communications, and the Civil Aviation Act 1946, nationalising Imperial Airways and bringing into existence British European Airways and British South American Airways. The most important act of the year in this respect was the Coal Nationalisation Act 1946, which at last removed the ownership of all but the very smallest mines from private hands and transferred it to the National Coal Board. In 1947, further nationalisation followed – the Electricity Act and the Gas Act – but since these public utilities were already run by large-scale enterprises, often municipal in nature, the ordinary consumer did not see much difference. The Transport Act of 1947 nationalised the railways, canals and some forms of road transport. There was considerable controversy over road transport, but little over the canals, or over the railways, where it was generally acknowledged there was a crying need for new investment and reorganisation. Lastly, iron and steel nationalisation was introduced in 1947, but caused a great deal of argument, since unlike the other measures the industry here was not a public utility, but a thriving, privately run industry in no apparent need of government aid or control. Here then at last was a real case of 'socialist exappropriation', a direct challenge to private enterprise, or so it seemed. Fears of the Bill being thrown out by the Lords led the government to pass the Parliament Act of 1949, which reduced the Lords' power to delay a Bill to one year; but, in the event, the Iron and Steel Act was passed in 1949 under the terms of the earlier Parliament Act of 1911, after a delay of two years. Nationalisation did not go very far: 80 per cent of industry was left in private hands.

How significant was nationalisation in the immediate post-war years? It does not seem to have played any obvious part in the government's overall control of the economy, or in any plan for industry as a whole. Other attempts to control industry through the Lord President's Committee and through the Development Councils achieved little. Much of it seemed inevitable, given the circumstances of each particular industry, the only exception being iron and steel. In a way, this was the one true socialist measure (that is, in the light of Clause Four), and it was certainly the most controversial; but it was inserted in the manifesto at the last minute, and by agreement did not come into effect until January 1951, and in fact was never fully implemented under the Conservatives. Apart from this industry, and also possibly the coal industry, nationalisation did not arouse any passionate defence or any special enthusiasm. However, the coal industry was different from all the others, in that nationalisation had been an issue since the Sankey Commission in 1919, and labour relations had been so bad in the industry over the years that taking it out of private hands was greeted with great satisfaction by the miners. Yet even here the results were disappointing. The compensation given the owners – £164.6 million – was regarded by many miners as excessive; and public ownership got off to a bad start on 1 January 1947 during an extremely harsh winter, when output was still inadequate, and transport difficulties due to the weather made it impossible to move coal to where industry needed it. The results of the hard weather was a severe fuel shortage, power cuts in industry and the home, temporary unemployment of two million, and a loss of £2 million worth of exports. Some wit scrawled on a poster announcing the coming of a Christian mission to London, 'For Christ's sake, bring some coal!' All this was scarcely a good advertisement for the benefits of nationalisation, even though the industry was not to blame for the weather. Subsequently things improved, but both production and productivity made slow progress: output which was 175 million tons in 1945 was still only 204 million tons in 1950, and even then the increase was due largely to an opencast output of 12 million tons, and an increased labour force. As for productivity, output per shift reached pre-war levels only by 1950, in spite of investment in new equipment. It may be that a better spirit prevailed in the mines after nationalisation, but this did not prevent strikes and disputes with the new management.

In long-term perspective, it is clear that nationalisation proved a grave ideological disappointment to many on the left, since it showed clearly enough that state control of sectors of capitalist industry brought little benefit to the workers. It was not the beginnings of a more efficient, planned economy which would ultimately be to the advantage of all the working classes. However, some would argue that it was not true nationalisation, in that there was no element at all of direct worker control. The workers, it was asserted, had simply exchanged one set of bosses for another, the officials of the NCB. At first, this argument appears to have some force. It is true that the model for control chosen by Herbert Morrison, Lord President of the Council, was the public corporation, based on his own 1933 plan for London Transport (Morrison was a great figure in the affairs of the London County Council, and had been Transport Minister in the second Labour government). It was a most unadventurous model, and made no provision for worker participation. But the trade unions failed to make any claim for a stake in running nationalised industries – they preferred to stay outside and preserve their right of collective bargaining, without sharing directly in the management. Of course, it would have been very difficult in any case to bring in direct worker control. In Sir Stafford Cripps' view, it would have been virtually impossible to have worker-controlled industry in Britain, even if it were on the whole desirable. It seems therefore that worker control was not the missing ingredient which would have made nationalisation a great success; and its apparent failure to demonstrate the inevitable superiority of state-run enterprise over private enterprise was a

severe blow to ideologues on the left, especially the botched hand-
ling of iron and steel, the one thriving industry to be nationalised
(it was rapidly denationalised for the most part by the Conservatives in the early 1950s). All this did not stop some on the left from
clinging to nationalisation as an article of faith for many years to
come.

To return to the first two years of the Labour government of
office: 1947 was the first year in which economic affairs suddenly
took a turn for the worse. By July, after what had been one of the
worst winters in living memory, the American loan had nearly run
out – there was only $400 million left unspent. Unemployment was
temporarily high, and exports were still only 17 per cent above the
pre-war figure. In October, the Chancellor of the Exchequer, the
ebullient Hugh Dalton of the booming voice, resigned after an
inadvertent and minor pre-budget speech disclosure, made to a
London evening newspaper. He was replaced by the ascetic Sir
Stafford Cripps, previously Minister for Economic Affairs. Under
Cripps, a new period of austerity was begun: new targets for production were devised, and imports were limited still further. Raw
materials were reallocated, and a reduction in the armed forces was
announced. In March of the next year, a policy of wage restraint
was adopted which was to last three years. Slowly things improved.
The economy was helped greatly in September 1948 by the generous grant of $1,263 million from Marshall Aid, itself part of a gift of
nearly $5,000 million by America to West Europe for rehabilit-
ation. By the end of 1948, the outlook was much brighter. During
the year, output increased by 36 per cent over 1939, and it seemed
that the battle for economic recovery was being won. Yet in 1949,
partly owing to the onset of recession in America, the pound began
to slide, and in the autumn it was drastically devalued by Cripps
from $4.03 to $2.80, a reduction in value of nearly 31 per cent. At
the same time, cuts were made in government expenditure, and
prescription charges were introduced under the National Health
Service (but in fact were not imposed). Once more the crisis was
weathered, and the economy improved again as American markets
recovered, exports became cheaper as a result of devaluation, and
in 1950 they were 75 per cent above pre-war figures.

When the period 1945–50 is surveyed as a whole, it is evident
that the Labour government cannot be said to have performed any
economic miracles, and there were the two periods of economic
crisis in 1947 and 1949; but the government were able to pull

through. They were successful on the whole in reviving industry, in maintaining the export drive, and above all in keeping a high level of employment throughout (the one exception was in the spring of 1947). Nationalisation had not brought the hoped-for gains, but at least it does not appear to have inhibited economic recovery. All in all, the government could congratulate itself on its success. A limited degree of government planning had achieved its aims. If anything, controls were maintained for too long, but a so-called bonfire of controls was carried out by the youthful President of the Board of Trade, Harold Wilson, in November 1948. The social consequences of all the economic problems, however, were considerable, and will be dealt with later in the chapter. It is fortunate for the government that the self-discipline and restraint learned in the war continued in the early post-war years. Still, whatever the shortages and inconveniences which had to be suffered during the period of austerity, there was some comfort for the working classes in the knowledge that substantial social reforms were taking place in the form of the creation of the welfare state.

Welfare Reforms: National Insurance and National Health Schemes

Labour's election manifesto *Let Us Face the Future* promised social security, a national health service, full employment, houses for the people, and the implementing of the Education Act 1944. All these promises were carried out to a greater or lesser degree, and the necessary legislation for the first two was passed early in the ministry, though it took two years for the national health scheme to be put into effect. A good beginning was made in 1946 with the National Insurance (Industrial Injuries) Act. Compensation for injury sustained at work went back to 1880, but existing schemes for compensation for injuries or illnesses resulting from working conditions were expanded by the 1946 Act, and made part of the national insurance scheme – that is, compensation was no longer payable by the individual employer. Curiously enough, the benefits payable under the Act were higher than those available when away from work due to sickness or being unemployed, possibly because industrial disablement had always been recognised as being in a different category from absence due to illness or unemployment.

The 1946 National Insurance Act had a far wider application, of course, and has been termed a cornerstone of Labour's welfare schemes. It was this measure above all which sought to provide the security from the cradle to the grave which was the essence of the Beveridge Report – literally so, in the sense that it included both maternity grants and funeral benefits. Generally speaking, it greatly extended the existing sickness and unemployment schemes, first brought into being in 1911, so that all were to be compulsorily insured (with some minor exceptions), and seven types of benefits were to be available. A new Ministry of National Insurance was set up to administer the new scheme, the first minister being James Griffiths. An important feature of the new set-up was that all contributions were to be at a flat rate – a good example of the universalism of Labour's reforms: not only was everyone, whether upper, middle or working class, to participate, but all paid the same rates. There was to be no targeting of those most in need, which would otherwise involve means testing, and an undesirable social differentiation. The contributions were also kept low so as to allow the lowest paid to afford them; at the same time, the rates of benefit were kept to subsistence levels. The results of all this was a much more comprehensive scheme than ever before which for the first time brought in the middle and upper classes, and in particular included the self-employed and lower middle classes, hitherto outside the scope of the earlier schemes.

Also in 1946 there was passed the National Health Service Act, designed to implement the recommendation of the 1944 White Paper and to introduce a free health service for all. In 1946 there did exist already some sort of a health service for the working classes under the 1911 Insurance Act, but it was confined to working people only, it was administered by so-called 'approved societies' (mostly insurance companies), and it made no provision for the dependants of contributors. Further, all hospitals except the poor law infirmaries charged fees, scaled on the basis of the patient's income. Any attempt to set up a national health service therefore involved a massive reorganisation, and finding a solution to at least two major problems – how to bring in the voluntary and local health authorities into the scheme, and how to persuade the medical profession as a whole to co-operate. The doctors had proved extremely difficult when the original health scheme was introduced by Lloyd George in 1911. The solutions to these problems were found by another brilliant Welsh member of the House of Commons, Aneurin Bevan, Minister for Health. In many ways he was an unexpected choice by Attlee for this post. He was an ex-miner from Tredegar, a trade unionist, a dedicated Marxist between the wars, yet on entering the House of Commons he soon acquired sophisticated and elegant tastes, and some wealthy friends, including the Conservative newspaper proprietor, Lord Beaverbrook. Brendan Bracken, also a member of the Beaverbrook circle, is supposed to have addressed Bevan to his face as 'You Bollinger Bolshevik, you ritzy Robespierre, you lounge-lizard Lenin . . .' He was an outstanding speaker in the House, and a constant and effective critic of Churchill during the war (Churchill called him 'a squalid nuisance'). It was this strange and gifted man, previously untested in office, who was to gain fame as the supreme architect of the National Health Service. For him, its creation was to be his finest hour.

In the first place, Bevan's scheme applied to all members of the public, not just the working classes. It was free to all contributors to the social security scheme, and it was to be administered by the Ministry of Health. Secondly, the problem of what to do about the hospitals was solved by nationalising them – something not included in the election manifesto, but a way of bringing the hospital consultants into the scheme. Henceforth they would be paid for their services in the hospitals (previously they had often given their services free in the voluntary hospitals which were run on a charitable basis), and they could also continue in private practice, even having their own patients in pay-beds in National Health hospitals. This suited them very well, and winning over the consultants was Bevan's first victory. Indeed, one of their leaders, Lord Moran, was very helpful to Bevan in his struggle with the doctors. As Bevan himself is supposed to have put it, rather crudely, 'I stuffed their mouths with gold.' Another important aspect of this was the need to rationalise the hospital system: some voluntary hospitals were very small, and many were already receiving grants from the Exchequer. Municipal hospitals, on the other hand, varied in size, dependent on the size of the controlling local authority. From the beginning, Bevan saw the need to produce a coherent plan for them all. As he put it

> The first fundamental from now on is to picture, plan and provide a hospital service on a broad national scale, and get rid once and for all of any purely historical impediments to doing so.

In this major aim, he was to prove very successful.

The second problem was not solved so expeditiously. The rank-and-file general practitioners were deeply suspicious of the new health scheme, principally because they thought they would lose their independence and become salaried state officials; and they also disliked the new prohibition on the private sale of practices, which in fact was essential if the distribution of doctors nationally was to be properly organised, and also to avoid (as Bevan put it) 'the sale of patients like cattle'. A long-drawn-out battle ensued between Bevan and the British Medical Association. In the course of time, but only just before the Act was due to come into force in July 1948, the doctors finally agreed to join the National Health Service, having been at last convinced that the system of paying them a small salary and then a much larger amount in the form of capitation fees avoided their becoming salaried civil servants and so preserved their independence.

The health service was to be financed from central funds (it was never intended that it should be paid for under the insurance scheme). There were to be three separate administrative authorities operating under the supervision of the Ministry of Health and Housing:

(1) Regional hospital boards (twenty in number) in charge of the voluntary and local authority hospitals.
(2) Local executive councils to run both dental and medical services. General practioners came under these councils, and were thus separated administratively from the hospitals.
(3) Local government authorities, who were left in charge of public health services such as the inspection of food, sewage disposal and scavenging, and welfare services such as home nursing and child care.

In addition, health centres were to be set up where a complete range of services (other than hospital services) would be available. Thus a rather odd three-fold division of responsibilities was devised, owing much (in spite of Bevan's desire to sweep away any 'historical impediments') to the way each branch of the health service had developed in the past. In practice, the new scheme worked well, except that initially it cost rather more than expected. In addition to the nineteen million people already insured, a further twenty-one million came under the scheme. The demand for dental services was badly underestimated: four million cases a year were expected – the actual figure turned out to be eight million. Again, the demand for ophthalmic treatment was also under-estimated. Its cost was expected to be about £1 million. In fact, in the first year it actually cost £22 million. Bevan's comment on all this was:

> The rush for spectacles, as for dental treatment, has exceeded all expectations ... Part of what has happened has been a natural first flush of the new scheme, with the feeling that everything is free now and it does not matter what is charged up to the Exchequer ... There is also, without doubt, a sheer increase due to people getting things they need but could not afford before, and this the scheme intended.

Later on, seeking to justify the possible imposition of prescription charges in 1949, Bevan claimed that the service needed by then to be protected against excessive demand:

> Now that we have got the National Health Service based on free prescriptions, I shudder to think of the cascade of medicine which is pouring down British throats at the present time. I wish I could believe that its efficiency was equal to the credulity with which it is being swallowed.

This was a somewhat barbed comment. In fact, charges were never imposed under the third Labour government, 1945–50, and the new health service as a whole operated very successfully. Somehow Bevan had managed to strike a fair balance between the need for overall state direction and the doctors' desire for professional independence, even though he did disappoint the Socialist Medical Association by failing to institute a salaried service and bring private medicine to an end. The NHS remains as a great monument to Bevan, and it was certainly his greatest achievement. Yet such are the ironies of history, he may be equally well remembered, by his political opponents at least, for the notorious remark in his speech at Manchester on the day before the NHS came into operation, that the Tories 'were lower than vermin' – a sudden and memorable return to his abrasive, hard-line style of the thirties.

National Assistance and Unemployment

Even after the passing of the National Insurance Act and the National Health Act in 1946, there were still some members of the community not catered for by either Act – special cases such as the blind, vagrants and the destitute. The last two categories were still the special concern of the poor law as administered by the Public Assistance Committees of the local government authorities. But in 1948 the National Assistance Act abolished the remnants of the old poor law, which dated back to the sixteenth century. In its place, the Act established a new national body, the National Assistance Board, which took over all the duties of the old Unemployment Assistance Board, set up in 1934. The purpose of the new Board is admirably set out in the wording of the Act:

> The existing poor law shall cease to have effect, and shall be replaced by the provisions of Part II of this Act as to the rendering, out of moneys provided by Parliament, of assistance to persons in need ...
>
> It shall be the duty of the Board ... to assist persons in Great Britain who are without resources to meet their requirements, or whose resources (including benefits receivable under the National Insurance Acts 1946) must be supplemented in order to meet their requirements.

Thus the idea was to underpin the social security system, and to help anyone not covered by other legislation who had a particular need for assistance. As for the old poor law, the PACs were abolished, and the only duty remaining with the local authorities in this connection was the duty of providing homes for the aged and infirm. Nye Bevan is supposed to have wanted to call these retirement homes 'Twilight Homes', but was persuaded that this was not a very tactful name for them.

The National Assistance scheme was never intended to be more than a safety net to support the relatively small numbers still in need in spite of the National Insurance Act; but in practice the rise in prices and the failure of benefit rates to keep pace with prices meant that for many the insurance allowances were too low. By December 1950 there were 1.34 million persons receiving allowances under the National Assistance Act, of whom 873,000 needed help because their benefits were too low. Over two-thirds of these claimants were old-age pensioners. It became necessary for the Board to subject applicants to a means test, which was much disliked, but unavoidable if allowances were not to be given indiscriminately.

Fortunately for the Board, unemployment remained low

throughout the years 1945–50. Earlier in this chapter, it was pointed out that the government faced great economic problems in 1945, yet it was committed to a policy of full employment. It is very much to its credit that this policy was fully implemented and, as it happened, with a minimum of government direction. In 1947 as a result of the severe winter and the shortage of coal, unemployment did flare up momentarily and reached a figure of two million, but rapidly dropped again as the economy recovered in the summer. The Control of Engagements Order issued at this time permitted the direction of labour, but very few workers were ever required to move jobs. A voluntary wages freeze by the unions between 1947 and 1951 also helped to stabilise the labour market. A mild shortage of labour characterised the economy throughout the period rather than a shortage of jobs, mainly because of the emphasis thrown on the newer industries rather than the old staples which had suffered so badly between the wars. The export drive, after a slow start proved very successful, and at this early stage of post-war development Britain had no competition to fear from its two formidable pre-war rivals, Germany and Japan. With the help of the American loan in 1945, and then Marshall Aid in 1948, the economy prospered.

The result was that the unemployment rate, which was 2.5 per cent in 1945, fell to 1.2 per cent in 1949, and was still only 1.8 per cent in October 1951. Although attention is customarily focused on the social legislation of 1946, together with the setting up of the NHS, the attaining of full employment by the government was as remarkable as any of its achievements. To have a job and at the same time the benefits of social security – this represented a striking increase in social well-being for the working classes, an unparalleled advance in the quality of life. Of course, there were snags, among them the housing shortage and the slow progress in education, two other aspects of the welfare state to which we now turn.

Housing and Education

There was obviously a great need for new housing after the war, partly because of the extensive damage caused by bombing, and partly because no domestic building had been permitted during the war. As the Labour manifesto had promised 'Homes for the People' – it could scarcely do otherwise – a great programme of house building was envisaged in 1945. The Minister responsible was Aneurin Bevan, whose ministry covered both Health and

Housing. The policy adopted was to permit building by licence only, and to build very largely for letting by local authorities; very few houses were built for private sale. It follows that the vast majority of houses put up were council houses, and waiting lists for tenancies grew longer and longer as ex-servicemen married and sought accommodation. The rise in the birth rate and the increased size of families put further strains on the housing stock. In London and elsewhere, the practice of squatting developed – larger houses, still empty for one reason or another after the war, were simply taken over and occupied illegally, usually by young people desperately seeking some form of roof over their heads. One kind of emergency accommodation provided took the form of prefabricated homes – prefabs, they were called – which could be erected very quickly, and were expected to last not more than twenty years. In fact, they were very well designed and were well equipped, including refrigerators, not normally to be found in working-class kitchens at the time. About 157,000 of these houses were erected between 1945 and 1950.

However, Bevan had no great faith in this kind of temporary accommodation, preferring the erection of good quality brick houses, about a quarter larger in floor space than pre-war council houses, and with an expected life of at least eighty years. They were relatively expensive to build and, including fixtures and fittings, cost £1,500 to £1,600 (the cost of a house built privately under licence was limited to £1,200). Bevan's plans immediately ran into difficulties. Building labour was scarce, materials (such as softwood timber) often lacking, and there were continuous interruptions in the supply of bricks and other materials, due to the division of responsibilities among different bodies for the actual building process – the Ministry of Works provided the basic building materials, the Ministry of Supply the fittings, while the local authorities put up the houses. There was much confusion as a result, and bottlenecks abounded. In addition, the shortage of skilled labour meant that the rate of erection was slower than expected. Bevan admitted to some of these difficulties in the Commons in 1947:

> We are having to close down brickyards because they cannot get orders, and the reason they cannot get orders is because the rate of bricklaying is not what we are entitled to expect it to be ... There will be found, on sites all round London, wherever one likes to look, stacks of bricks.

Added to these practical difficulties of organisation were financial problems. For example, in 1947 there was a £10 million cut in timber imports. Then in the financial crisis of 1949, cuts in government expenditure forced a severe reduction in local authority building. For all these reasons, the rate of construction was disappointingly slow. The figures are as follows for new houses completed:

1946	55,400	1949	217,240
1947	139,690	1950	210,253
1948	227,616	1951	204,117

Meanwhile, Housing Acts of 1946 and 1949 extended local government building powers, the Rent Control Acts in the same years strengthened rent controls and the powers of rent tribunals, while the 1947 Town and Country Planning Act gave further planning powers to local councils.

Although at the outset there were proposals for building four million houses, by 1951 only just over one million houses had been built, and there were still 750,000 fewer houses than households in that year. Bevan's record in the field of housing has therefore been judged by some historians to have been far less successful than his achievements as Minister for Health. Various reasons have been put forward to account for this – for example, the simple fact that his duties as Minister for both Housing and Health were too heavy for any one man to bear; and again, his long-drawn-out struggle with the BMA (it is suggested) was a distraction from his duties as Housing Minister. Bevan himself contributed to this view by lightheartedly remarking that he spent just five minutes a week on housing. More recently, historians have laid greater emphasis on the difficulties which Bevan faced, and also upon the numbers of houses actually built (these numbers appear to have been revised upwards in the course of years). Further, as will be seen in the next chapter, the unfavourable comparison often made with the numbers built by Macmillan in the 1950s has also been challenged. It is undeniable that the building programme was slow off the mark in 1945 and 1946, but admittedly 1947 was a year of economic crisis, and after the boom year of 1948, so was 1949. In this last year, 300,000 houses were planned, but cuts reduced the figure considerably. All in all, the record does not seem too bad, and a distinguished historian of the post-war Labour governments has suggested that after a slow start the government's record constitutes a competent overall performance, if not outstanding; and, in view of all the difficulties, housing 'deserves its honoured role in the saga of Labour's welfare state'. This may be thought a fair judgement, though at the time for young married people sharing homes with their parents, the housing waiting lists seemed unconscionably long.

As for education, the government's main task as they saw it was to implement the Butler Act of 1944 by abolishing all fees in local educational authority schools, and by providing secondary education for all. This they duly did. The new tripartite secondary system of grammar, technical and secondary modern schools was put into operation, together with the new selection procedures at 11+. In 1947 the school-leaving age was put up to fifteen in accordance with the Act, and the General Certificate of Education replaced the old School Certificate as a leaving certificate. In the field of further education, once more the idea of so-called county colleges (for part-time, compulsory attendance for the fifteen-to-eighteen age range) failed to materialise. The shortage of teachers was met in part by an emergency one-year teacher-training scheme (followed by further part-time study), and also by extending the FETS (Further Education and Training Scheme) grants for ex-servicemen and women to those who wished to take university degrees with a view to teaching. For a time, the universities became crammed with ex-service students who occupied 90 per cent of the places.

The Labour government is usually criticised for failing to do more in the field of education, and indeed the Education Minister, Ellen Wilkinson, is much better known as the fiery author of *The Town That Was Murdered* than for anything she achieved as Education Minister (but at least she is better known than Butler's wartime predecessor, Mr Herwald Ramsbotham). Certainly Labour failed to supply any new ideas, or any new emphases or changes in direction. Even before criticism began to mount against the three-fold system of secondary schools (as already described in Chapter Two), nothing was done about technical education or the apprenticeship system, both of great importance to the working classes the government was supposed to represent. The few technical schools often took their entry at 13+, and appear to have been the main beneficiaries of the 13+ transfer scheme, which was supposed to reallocate those children wrongly selected by the 11+. In practice, the grammar schools were reluctant after two years to transfer children unsuited to their regime; while secondary modern schools were similarly slow to transfer their best pupils to the grammar schools. So the 13+ system did not work very well to remedy the deficiencies in the 11+ selection procedures.

The explanation for Labour's lack of real and positive success in education is commonly thought to be the very conservative educational attitudes of their leaders. It is true that only a small minority had left school at fourteen or earlier (such as Shinwell and Bevin). Most seem to have had a great faith in the local authority grammar school as a means of promoting social mobility for the working classes. These schools were to be free, and entrance to them obtainable through the 11+ examination, which seemed to offer fair opportunities to working-class children with ability. These views appeared not unreasonable at the time, of course. In any case, the 1944 Act had been passed only the year before Labour took office, and itself required a considerable amount of change, without any further reforms being introduced. There is the additional point that the government had many other areas of welfare to deal with apart from education. When all these points are taken into consideration, the government's record in education appears sound enough, though certainly not very exciting or adventurous.

Working Conditions

Once the war was over, the long hours made necessary by the demands of war production were reduced to their pre-war number, and indeed were reduced somewhat further, though not on the scale of the shortening of hours which occurred in 1919. By the end of 1946, the normal week in a large number of industries had settled down on the basis of national agreements to forty-five hours (the engineers settled for a 44-hour week from 1 January 1947). Nearly all the 45-hour-week factories worked a five-day week; some factories even reduced the week to forty-two and a half hours, so as to have five equal working days of eight and a half hours each. Thus the five-day week which had begun to appear between the wars, now became the rule in the majority of cases. Its social significance is considerable. Whereas the First World War had brought about a marked reduction in the total of hours worked in the week, the Second World War altered the pattern of the week's work for most of the working classes. The advantages of the long weekend are very clear, and are well set out in the annual Report of the Chief Inspector of Factories for 1947:

> Its popularity with the work people is great: the opportunities it gives to women to shop on Saturday morning when all the best available foodstuffs are displayed in the shops, the freedom for the men and boys to attend sports meetings, even at a distance, or to follow other spare-time occupations, and the long break from work each week, combine to make it the most valued advance of modern times.

The general adoption of the five-day week was not accompanied, of course, by any reduction in production – this would be unthinkable, given the need for the export drive – and production levels were maintained by increased productivity and full employment. Overtime also made some contribution here, but only to a limited extent at first. In 1946 and 1947 there was some reluctance to undertake it. This was understandable enough at the time as a reaction to the long hours during the war, but the PAYE scheme made sure that income tax was duly paid on additional earnings, and in any case there was a lack of consumer goods in the shops on which extra cash might be spent. Following the financial crisis in 1947, the Prime Minister actually had to appeal for longer hours to be worked. This was easier said than done in view of the existing statutory and other restrictions on working hours, and in December 1947 two government orders were issued temporarily permitting longer hours in the coal and cotton industries. However, by 1949 manufacturing industry had attracted an additional 200,000 men and women, and in the next year there was a considerable increase in overtime all over the country, due in part to the effect of rearmament on the engineering and aircraft industries. There were still some complaints from women workers about the inflexibility of working hours, since some would prefer to work overtime on Sundays rather than on Saturdays or on the two evenings a week when it was permitted; but Sunday working was barred to them by law. One way or another, production went up, and, as was noted earlier on, in 1950 output was 75 per cent above pre-war, which was precisely the target figure aimed at when Labour took office.

Conditions on the shop floor do not appear to have altered much during the early post-war years, though it was a great relief to have done with the black-outs and to secure better ventilation as a result. Conditions were at their worst during the great freeze-up of 1947, with the shortage of coal for both heating and industrial purposes, and with frequent power cuts which affected lighting and heating as well as the operation of machinery. The trend towards the use of powered machinery continued, though there is no evidence of any widespread increase in the size of the individual factory. As for accidents, after an initial improvement the accident rate did not change very markedly. In 1946, there were 826 fatal accidents, 180 of them in the building industry. In 1950 there were 799 deaths, with a rather larger work force. A tiny minority of deaths and accidents were due to skylarking, as when a youth of nineteen pretended to throw another lad of fourteen over a rail into the harbour; both fell in, and were drowned. In another incident, a boy of fifteen lost an eye when playing with others at spearing frogs with sharpened files during the dinner hour. Many accidents were due to what might be called traditional causes – the failure to operate safety guards correctly (or ignoring them completely), and women's hair becoming caught up in machinery or in overhead banding where it was still employed in old-fashioned establishments. Among the biggest improvements of the time was the adoption of fluorescent strip lighting. The 1948 Factory Act brought only minor changes; it simply amended the 1937 Act by extending the age limits of the medical examination of young people on entering factory employment. It also included male workers in the regulations for seating facilities, and issued extensive new building regulations. The number of factory canteens increased, but in 1948 there were still only 14,717 hot-meals canteens in a total of 243,369 factories and workshops.

On the whole, no outstanding changes took place in the working environment in the immediate post-war period, though useful progress was made in a number of directions. Work discipline remained as before, and trade disputes were comparatively rare. The wartime regulation, Order 1305, forbidding strikes and requiring disputes to go to arbitration, was still in force, but since pay awards under it permitted wages to rise in step with prices, most unions found this procedure acceptable. In fact, strikes did occur at times, as one might expect, but there were no prolonged national stoppages; and the number of working days lost was comparatively small, certainly when compared with stoppages after the First World War. In 1947, the figure was about 2,430,000, and throughout the period 1945–50 it was around two million. As for the unions, membership was greatly helped by conditions of full employment. In 1945, membership stood at 7,875,000. At the end of 1946 it had increased by 11.5 per cent. In 1947 it was over nine million (the highest ever up to then), and in 1950 it reached 9,243,000, representing 43 per cent of all employees. One of the first moves by the government on assuming office had been to repeal the punitive 1927 Act, so that general strikes again became legal, 'contracting out' replaced 'contracting in' and restrictions on trade union membership by civil servants were lifted; but these changes did not have much effect on the day-to-day lives of workers.

The Standard of Living

The largest element in any cost-of-living calculation is usually money wages in relation to prices, and throughout the period 1945–51 money wages remained remarkably stable, assisted by a government policy of voluntary wage restraint from 1947 onwards. Table 3.1 gives the index figures in summary form. From these figures it will be seen that the cost of living kept ahead of wage rates over the five years, but earnings just managed to stay ahead of the cost of living. This is because earnings were boosted by piece-rate earnings, by overtime and by the upgrading of work processes. In fact, though the cost of living had nearly doubled since 1938, earnings had increased by nearly two and half times. So, although the government showed no undue preference to the unions over the level of wages, in fact real wage levels were maintained and indeed enhanced during the period.

Table 3.1 Earnings, Wage Rates and the Cost of Living, 1946–50

	Average weekly earnings	Wage rates	Cost of living
1946	100	100	100
1947	107	105	107
1948	116	112.5	115
1949	120.5	116	119
1950	126	118	123

Source: Pollard, *The Development of the British Economy, 1914–1990* (3rd edn, 1983).

However, the standard of living does not depend solely on the level of real wages. Housing, for instance, must also be taken into account. It has already been pointed out that the housing shortage made life miserable for those sharing accommodation, though this problem was beginning to ease a little by 1951. Again, food rationing did not cease when the war ended. It not only continued, but grew more stringent under the Labour government. By 1948, rations were even more limited than they were in wartime. In one week in 1948, the meat allowance was down to thirteen ounces, cheese down to one and a half ounces, butter and margarine to six ounces, cooking fat to one ounce, and milk to two pints, with one egg. Some found it a good policy to register as vegetarians, forgoing the meagre meat ration for a better supply of dairy products. In addition, a world wheat shortage in 1946 forced the government first to reduce the size of the standard loaf, then to introduce bread rationing: the allowance was two large loaves a week for adults. Rationing was preceded by a mad rush to stock up before the official commencement of the scheme. According to *The Times*:

> Shops were besieged by customers asking for six, seven, even ten loaves each – twice or thrice as much bread as their families could eat at the weekend. 'The women have gone mad,' said a baker.

Bread rationing went on for two years, till July 1948. Potatoes were also rationed for a time. It is much to the credit of the British people that even in these straitened circumstances they could still send food parcels to their starving ex-enemies in Germany, and that among the leaders who organised this service was one whose race had suffered grievously at the hands of the Germans, the Jewish publisher Victor Gollancz.

Shortages were not limited, however, to housing and foodstuffs. At the time, it was as if most things were either on coupons, or points, or dockets, or just not obtainable at all. It was Sir Stafford Cripps, Chancellor of the Exchequer, who popularised the use of the word 'austerity' in connection with the need for economies in the late forties. Certainly young people getting married found there were problems in setting up home: furniture was rationed, and so was curtain material and bedding. Most suites of new furniture were constructed to certain government-approved standards (the so-called 'utility furniture'), and there were also government standards for bed linen and clothing. Young couples might find difficulties in getting together sufficient food for the wedding breakfast. In these circumstances it is not surprising that a black market developed in goods which were in short supply. Such goods would appear surreptitiously in pubs, or be produced from suitcases on the pavements of busy thoroughfares before the police arrived to stop the trading. The key figure in these dubious proceedings was the 'spiv', a word that came into popular use at the time, and applied to anyone living by his wits without regular work. So the continued shortages of all kinds begat the spiv, who was to linger on for many years, even into the years of affluence of the 1960s. His successor is still with us today in the form of the equally shady but rather better-off urban entrepreneur and second-hand car dealer, Arthur Daley, a key figure in the long-running TV series *Minder*.

How far the working classes were seriously affected by the period of austerity is difficult to say. As we have seen, their standard of living was maintained or even improved at the time. For those who had slogged through six years of war, the post-war years were not exactly years of severe hardship. In any case, full employment and the safety net of the welfare state had transformed the scene, so the inconveniences and deficiencies of austerity did not figure very prominently in their lives. They had been schooled by war conditions to put up with shortages (the usual cry was, 'Don't you know there's a war on?'), to make do and mend, and this they continued to do when peace returned. In the words of the song sung by so many servicemen:

> When this bloody war is over
> Oh, how happy I shall be
> When I get my civvy clothes on
> No more soldiering for me . . .

For most, it was enough to be home in one piece, to have a job, and to enjoy the pleasures of everyday life. Most of the leisure activities of the pre-war period had continued in an attenuated form during the war, and they were now able to expand again. People still went out to the pub, club, dance hall and cinema, and still ended the evening with fish-and-chip suppers. Certainly, attacks on government policy, on the number of government controls, and on the effect of austerity came usually not from the working classes but from the middle classes. It was they who were increasingly impatient with petrol rationing, the scarcity of new cars (they were all going for export, and the proud owner of a new car purchased on the home market had to promise not to resell it within two years), the restrictions on public dinners, and so on.

Finally, the effects of the years of Labour rule on the working-class standard of living were to be seen in a remarkable survey of York carried out by B. S. Rowntree and G. R. Lavers in 1950. As in the previous social surveys of this city, they sought to establish the extent of poverty among the working classes, and found that, whereas in 1936 the proportion was 31.1 per cent (17.7 per cent of all classes), in 1950 it was only 2.8 per cent. Such was the effect of full employment, together with the new social services. Whereas in 1936, one-third blamed their poverty on unemployment, not one did so in 1950; but 68 per cent thought their poverty in 1950 was due to old age. Further, if only the welfare allowances of 1936 had been available in 1950, the proportion of those in poverty would have been 22 per cent, not 2.8 per cent. This survey of York therefore provides a striking illustration of the results of Labour's policies for a working population which had seen a marked decline in poverty since the 1930s.

The End of Labour Rule

In February 1950 a general election was held in which Labour scraped home with a majority of five seats. Clearly, some voters who had supported them in 1945 were looking for a change; the strain of austerity on the middle classes was beginning to tell. The fourth Labour government which was then formed, again under the leadership of Clement Attlee, lasted less than two years. Proposals to nationalise a further list of industries, including cement and sugar, were never carried out. Industrial disputes started to mount as the wages freeze began to melt. A number of communist-led strikes led to prosecutions under Order 1305, while up to 3,000 troops were used to transport meat in a strike at London's Smithfield market. The outbreak of the Korean War in June 1950 had severe financial repercussions in that defence expenditure was greatly increased, and charges for both teeth and spectacles under the NHS were introduced in the 1951 budget by Cripps' successor as Chancellor of the Exchequer, Hugh Gaitskell. This led to the resignation of Bevan, now Minister of Labour, who argued that the

charges were wrong in principle (and also that the defence estimates were unrealistic). Harold Wilson, President of the Board of
Trade, and John Freeman, junior Minister of Supply, also
resigned. By midsummer 1951 the government was worn out:
Cripps and Ernie Bevin had both died, Attlee had been in hospital
with a duodenal ulcer, Herbert Morrison was proving a somewhat
unsuccessful Foreign Secretary just when great problems were
looming in Egypt, Iran and Central Africa. There was in addition a
balance of payments crisis lasting from July to September.

The one bright spot of the time was the Festival of Britain, a
kind of middle-class celebration of British achievement, held on
the South Bank in London, and visited by eight and a half million
people (it was described, rather wickedly, as 'all Heal let loose', a
reference to the fashionable furniture store in Tottenham Court
Road). In Battersea Park nearby, Pleasure Gardens and a Funfair
were opened in imitation of the eighteenth-century pleasure gardens of Vauxhall. The attractions included the Emmet Railway,
the Guinness Clock and an elevated walk (floodlit at night) through
the trees. The Pleasure Gardens drew over eight million visitors,
and were perhaps rather more to the taste of the average working
man and woman than some of the more recherché exhibits on the
South Bank. There were queues for both nylon stockings and festival rock (for which points had to be surrendered). The Festival of
Britain closed at the end of September 1951. Its closure was
followed almost immediately by the dissolution of Parliament on
5 October, and another general election. The results are given in
Table 3.2 The Conservatives were home at last, on a very high poll
of 82 per cent. However, Labour could draw consolation from the
fact that they had won the popular vote, and they had gained the
largest vote ever given to a political party in a general election.

Table 3.2   The General Election of October 1951

Party	Votes gained	No. of MPs
Conservative	13,717,538	321
Labour	13,948,605	295
Liberal	730,556	6
Communist	21,640	0
Others	177,329	3

Social Change Under Labour

How significant for the working classes were the social changes of the six years of Labour rule? It is easy to detect flaws in the achievements of the Labour governments. In the first place, the welfare state was obviously not their exclusive creation. It rested on the earlier Liberal reforms before the First World War, on extensions to those reforms between the wars, and then on the Beveridge Report, itself the work of a Liberal civil servant and university figure. One critic, Professor Titmus, even went so far in 1965 as to suggest that Labour's welfare state was 'little more than an administrative tidying-up of social security provisions'. Another critic has commented more recently that, perhaps inevitably, Labour set about planning to avoid the 1930s, when that decade of the world's history was not going to return anyway. He continues: 'Obsessed by a vision of a socialist future, and dominated by memories of the past, Labour tended to by-pass the present.'

We have seen already that criticism can be levelled at the slow start in housing, and at the inadequacies of the housing programme even in 1951, and at the unadventurous nature of Labour's policy in education. On the largest issue of all, perhaps, it can be argued that Labour singularly failed to introduce the socialist economic change which would have allowed a real reorganisation of society; nationalisation was half-hearted and a virtual failure. There was very little redistribution of income, and in the early 1950s 1 per cent of the population owned over 50 per cent of the private capital in England and Wales. The basic class structure of society remained completely unchanged. In matters of detail, too, it is easy to find fault. The National Health Service was well-meaning enough, but it was given a clumsy administrative system, private medicine was allowed to flourish, and the projected system of local health centres failed to materialise except in one or two isolated instances, such as the William Budd Centre in Bristol. Again, the level of allowances under the social security scheme, as was noted earlier, was too low, so that those in need had to resort to the National Assistance Board, and were subject once more to the humiliation of means testing.

This is a lengthy catalogue of faults, but left unqualified it scarcely permits a fair estimate of what Labour achieved. It is of course perfectly true that Labour built on foundations laid by others – it would be strange if they did not – but to say that they

merely tidied up existing social security provisions seems a remarkable understatement; and the idea that Labour were so preoc-
cupied with the past and the socialist future that they 'tended to
by-pass the present' is a quite baffling judgement in view of the
mass of social legislation which was passed (quite apart from the
achievements in the field of economic, foreign and Commonwealth
policies such as the grant of independence to India). In fact,
Labour carried out all its major election promises, and it is at least
doubtful whether the Conservative Party would have done as
much. This does not sound like by-passing the present. Kenneth
Morgan, himself a Labour supporter, has provided an assessment
of Labour's social policy in the following words:

> Labour's welfare state then, was a mosaic of reform and
> conservatism. Innovation in health and social insurance,
> partial change in housing, relative quiescence in education
> covered the spectrum of social policy.

This seems a not unreasonable assessment of what Labour actually
achieved in social policy (though Professor Marwick prefers 'crazy
paving' to the word 'mosaic'), and Morgan does go on to consider
further aspects of Labour's welfare state, such as food subsidies,
the policy of fair shares and full employment.

What really is left when the smoke of debate has cleared, and the
changes of forty years ago are seen in perspective? Surely, three
changes wrought by Labour stand out, and remain as important
landmarks in the social history of the English working classes: the
first is full employment – something which contrasts so sharply
with the miseries of the 1920s and 1930s, and something which was
to persist under subsequent governments for nearly thirty years till
heavy unemployment returned again in the 1980s. This was a truly
remarkable achievement, and worth recalling today in the light of
the unemployment figures of the last decade. The second is the
creation of the system of social security – imperfect even in its own
day, and certainly so today, but a monument to the desire for
fairness and compassion which characterised not only the Labour
governments of the time, but indeed much of the contemporary
thinking on social matters in the immediate post-war years. The
third is the establishment of the National Health Service – again, in
the nature of things, certainly not without imperfections, and the
subject of hot debate still in the early 1990s. Nevertheless, these
three changes helped to shape the social history of the working

classes to a marked degree in the following decades. Kenneth Morgan makes the point very well in stressing the importance of the post-war Labour governments when he says of Attlee's government that:

> It was without doubt the most effective of all Labour governments, perhaps the most effective of any British government since the passage of the 1832 Reform Act ...

The grammar may be questionable here, but the sentiment is clear. There is one last important point to be made in this connection: the effects of the new directions in social policy begun by Labour were to be seen for years to come, whichever party was in power. The Conservative Party was forced to modernise its policies, as will be seen in the next chapter, so that the welfare state and the maintaining of full employment were to become cardinal tenets in that party's social policy. R. H. S. Crossman was later to remark that Churchill's 1951 government was only 'slightly to the right of Attlee's cabinet'. For the next quarter of a century or more there was substantial agreement between the parties on the fundamentals of social policy. It is hard to think of a more telling proof of the significance of Labour's achievements. The working classes had indeed taken a major step forward.

In conclusion, social change in this country has been brought about in a variety of ways. It may be worth remarking that in this case, oddly enough, it came as the result of the endeavours of a predominantly middle-class cabinet. Attlee himself was an Old Haileyburian, and took pride in the promotion to ministerial rank of fellow Haileyburians. Both Dalton and Cripps were Wykehamists (Cripps was the son of Lord Parmoor, a former Labour minister). Four members of the original team were peers of the realm – Viscount Jowett, Viscount Addison, Lord Penthick-Lawrence and Lord Stansgate. Of the senior members in the cabinet, only four – Morrison, Bevin, Shinwell and Bevan – came from strongly working-class backgrounds. Of course, whatever their social background, they were all members of a party which owed its existence to the trade union movement, an undeniably solid working-class body. In this sense it could certainly be said that they all represented the working-classes. Yet at the same time it could also be argued that the successes of the Attlee government showed that middle-class paternalism was still alive and well in the middle of the twentieth century.

Chapter 4

The Growth of Affluence
1951–1974

The Political Scene

Given the successes of the post-war Labour governments, it was assumed within the Labour Party that after a suitable period for recuperation, Labour would be called upon to form another government and continue with its programme of social reform. Indeed, it seems that at first many Party members were simply prepared to wait for the new Conservative administration under Churchill to come to grief: they were convinced that the application of undiluted Conservatism would soon lead to the Labour Party's being returned to power by the electorate in order to put things right. In fact, this expectation was to prove quite unfounded. Once back in office, the Conservatives remained there for thirteen years; and over the period 1951–74 the Labour Party was in office for only six years, between 1964 and 1970 – that is, for little more than a quarter of the entire period. This is somewhat surprising in view of Labour's achievements earlier on. Broadly speaking, there appear to be two major reasons why this happened.

The first reason is that when the Conservatives returned to power, they had no intention whatever of dismantling the welfare state or even of reversing the process of nationalisation, other than in the steel industry. A new Conservatism had emerged in the late 1940s, mostly through the work of younger Tories such as R. A. Butler, the author of the 1944 Education Act. This newer, more progressive Conservatism, as was noted at the end of the previous chapter, was not markedly different from the policies pursued by Labour. In both home policy and foreign affairs, a broad consensus emerged. Of course, some differences remained, especially between moderate and right-wing Conservative views and the outlook of those on the left of the Labour Party; but there was enough in common for the word 'Butskellism' to be coined as a useful label for the consensus views of the time, the word being formed from the surnames of R. A. Butler and Hugh Gaitskell, who succeeded Attlee as leader of the Labour Party in 1955. Attlee retired full of honours, both literally and metaphorically. He is supposed to have composed a shrewd self-appraisal in the form of a limerick just before he was made a Knight of the Garter:

> Few thought he was even a starter
> There were many who thought themselves smarter
> But he ended PM
> CH and OM
> An earl and a Knight of the Garter.

The second reason why Labour was out of office for so long is that, while the new-look Conservatives remained in office, the standard of living improved and unemployment remained remarkably low. Instead of presenting an equally or more attractive programme to the electorate, Labour was rent by internal disputes as to what their programme should be. Clearly, the welfare state was firmly established and appeared to be in no danger from the Conservatives. Should then the Labour Party extend nationalisation? Should it aim at implementing Clause Four? In the 1950s there was a good deal of revisionist thinking on these issues, together with much criticism of the leadership by a group of left-wingers led by Aneurin Bevan (the 'Bevanites'). Anthony Crosland, in his book *The Future of Socialism* (1956), spoke for many progressive thinkers in the Party in suggesting that Clause Four was outmoded, and that the Party should concentrate rather on maintaining the welfare state, on the abolition of poverty and on promoting greater social equality. Not all revisionists accepted the idea of abandoning Clause Four, though they still urged the necessity of new thinking. Among these would-be reformers was R. H. S. Crossman, a highly intelligent ex-university teacher and maverick of the left. The revisionists failed to convince the traditionally minded members of the Party, who regarded Clause Four as the letter of the law; for them, it was a fundamental precept of socialism, never to be abandoned by the true believer. Even after three election defeats in succession (1951, 1955 and 1959), there were calls from the left for a return to basic socialist principles – the Clause Four Bourbons, as their opponents called them, alleging that they had learned nothing and forgotten nothing. When Gaitskell boldly attempted to get rid of Clause Four in 1959, his efforts ended in failure. Harold Wilson, who became leader of the Party following Gaitskell's premature death in 1963, was too astute a politician to raise the issue again, remarking somewhat disingenuously that tampering with Clause Four was like trying to remove the book of Genesis from the Bible. Presumably he was implying that no one was under any obligation to believe in Clause Four (or the book of Genesis), but that it would be impolitic to try to get rid of it because it would frighten the traditionally minded.

Other subjects which caused dissension among Labour Party supporters (and perhaps weighed rather more heavily with the average voter) were whether Britain should join the Common Market or not, and whether Britain should dispense with nuclear armaments and disarm unilaterally. Although entry into Europe was opposed officially by the Labour Party, it was finally achieved by the Conservatives under Edward Heath in 1973; but the arguments over unilateral nuclear disarmament dragged on, and for a short while it became official Labour Party policy at the Scarborough Party Conference in 1960. Interestingly enough, Bevan the arch-critic and rebel opposed unilateralism earlier on at the 1957 Conference, declaring that if it were adopted he as the next Labour Foreign Secretary would be sent 'naked into the conference chamber'. The arguments of the unilateralists, he declared, constituted not statesmanship, but 'an emotional spasm'. Gaitskell similarly spoke against unilateral nuclear disarmament, and although narrowly defeated on the issue at Scarborough, declared in his most famous speech that he could never accept the Conference decision:

> It is not in dispute that the vast majority of Labour
> Members of Parliament are utterly opposed to unilateralism
> and neutralism. So what do you expect them to do? Change
> their minds overnight? ... There are some of us, Mr
> Chairman, who will fight and fight again to save the Party
> we love. We will fight and fight and fight again to bring back
> sanity and honesty and dignity, so that our Party with its
> great past may retain its glory and its greatness.

The following year, Conference's decision was reversed.

All these disputes clearly weakened Labour's support by the electorate, and the arguments over defence policies in particular were to resurface later, especially in the 1980s. In addition, there were the beginnings of certain social trends which will be examined later in this book. The most important was the rise in prosperity and the increase in real wages. In the period 1951–9 there was a 20 per cent rise in consumption. The better-paid working man began to enjoy a more affluent way of life, and to adopt a lifestyle more characteristic of the lower middle class. House ownership as opposed to renting accommodation increased. At the same time, the service industries were expanding, while manufacturing industry remained static or contracted, so that white-collar jobs increased at the expense of manual labour. All this should not be over-emphasised for the 1950s, and these changes were to assume much greater importance later on. Nevertheless, even in the 1950s class solidarity was beginning to weaken, and the social basis for Labour's electoral support was not what it had been in the 1940s.

The Labour Governments 1964–1970

What then was actually achieved by the Labour Party when they were in office between 1964 and 1970? This is not a political history, but some account is necessary of those political events which affected the social history of the period. The contrast with the great achievements of 1945 to 1951 is very marked, but of course the tasks facing Labour in the two periods were very different. In 1945 Labour was confronted by massive economic and social problems, but had a substantial majority and widespread support for introducing the welfare state. In 1964, the Labour majority in the House initially was only five at the maximum. The welfare services were firmly established, and Harold Wilson's main aim appeared to be to achieve some kind of technological revolution which would keep Britain ahead of her rivals rather than a further major instalment of social reform. In 1966 the general election transformed his small majority into a much more comfortable overall majority of ninety-six. The most striking feature of Labour's six years in office is probably the continual struggle to keep the economy on an even keel, and as part of this there were repeated attempts to hold down prices and wages, and to curb excessive wage demands and wildcat strikes. In addition, some useful social reforms were passed, but in a pragmatic spirit, and not as part of any wide-ranging, overall plan of reform. Perhaps the most challenging attempt at economic reform was the proposed renationalisation of steel. A White Paper in 1965 planned to take fourteen of the largest steel companies into public ownership, but nothing was done to further the proposal. A Bill to reform the House of Lords was also abandoned.

On the economic front, the Labour government of 1964 inherited a balance of payments problem which was solved at least temporarily by a 15 per cent surcharge placed on imports. Six years later in January 1970 there was a trade surplus of £39 million, and the economic situation looked promising. In between these dates, economic fluctuations were very marked, and there were numerous financial crises, the worst being in the summer of 1967 when the trade gap widened and the reserves fell. It was thought necessary to devalue the pound by 14.3 per cent. Wilson observed cryptically that 'This does not mean that the pound in your pocket ... has been devalued.' What it did mean was that devaluation was followed by further cuts in the armed forces, and then by a tranche of economies of a kind hardly to be expected from a Labour government. Thus prescription charges were brought back (they had been abolished by Labour back in 1964), charges for dental treatment were raised, free milk was withdrawn from secondary schools, the housing programme was curtailed, and the raising of the school-leaving age was postponed from 1971 to 1973. None of this was entirely unprecedented, of course, for in the previous year there had been counter-measures to inflation such as raising hire-purchase terms, placing a £50 limit on holiday spending overseas, increasing purchase tax by 10 per cent, and putting more duty on wines and spirits. Efforts were also made from 1964 onwards to impose a voluntary prices and incomes policy. In 1964 this became a mandatory prices and wages freeze for six months, followed by a period of severe wages restraint.

All this was unpopular with the trade unions, who treasured their right to negotiate wages freely in the best interests of their members. In 1968, the Trades Union Congress voted by 7.7 million votes to 1 million against the government's wages policy, while the Labour Party's annual Conference in that year rejected that policy by nearly five to one. It was in this year that the government was particularly unpopular with the unions. The Donovan Commission Report on trade unions was published early in the year, and was followed by a White Paper commissioned by the Employment Secretary, Barbara Castle, entitled *In Place of Strife*. This sought to limit the freedom to strike in certain cases by providing for a 28-day 'cooling off' period and a secret ballot of members. There were also to be penalties imposed on unions who broke the new law. Strikes in themselves were not barred, and the conciliatory period and holding of a ballot were for discretionary use only. The whole idea was to stop lightning, unofficial strikes, and so actually to strengthen official trade union procedures. Nevertheless, Barbara Castle was fully aware of the difficulties she faced. She assured George Woodcock, secretary of the TUC, that she was not hostile to the unions – 'You know, George, I am not out to clobber the unions' – but she observed gloomily to another friend, 'It would be I who first shackled the unions' (the grammar is admirably correct, but the statement turned out to be quite false). Later she remarked in her diary:

> I found the TUC was less enthusiastic about Donovan than it had made out to be ... it remained deeply suspicious of any interference in the running of union affairs or any kind of sanctions against unions. I was soon in difficulties, therefore, over the Donovan proposals ...

The White Paper was immensely unpopular on the left – it was opposed within the cabinet by James Callaghan (who actually spoke against it at a meeting of the National Executive Committee of the Party), by Labour backbenchers (over a hundred abstained or voted against it), by the National Executive Committee itself, and by the General Council of the TUC. Under pressure, the TUC produced their own relatively toothless 'Programme for Action' for trade union reform, which was accepted at a special meeting of Congress in June 1969. The cabinet clearly risked defeat if they persisted with the Bill which had been drafted. On 18 June they capitulated, accepting the 'Programme for Action', providing that the TUC undertook 'a solemn and binding undertaking' to enforce it; this meant very little. The government's plan to introduce the unions, kicking and screaming, to the changed economic realities of the post-war scene, which made industrial peace so vital, resulted in almost complete failure. Perhaps inevitably, it was left to the Conservatives to resume the challenge to the unions after 1970.

On the whole, the record of the Labour governments of 1966–70 in economic affairs was somewhat inglorious. It must be said,

however, that every government since the war has had to deal prag-
matically with economic problems as they arise, and the Labour
governments were conventional enough in their policies, relying
for the most part on the well-known principles of Keynesian demand management. In fact, the economy was not in a bad shape by
1970, and by then a number of useful social reforms had been
passed which can be conveniently dealt with here. They include
the Rent Act of 1965, fixing fair rents and giving increased security
of tenure; the Trade Disputes Act of 1965, protecting trade union
officials against legal actions arising out of breaches of contract,
thus effectively overturning the decision in the recent case of *Rook*
v. *Barnard* (1964); and the Redundancy Payments Act of 1965. In
the field of race relations, the Race Relations Board was set up by
the Race Relations Act of 1965, and this Act was extended by
another in 1968, increasing the powers of the Board and banning
discrimination in housing, employment, insurance and other services. It was this Act which provoked Enoch Powell, Conservative
MP for Wolverhampton, into a notorious prediction of racial strife
to come: 'As I look ahead, I am filled with foreboding. Like the
Roman, I seem to see the River Tiber foaming with much blood.'
This was a testimony to Mr Powell's classical erudition, but
scarcely a helpful prediction at the time.

The Immigration Appeals Act of 1969 further amended the law
on the subject, while useful advances were made in the field of
education as comprehensive education was encouraged by Circular
10/65 in 1965, the Certificate of Secondary Education was introduced, and the Open University was established in 1970, this last
achievement owing much to Nye Bevan's widow, Jennie Lee. It
must also be noted that the Wilson governments passed several
liberal and humanitarian Acts such as the Murder (Abolition of
Death Penalty) Act of 1965, abolishing the death penalty for murder, at first for a trial period, and then permanently. Homosexual
practices between consenting adults (that is, over eighteen) were
also legalised by the 1967 Sexual Offences Act. The age of consent
was reduced to eighteen, while the laws on divorce and abortion
were amended by Acts passed in 1967 and 1969. We shall return to
the subject of changing moral standards in the next chapter.

In concluding this section, it must be remarked that the social
history of the English working classes was not significantly altered
between 1951 and 1974 by the direct action of the so-called People's
Party. Indeed, some of their legislation, such as the return of

prescription charges, came somewhat oddly from the party which had created the welfare state. The major influence on the lives of ordinary people was probably the continuance of a high level of employment, and the rise in the standard of living – that is, it was the improvement in the economy as a whole which had the greatest effect. To this subject we may now turn.

The Economy

Much more important in the post-war decades for the general well-being of the working classes than Labour legislation was the continued growth of the economy. 'Growth' was the keyword of the time: it was well known not only that the economy was growing, but that it was vital for everyone's standard of living that this growth should be maintained. Circumstances in the 1950s and 1960s were very favourable for Britain to advance internationally. Britain alone had escaped invasion, and competition from war-ravaged Germany and Japan was at first very limited. Marshall Aid and then increased public expenditure helped to stimulate economic activity. Industrial output grew annually by 3.7 per cent in the period 1948 to 1960 (the figure for the inter-war period was 3.1 per cent). Physical output per head also rose. Most strikingly, gross domestic product (GDP) per head, which had risen by 29 per cent between 1920 and 1936, in the post-war period of 1950–60 rose by 40 per cent.

This did not mean, of course, that the ailing staple industries of the inter-war period had miraculously revived. They continued to decline, and production decreased in coal, iron and steel, shipbuilding and textiles; but this decline was more than offset by the further rise of the new industries such as chemicals, oil, the electrical industry and the motor industry. There was also a further shift of employment into the service sector, where production increased in gas, electricity, water, food, drink and tobacco. So two distinct movements may be discerned, one away from the old staples and into the new industries, and the other into the service or tertiary sector. The latter was particularly significant in signalling a move away from manufacturing industry as an employer of labour, a process of deindustrialisation which was to become increasingly prominent by the 1980s. By 1981 there were 11.2 million workers in the tertiary sector, which represented 54 per cent of the total work force, and nearly double the numbers employed in manufacturing industry.

As we have seen, all this did not go unattended by sudden crises in the national finances. Nevertheless, up to the early 1970s the overall pattern was one of economic success, due largely to the skilful practice of Keynesian principles of management of the economy. Here Butskellism seemed to work well. What was less emphasised at the time was the extent to which Britain's share in the world's manufacturing exports was declining. The figures in Table 4.1 for the years 1950 to 1975 are instructive. Thus, Britain's share in the world export of manufactures had declined very markedly. Of course, healthy economic activity need not take the form exclusively of manufacturing – man does not live by manufacturing alone – but the figures for GDP, set out in Table 4.2, exhibit a similar alarming relative fall. This is not the place for an extended discussion of the implications of these figures, but the evidence seems clear enough that under the glossy exterior of the British economy there lurked deeper problems of low growth and low productivity that were to come to the surface after the oil crisis of 1973.

Table 4.1 Percentage Share of World Exports of Manufactures, 1950–75

	1950	1960	1965	1970	1975
United Kingdom	25.5	16.5	13.9	10.8	9.3
France	9.9	9.6	8.8	8.7	10.2
Germany	7.3	19.3	19.1	19.8	20.3
Japan	3.4	6.9	9.4	11.7	13.6
USA	27.3	21.6	20.3	18.5	17.7

Source: B.W.E.Alford, *British Economic Performance, 1945–1975* (1988).

Table 4.2 GDP per Person Employed 1955–1973 (average rates of growth per annum)

	UK	Austria	Belgium	France	Germany	Italy	Netherlands
1955–60	1.8	4.2	2.1	4.9	5.0	4.6	3.5
1960–4	2.2	4.6	4.1	5.0	4.7	6.3	3.4
1964–9	2.5	5.2	3.6	5.2	5.0	6.3	4.8
1969–73	2.8	6.4	4.2	5.0	4.2	4.5	4.4

Source: Alford, *British Economic Performance, 1945–1975* (1988).

In the meantime, the phrase 'affluent society' was used more and more to describe Britain in the sixties. The figures warning of the country's relative decline were of little interest to the average working man and woman who understandably enough were more concerned with job prospects, conditions at work and standards of living. In all these respects, affluence was a reality for most workers. Jobs were plentiful, wages kept ahead of prices, welfare services were maintained, and the entertainment and leisure industries expanded. Indeed, there was a shortage of labour, and a steadily increasing stream of immigrant labour, at first mostly from the West Indies, made itself available for the less attractive jobs, for example, as porters on British Rail, bus conductors, sweepers and cleaners. West Indian help in the hospitals, in particular, was invaluable. All in all, whatever criticisms are made of British economic performance at this time, the remark of the Conservative Prime Minister, Harold Macmillan, made in 1957, that 'Most of our people have never had it so good' (he liked to affect a demotic mode of speech at times) seems to be justified. For the masses, they certainly had never had it so good.

Work and Its Rewards

Conditions at work improved without changing very significantly during the period covered by this chapter, but the typical place of work underwent important changes. Between the wars, the majority of workers were still employed in manufacture in factories or workshops; after 1951 the numbers so employed were reduced until, as noted earlier, they were only half as many thirty years later as those in the service sector. There was also a steep decline in agricultural employment, which was reduced sharply by about one-third between 1950 and 1980. Moreover, when a worker was still engaged in manufacturing industry, his place of work usually became much larger in the course of time. Meanwhile, the Factory Inspectorate concentrated more and more on safety regulations, especially when potentially dangerous products such as chemicals were in use. In the report of the Chief Inspector of Factories for 1954 there was for the first time a section on 'automation' – described as 'a transatlantic term of which we are going to hear much in the future'. In the same report there was an explanation of a device called a 'computer'. Another sign of the times was a chapter in the 1958 report on Nuclear Energy and Ionising Radiations.

To consider some of these developments in more detail: the change in the size of the factory is well illustrated by comparing the Chief Inspector's report for 1951 with the report for 1971, twenty years later. In the former report, it is emphasised that the great bulk of premises subject to inspection remained small. This was so in the Black Country, while in London hand embroidery, mostly for masonic regalia, was carried on as before in small workshops in Bethnal Green and the City. By way of contrast, the 1971 report pointed out that while well over half of the factories registered still remained very small (about 130,000 out of a total of 198,000), they employed in the aggregate only about 7 per cent of the working population. More than half the workers were employed in fewer than 5,000 premises. According to Professor Pollard, the share of small firms of total manufacturing output dropped from 35 per cent in 1935 to 16 per cent in 1963. At the other end of the scale, the largest hundred manufacturing firms in 1948 were responsible for 21 per cent of output, 38 per cent in 1963, and 47 per cent in 1976. By the 1970s, therefore, Pollard suggests that the giant firm had become typical for manufacturing as a whole: in 1972, 45 per cent of manufacturing employees worked in enterprises of 5,000 or over, compared with only 35 per cent in enterprises employing 999 or less. Almost 60 per cent worked in individual plants employing 500 or more.

How far this growth in the size of factory premises made working conditions safer or more pleasant is not easy to judge, since the raw figures for accidents must be seen against a declining factory population. Nevertheless, after some increases in the early 1960s, by 1970 the figure for the year for fatal accidents was the lowest for the century (see Table 4.3). The 1970 report also records the fact that the first chair in Industrial Safety and Hygiene had just been established at Aston University in Birmingham.

Table 4.3   Fatal Accidents, 1967–70

	1967	1968	1969	1970
Factory premises	342	359	357	325
Construction sites	197	238	265	203
Docks and inland warehouses	25	28	27	28
Total	564	625	649	556

Source: Annual Report of the Chief Inspector of Factories, 1970.

However gratifying this decline in fatal accidents might be, the 1971 report still records dissatisfaction with the continued indifference of some companies to the safety of their workers. This was particularly noticeable in the construction industry. To quote the report:

> The construction industry has been faced by the inherent dangers of excavation work for many years. There is plenty of knowledge of how to cope with these dangers as the high standard of timbering provided by many companies clearly demonstrates. Unfortunately, however, some companies either remain ignorant of the methods of protecting their workers or are less scrupulous about doing so. The price for this during the last ten years is the lives of 159 men killed in excavation collapses. This means that part of our industrial activity is being conducted on the wholly unacceptable basis that 15 men will meet their deaths each year by being buried alive in circumstances which should never occur.

Meanwhile, the health and welfare provisions of the Factory Acts were extended to other workplaces by the Offices, Shops and Railway Premises Act 1963, while the Health and Safety at Work Act 1974 (according to the Inspectorate, the most radical piece of legislation since the Factory and Workshop Act 1878) set up a Health and Safety Commission, and brought together five inspectorates – those for Factories, Explosives, Mines and Quarries, Nuclear Installations, and Alkalis and Clean Air.

All in all, the period 1951–74 appears to have witnessed an appreciable improvement in safety at work, though the total of non-fatal accidents notified actually went up in the 1960s, reaching a peak in 1969 of 322,390 but declining to 256,960 in 1974. As the scope of the Factories Act widened, while at the same time the size of the work force in manufacturing industry declined, it is not possible to make exact quantitative judgements; but it is reasonable to suppose that much more care and attention was given to safety matters by employers and staff alike in the 1970s. The early post-war years were in turn much safer than the similar period after the First World War, when medical attention could be extraordinarily crude. In the furniture trade, for example, shavings, or shellac finished off with shavings, would be applied to flesh wounds, while girls in the Birmingham cycle trade, affected by the vapour from rubber solutions, were simply laid on the ground in the fresh air till they recovered. Things had improved greatly by 1974, but this did not prevent one of the most disastrous industrial accidents ever in that year when the Nypro (UK) Ltd chemical works at Flixborough blew up, killing twenty-eight and injuring thirty-six; 1,821 houses and 167 retails shops were damaged or destroyed.

What happened to working hours? In the broadest of terms, the normal week remained at about 44.6 hours during the 1950s, but was gradually reduced during the 1960s until it had reached 40.0 hours in 1974. Table 4.4 sets out the picture in more detail. If overtime is taken into account, the reduction is from between 46 and 47 hours in the 1950s to an average of 43.6 hours in 1970–4 – a similar reduction to that in normal working hours of about four hours weekly.

So far the picture is rosy enough: life at work became safer in the fifties and sixties and there was a significant reduction in the hours of work. One other factor must be examined before estimating changes in the standard of living: this is unemployment. Between the years 1945 and 1965 unemployment remained low, averaging about 1.8 per cent of the work force, or round about 400,000. This figure could be assumed to represent the small proportion of the working population who were merely passing from one job to

Table 4.4

Year	Normal weekly	Actual weekly
1960	43.7	46.2
1961	42.8	45.7
1962	42.2	45.3
1963	42.4	45.4
1964	42.2	45.8
1965	41.4	45.3
1966	40.7	44.3
1967	40.5	44.3
1968	40.5	44.5
1969	40.4	44.6
1970	40.3	43.9
1971	40.2	43.2
1972	40.1	43.5
1973	40.0	43.9
1974	40.0	43.4

Source: A.H.Halsey (ed.), *British Social Trends since 1900* (1988).

another, or were the chronically unemployed or unemployable. During this period it could very reasonably be taken for granted that anyone who really wanted to find a job could do so. It will be recalled that Beveridge considered that an unemployment figure of 3 per cent represented full employment. Throughout the 1950s the figure was about 1.5 per cent, and in the 1960s about 2 per cent. However, the recurrent peaks of unemployment crept up during these two decades. The peak of 400,000 in 1952 was followed by a peak of 500,000 in 1958, then of 600,000 in 1963. By 1972 the peak of 950,000 or 3.8 per cent was reached, and thereafter the figure never dropped below 500,000. In 1975 the ominous figure of one million unemployed was attained (4 per cent). Clouds were obviously gathering by the mid-1970s, but for the greater part of the period under review in this chapter, unemployment was scarcely a problem. Both the major political parties were pledged to keep unemployment at a minimum, and this they appeared able to do until the onset of the 1970s.

To turn now to the standard of living: during the 1950s the cost of living rose by about 41 per cent. In the 1960s the rise was a little steeper – 57.5 per cent, with a marked acceleration in 1971–4 of 45 per cent. Over the whole period 1951–74, the cost of living went up by just over three times. Weekly money wages, on the other hand, over the same time increased by a little over six times, so that real wages just about doubled. Taking the slightly longer period of 1950–75, Professor Pollard has reached a very similar conclusion, based on a rise in average weekly earnings from an index figure of 63.5 in 1950 to 115.8 in 1975, that real wages very nearly doubled. These are remarkable conclusions. There were, of course, some pockets of poverty untouched by the welfare state, and they will be considered later. Again, another qualification is that all wages figures quoted are averages, and not those of the poorest paid; though from the mid-sixties onwards unskilled wages settled at around 85 per cent of skilled wages. Women's wages remained much lower than men's. Nevertheless, once necessary caveats of this kind have been issued, it is evident that the working classes experienced a period of unparalleled prosperity for nearly a quarter of a century in the post-war period.

Undoubtedly most of this prosperity is attributable to full employment and the rise in real wages (Professor Cairncross has remarked that much of what happened over the three post-war decades can be traced to the effect of full employment). When all this was accompanied by a shorter working week and a better working environment, Macmillan's famous dictum once again comes to mind. This is not to say, of course, that working conditions everywhere had become idyllic; a good many work processes were still both dirty and dangerous, as in iron foundries, or simply tedious and exhausting as on the assembly lines at Longbridge, Cowley and Dagenham. Nevertheless, it remains true that on the whole life at work had improved, and so had its rewards. Among the latter is holiday entitlement, which had increased to the extent that by 1974 38 per cent of manual workers had three weeks' paid holiday, and just over half (52 per cent) had three to four weeks off. Yet all this was achieved against a background of continual changes in government economic policies, often directed at limiting wage demands in order to control inflation. Co-operation with the trade unions therefore became a prime necessity, and the unions gained a political prominence without precedent in the 1970s.

The Trade Unions

Undoubtedly the prosperity of the time had a great deal to do with the increase in membership and in the power of the trade unions in the fifties and sixties. The membership figures in Table 4.5 speak for themselves.

Table 4.5   Trade Union Membership, 1950–75

Year	Membership	Density of membership (%)
1950	9,289,000	44.1
1955	9,741,000	44.5
1960	9,835,000	44.2
1965	10,325,000	44.2
1970	11,187,000	48.5
1974	11,764,000	50.4
1975	12,026,000	51.0

Source: Halsey (ed.), *British Social Trends since 1900* (1988).

It will be observed that membership increased in the period by over 2.5 million, and that by 1975 the unions had recruited just over half of all workers eligible for union membership. In fact, by then total membership represented slightly under half of the total occupied population of the country (12,026,000 out of 25,021,000). It should be added that membership was to mount even higher and finally peak in 1979 at 13,289,000. Notable features of this growth earlier on included the amalgamations which followed the Trade Unions (Amalgamations) Act 1964, such as that of the Engineers and Foundry Workers, and the formation of the National Graphical Association. Three craft unions merged to form the Amalgamated Society of Boilermakers, Shipwrights, Blacksmiths and Structural Workers; the Electricians and Plumbers also combined to form one union. The Amalgamated Society of Technical and Managerial Staff (ASTMS), a new white-collar union, was created under the leadership of the highly articulate and skilful Welsh unionist, Clive Jenkins. At the same time there was an increase in the numbers of the largest unions. By 1968 there were nine unions with more than a quarter of a million members each, and eleven in 1979. Membership was also influenced by the growth of the 'closed shop' principle. This affected about 3.75 million workers in 1962, and 4 million in 1974. Another feature of trade union expansion was the spread of unionism among white-collar workers, partly because of their growth in numbers as a proportion of the total work force, and partly because they felt they were being paid relatively less than manual workers. The result was the growth of substantial unions such as the National Association of Local Government Officers (NALGO) and the National Union of Teachers (NUT), both of which joined the TUC in the 1960s. At the same time, some of the long-established trades shrank in numbers, so that their union membership was reduced accordingly; for example, in 1968 the miners had only 54 per cent of their membership in 1959, while the National Union of Railwaymen were down to 60 per cent of their previous strength.

This increase in the numbers and influence of trade unionists before 1974 was not always welcome to those outside the movement. Certainly the general public was frequently reminded of their importance during the periodical clashes between the unions and the government over wages policy. Professor Pelling refers to the unions' 'loss of popular repute' in the late 1950s, though he thinks there was some recovery of this loss in the early 1960s. At the time the great struggle to free the Electrical Trades Union from communist domination which began in 1956 produced a number of unsavoury revelations of ballot-rigging. These inevitably tarnished the image of the movement. Eventually the two ex-communists who led the campaign for reform, Frank Chapple (now Lord Chapple) and Les Cannon, sued the union in 1960, and in the same year the union was expelled from the TUC and the Labour Party. Fresh elections for union officials were held under new rules, and the reformed union was readmitted to both the TUC and the Labour Party in 1962. This was a necessary cleaning-up operation, and after all its travail the union eventually emerged with some credit, though the whole episode gave considerable satisfaction to opponents of trade unionism.

Other aspects of union activity which undoubtedly attracted criticism included the speed with which some union officials called men out on strike, often on the basis of a show of hands at a mass meeting (the 'wildcat' strike); then there was the practice of over-manning, and the persistence of inter-union demarcation disputes. Occasionally there was violence on the picket lines, when blacklegs or scabs were attacked. Middle-class prejudice against unionism was strengthened by films such as *I'm Alright, Jack* (featuring Peter Sellers as a self-important shop steward), and *The Angry Silence*, portraying the treatment meted out to a blackleg. A popu-lar TV comedy, *The Rag Trade*, amusing and harmless in itself, featured Miriam Karlin as a militant shop steward in a small clothing workshop whose strident blast on the whistle and cry of 'Everybody out!' would bring work to an abrupt end, to the dis-may of the bumbling and inefficient proprietor, played by Peter Jones. In fact, the majority of strikes were conducted properly enough, and were based on perfectly legitimate grievances; the real problem was the increase in unofficial strikes which did not follow the conventional procedures. Although the belief grew up at the time that England was particularly strike-prone, there is actu-ally no reason to suppose that workers here went on strike more readily than workers elsewhere in Europe. Further, three-quarters of all strikes lasted less than three days for most of the 1960s. In the late 1960s this proportion was reduced, but still remained at about half in the 1970s. Earlier on, the coal industry was more strike-prone than other industries – 70 per cent of all strikes between 1952 and 1957 were in the coal industry. Later on, the metal industry and the motor industry became the commonest industries for strikes. Yet even then, in the period 1971–3 there were no strikes at all in 95 per cent of manufacturing plants. However, by then strikes were becoming more serious, not necessarily because they were more numerous, but because they were lasting longer and the number of days lost at work was growing. The official figures – set out in Table 4.6 below – are thought to understate the true figures very considerably, but they show the trend from 1964 to 1974 clearly enough.

Table 4.6   Industrial Disputes, 1964–1974

Year	No. of stoppages	Workers (000s)	Days lost (000s)
1964	2,524	883	2,277
1965	2,354	876	2,925
1966	1,937	544	2,398
1967	2,116	734	2,787
1968	2,378	2,258	4,690
1969	3,116	1,665	6,846
1970	2,906	1,801	10,980
1971	2,228	1,178	13,551
1972	2,497	1,734	23,909
1973	2,873	1,528	7,197
1974	2,922	1,626	14,750

Source: Halsey (ed.), *British Social Trends since 1900* (1988).

It is no coincidence that the overwhelming majority of strikes were concerned with pay in a period when successive governments, both Conservative and Labour, struggled to keep wage levels down in order to reduce inflation. In fact, as was seen in the last chapter, efforts to restrain wage increases began even in the late 1940s. They were resumed very mildly in the early 1950s when the Chancellor of the Exchequer, R. A. Butler, sought but failed to reach an agreement with the TUC that wage increases should be linked with productivity. Further efforts were made in 1957 by both the engineering and the dock employers to agree on a voluntary wage restraint, but without success. In the same year, the government set up the Council on Productivity, Prices and Incomes to give advice on wage claims; it was viewed with great suspicion by the TUC, which in effect boycotted it until its abolition in 1962. The 1950s ended without any firm wages policy being pursued by the government, which sometimes attempted to prevent wage increases while at other times refrained from intervening in the interests of keeping industrial peace.

Why should such difficulties have arisen? That there were great difficulties is undeniable. Professor Phelps Brown, the distinguished historian and expert on trade unionism, has remarked: 'So incomes policy is inescapable; but it has also proved impracticable. Again and again, after a time it has broken down.' Denis Healey, Labour Chancellor of the Exchequer in the 1970s, puts it another way in his autobiography:

> Adopting a pay policy is rather like jumping out of a second-floor window. No one in his senses would do it unless the stairs were on fire. But in post-war Britain, the stairs have always been on fire …

There was indeed no alternative under conditions of full employment to attempting to enforce some form of wages policy if inflation, with all its dire consequences, was not to get out of hand. It was obviously in the interests of all for this to be done. On the other hand, the trade unions were very suspicious of efforts to hold wages down, especially when the cost of living was rising and when ample profits were being made by the employers. Why should the workers suffer wage restraint in these circumstances? The very essence of trade unionism has always been to exercise the collective strength of labour in order to achieve a fair day's pay; so that to take away trade union rights to collective bargaining in the higher interests of the community as a whole seemed to many to be a most dubious proceeding – a sell-out to the employers, in fact. Of course, this might be considered an absurdly short-sighted attitude, but even when trade union officials were prepared to accept some form of wage restraint, their difficulty was often that they could never be sure that other unions would not defy the government and secure an advance for their own members (in games theory, the classic case of the 'prisoner's dilemma'). So the chances of anything other than a compulsory policy having any effect were remote. Yet a compulsory policy, as we have seen, was deeply repugnant to the unions, and in practice often broke down. For these reasons the whole business of incomes policy, wage restraint and trade union power remained a problem throughout the fifties and sixties, especially when full employment and the shortage of labour encouraged instant strikes.

In 1962 the National Economic Development Council (the NEDC, or 'Neddy') was established in a further attempt to regulate the economy, together with another body, the National

Incomes Commission. A severe pay freeze had been introduced the previous year, but this was relaxed in 1962, followed by a 'guiding light' of a permitted 2 per cent pay increase. Economic conditions eased later in 1962, and again in 1964, Labour taking office under Harold Wilson in the October of that year. The main events of Wilson's two ministries, 1964–6 and 1966–70, have already been described, though it should be mentioned again that efforts were renewed to achieve some sort of wage stability: the employers and unions signed a Declaration of Intent on Productivity, Prices and Incomes in 1964, a National Board for Prices and Incomes was established in 1965, and both voluntary and compulsory wages freezes were tried. In spite of all this, Barbara Castle felt compelled to introduce the ill-fated White Paper, *In Place of Strife*, in 1968. Meanwhile industrial unrest increased, three times as many workers being involved in stoppages as in 1967. In 1969, days lost through disputes were more than three times what they had been when Labour took office in 1964.

Hence, when the Conservatives under Edward Heath replaced Labour in 1970, they were faced with a uniformly hostile trade union movement. The hostility increased with the government's Industrial Relations Act of 1971, which made another attempt to reform union procedures. A National Industrial Relations Court (the NIRC) was set up with power to impose a 'cooling-off' period and to require a strike ballot when the Court considered it necessary. The Court could also impose fines on unions for 'unfair industrial practices'. The unions were to register with a new Registrar of Trade Unions and Employees' Associations. The pre-entry closed shop became illegal. These provisions provoked roars of protest from both the trade unions and the Labour Party (though there were obvious similarities between some of the terms and Barbara Castle's earlier proposals). The TUC boycotted the NIRC, suspending thirty-two unions in 1972 and expelling twenty in the next year for registering. Meanwhile, the economic situation grew worse as unemployment increased and inflation intensified (the average annual increase between 1970 and 1973 was 8.6 per cent).

The government's trade union legislation worked very badly. When a conciliation period was imposed on the railway unions by the NIRC, and a secret ballot ordered, the effect was to strengthen the railway workers' determination to strike; they voted six to one in favour of striking (the Railway Board conceded their claims almost in full). The Court had as little success when the London dockers were ordered to stop blacking certain lorries and five dockers (the 'Pentonville Five') were jailed for disobeying the order. Thirty thousand dockers then came out on strike. The five dockers were finally released on a technicality by the intervention of a hitherto little-known government official, the Official Solicitor. The engineering workers also attracted the displeasure of the Court, which fined them first £5,000 and then £50,000 in 1972, and then £75,000 in 1973. But perhaps the most significant event of all took place in January and February 1972 with the first national miners' strike since 1926. A particular feature of this strike was the use of flying pickets, who moved from one industrial site to another: parties of miners picketed coal-fired power stations so that coal supplies could not get through. The railwaymen also refused to move coal trains. One notorious episode occurred at the Saltley coke depot in Birmingham where amid scenes of considerable violence 6,000 unionists prevented coke lorries from being moved. A Committee of Enquiry was appointed by Heath's government (the Wilberforce Committee), and the miners secured rises of 17–20 per cent, three times greater than those offered by the Coal Board. Well-organised, all-out tactics that did not flinch at violence seemed to be winning the day.

By 1973 there was still no solution in sight to the problems of rising inflation and continued large-scale pay demands. The Conservative government's efforts to regulate wage demands through a tighter control of trade union activities had failed. The government fell back again on a wage and price freeze from November 1972 onwards, with a new Pay Board and Prices Commission. Stage III of this policy came into operation in October 1973 just when Arab oil producers were restricting supplies and the price of oil imports was trebled. During the following month the National Union of Mineworkers (President, Joe Gormley, secretary Lawrence Daly) put forward a pay claim which breached Stage III, at the same time banning overtime and weekend working. Problems increased when the electricity power engineers began a work-to-rule, and the railway union, ASLEF, banned Sunday, overtime and rest-time working. Faced by these new threats, the government declared a State of Emergency on 13 November: to conserve fuel, the use of electricity for heating was restricted, and from January 1974 electricity was supplied to industry for only three days a week. Further, a 50 m.p.h. speed limit was introduced, and television broadcasting had to stop at 10.30 p.m. Thus the combination of an economic crisis and the intransigence of certain unions (the NUM in particular) had produced a national crisis.

Over the next two months, strenuous efforts were made to bring about a settlement of the miners' dispute, both by the government and by the TUC, which at one stage suggested that if the government brought the miners and the Coal Board to an agreement the TUC would see to it that the other unions would not take the miners' settlement as a precedent; for the miners, they argued, were clearly a special case requiring special consideration. This conciliatory offer came to nothing. Further proposals in January 1974 by the Pay Board based on the relative differences in pay between different groups of industrial workers also proved fruitless. On 1 February, the results of a miners' ballot on national strike action was announced: 81 per cent were in favour of striking. On 7 February, the Prime Minister announced that a general election would be held at the end of the month.

What were the issues which faced the electorate in this election? For Heath, the basic issue was quite clear: in his view, the trade unions had now become so powerful that they were dictating to the country – that is, unelected bodies were seeking to impose their will by industrial action on the properly elected government of the nation. In Heath's own words, 'The challenge is to the will of Parliament and a democratically elected government.' From this point of view, it was a simple question of who was to rule the country, Parliament or the trade unions. Fundamental issues were at stake, as they had been in 1926. Labour did not choose to face this argument directly, but concentrated rather on the state of trade and industry, the damage inflicted by the three-day week, the gloomy trade figures and so on, claiming that if Labour was returned to power, they would clear up the disastrous mess resulting from Heath's policies. On the whole, the election campaign did not go well for the Tories: the Pay Board disclosed figures which seemed to show that the miners' pay had been overestimated in the past in relation to other earnings, while the Industrial Relations Act, which admittedly had been rushed through by the government, was even criticised by the Director General of the Confederation of British Industry. How far incidents of this kind actually influenced voting behaviour is hard to say, but the election results showed a distinct swing to Labour, as Table 4.7 illustrates. In fact, the Conservative vote was down by 1.2 million votes, and they lost thirty-six seats. Labour had the largest number of seats,

Table 4.7　The General Election, February 1974

Party	Votes	Seats
Conservative	11,868,906	297
Labour	11,639,243	301
Liberal	6,063,470	14
Plaid Cymru	171,364	2
Scottish Nat.	632,032	7
Others (GB)	240,665	2
Others (NI)	717,983	12
Total		635

but no clear majority, and their vote dropped by half a million votes or so. Both the Liberals and the Nationalists profited from the loss of votes by the two major parties.

Whatever interpretation is placed on these figures, it is clear that the electorate had voted against the policies of the Heath administration. How far the average voter was impressed by the constitutional issue as Heath saw it, is hard to say. Probably the more than a million who withdrew their votes from the Tories were more concerned about the state of the country, that is, about the three-day week, which had been in force since the beginning of the year; power cuts, which extinguished not only the household lights but also the TV, tried people's patience. There were certainly many voters who, in spite of growing uneasiness at the strength of the trade unions, thought that Labour would handle them better than Heath. At all events, the Tories were out, and Labour were in, with a precarious majority (soon to be strengthened by another election in October of the same year). Among the new government's first actions was to scrap Heath's pay policy, repeal the Industrial Relations Act, and see that the miners got the pay rise they had demanded. Militant trade unionism had triumphed.

Or so it seemed. It is appropriate to break off the story of the successes of trade unionism at this point because the fall of the Heath government can be interpreted as the greatest political achievement of trade union power in the post-war period. After all, the situation in early 1974 was quite extraordinary: on the one hand the country was crippled economically by power cuts, with manufacturing output reduced by nearly a half, while on the other hand the Conservative government appeared unable to do much about it – hence the appeal to the electorate. It is hard to imagine a

137

more dramatic assertion of power by the unions; and at the time there was no lack of political commentators who pointed out that the political map had been changed by the events of spring 1974. There was now a new political power in the land – the trade unions – who by direct action could topple the government. What could stop them from doing it again? The extension of the closed-shop policy had consolidated their hold on the workplace. The use of aggressive picketing certainly intimidated the faint-hearted, while flying pickets strengthened sympathetic strikes, bringing vital sectors of the economy to a standstill. No longer did strike action depend on how long a union's strike funds would last out, for strikers' families could obtain support from social security. It must also be remembered that the unions continued to exercise a strong influence over the Labour Party, not only through the political levy on their members, which provided most of the Party's funds, but also through the sponsoring of individual Members of Parliament. About 40 per cent of Labour MPs were sponsored by trade unions in October 1974.

For all these reasons it seemed in 1974 that a new era had begun in which the trade unions had to be admitted into partnership with the government of the day, of whatever political complexion. Direct attempts to fetter their power by the *In Place of Strife* proposals and by Heath's Industrial Relations Act had obviously failed. True, from the perspective of the 1990s, all this might appear to present a somewhat lurid scenario, and one which fails to take sufficiently into account the basic aims and objectives of the unions. They were by no means a united body, bent on forcing the maximum concessions from government and employer alike. From their point of view, they were merely maintaining traditional postures in face of what they saw as an abrupt and headlong attack on their established rights. Certainly Heath had done little to secure their co-operation when introducing the Industrial Relations Act. However, at the time it seemed otherwise, and certainly the aggressive tactics of the NUM gave cause for alarm. It remained to be seen how far the new Labour government could itself reach agreement with the unions.

Housing

In 1951 there was still an urgent need for additional housing for the working classes, Labour's achievements in this field immediately after the war being somewhat limited. During the next quarter of a century, successive governments attempted to meet this need by continuing to support both local authority and private building, though with different degrees of emphasis. The continued rise in population (by 2.3 million in the 1950s, and by 2.6 million in the 1960s), together with the increasing deterioration of the older, nineteenth-century section of the housing stock, did not make this any easier. There was also the additional complication of the marked growth of smaller households. Professor Burnett has called this 'a spectacular increase in small households' of one or two persons. In 1911 such small households constituted only 21.5 per cent of all households; in 1966 they were 45.9 per cent. Whereas the population grew by 7 per cent in the sixties and seventies, the number of small households went up by 20 per cent. The reasons for this – more and earlier marriages, more one-parent families – will be examined in the next chapter; for whatever reasons, this expansion put additional and novel strains on the housing stock. On the whole, builders did not respond very positively to this need, though it is true that more local authority flats and maisonettes were provided after the war than before. The overall picture for houses built in England and Wales is set out in Table 4.8.

Table 4.8   Houses Built, England and Wales, 1950–74

Years	Local authority	Private	Total
1950–4	912,805	228,616	1,141,421
1955–9	688,585	623,024	1,311,609
1960–4	545,729	878,756	1,424,485
1965–9	761,174	983,338	1,744,512
1970–4	536,560	830,047	1,366,607

Source: A.H.Halsey (ed.), *British Social Trends since 1900* (1988).

It will be seen that the Conservative government of the early 1950s built large numbers of council houses, Harold Macmillan as Housing Minister actually producing a record 319,000 in 1953, and 348,000 in 1954. This was achieved by providing more generous subsidies to local authorities and by making available more licences to build. These licences were abolished altogether in 1954. Thereafter private builders built more houses than local authorities, and continued to do so for the rest of the period, even in 1965–9, when council house building received a boost under the Labour administration of Harold Wilson. As for the basic housing policies of the two major political parties, the Conservatives accepted the need for council house building, but also encouraged private enterprise in building and the growth of owner-occupancy. For this reason, even in the 1950s the Conservative governments were prepared to help council house tenants to buy the houses they were renting, and on advantageous terms. At first, Labour resolutely opposed this, partly because of their suspicion of private ownership of property and their belief in public ownership, and partly because council house sales might mean less available rented accommodation. However, by the mid-sixties, they were forced to change their minds as the numbers grew not only of those wishing to buy their council houses but of the better-paid workers who wished to buy privately. The Labour government's White Paper *The Housing Programme, 1965–70* was at last prepared to recognise owner-occupancy as the 'normal' tenure, and rented public accommodation as merely a short-term expedient. Certainly by this time, the increase in house ownership among the working classes had become very noticeable, as Table 4.9 bears out. Thus by the mid-seventies, over half the houses in England and Wales were owner-occupied. A good proportion (that is, more than a quarter) were still rented from local authorities of one kind or another, but the proportion rented from private landlords had been halved – something to be discussed a little later.

What changes are to be seen in the council house estates which were home to so many working-class families at this time? Broadly speaking, there were three major developments which require comment. The first is a general improvement in the standard of amenities provided. The Dudley Report of 1944, for example,

Table 4.9   House Tenure in England and Wales (Percentages)

Tenure	1951	1960	1971
Owner-occupied	31	44	55
Rented (local authority, or new town)	17	25	28
Rented (private landlord, and miscellaneous)	52	31	22

Source: Halsey (ed.), *British Social Trends since 1900* (1988).

recognised that living space in council accommodation was often too cramped, and kitchens and bathrooms needed to be improved. Recommendations in this report were incorporated into the official Housing Manual in 1944. The highly influential Parker Morris Report, *Homes for Today and Tomorrow* (1961), went further in suggesting improvements in the size of rooms and in amenities. In 1967 its recommendations became mandatory in new town houses, and in 1969 generally in local government building. The result was to put up the cost of new houses by a fifth. The second major development was a specialised aspect of the first: increasingly council houses were built with some form of central heating – a hitherto unknown luxury for working-class tenants, who previously employed local heating in the form of coal fires, or electric, gas or paraffin heaters. The arrival of central heating was a sign not only of the changing idea of what was a minimum standard of comfort necessary in the house, but also of the tenants' improved ability to pay (sometimes underfloor electric heating would be installed, which could prove ruinously expensive for many elderly tenants on pensions). Along with central heating went another sign of improving standards and affluence – garages were increasingly provided with council accommodation. Critics no longer suggested that council house tenants kept coal in the bath. Instead, they could allege that they kept a Jaguar in the garage or on the drive (though this jest, too, fell out of fashion by the 1980s). Certainly in the 1970s the newer council housing was very different from that built in the 1920s, when the WC might still be out in the yard at the back, and the internal walls might still be unplastered brick.

The third and most important development is more complex and on a different scale. Dissatisfaction grew after the war with the planning of the first inter-war estates. They were criticised for being boring and monotonous in design, with rows and rows of identical houses, often built at a distance from town centres, with only a limited range of accommodation available, and often with no real community spirit. What was needed, it was thought, was a much more flexible approach, with a variety of building styles – semi-detached, terraced, maisonettes, flats and so on. In particular, there developed the belief that lofty blocks of flats would be the most economical use of land, and modern building techniques could make this possible. Enthusiasts for this kind of building envisaged the creation of new communities or even of cities in the sky. Corbusier's idea of the house as a machine for living in could be put into practice for the purpose of housing the working classes. So the idea of high-rise building or tower blocks on council estates was adopted, and the now familiar matchbox shapes began to appear on the horizon.

The first of these buildings appears to have been built in Harlow in 1950. In the following year, the Alton Estate at Roehampton near London included a group of eleven-storey blocks. High-rise blocks of council flats began as part of mixed estate developments, but more and more they were seen as a cheap and easy method of providing accommodation in the form of one- and two-bedroom flats. In the period 1953–9, they accounted for 9 per cent of local authority building; in 1966, they peaked at 26 per cent. In the mid-1960s, government grants were increased for blocks over six storeys tall. The result was that blocks grew taller – they reached twenty-two storeys in Sheffield and Salford – though additional subsidies for height were withdrawn after a year or two. By the late 1960s, some complaints were being heard about the quality of life possible in the new tower blocks, but many housing authorities regarded them as inevitable because of the need for higher densities of housing made necessary by the scarcity and cost of suitable land for building. In 1968, however, the gas explosion in a London tower block, Ronan Point, caused a revulsion against buildings of this type. Investigation showed inherent faults in the structure of the block, and similar tower blocks had to be evacuated.

From then on, high-rise flats were regarded with disfavour, though 10 per cent of all local authority building in 1970 was still in this form. It would be fair to say that some tenants, usually younger tenants, actually liked living in them, but many did not. They were obviously unsuitable for families with young children, and play areas at ground level were difficult to supervise. Lifts frequently broke down or were vandalised, long concrete passageways were windswept and unfriendly, and security was difficult to maintain. Some inner-city estates became ghettos approached by the police only with caution. In many cases, graffiti and the stench of urine contributed to a depressing environment for the occupants. Again, it was the worst of the tower blocks which got into the news, but the failure of the high-rise experiment is seen in the fact that by 1990 a number of authorities have either sold off some of their tower blocks for private development, or have simply blown them up.

Only a proportion of the working classes lived on council estates. A substantial number rented from private landlords – indeed, well over half of houses were rented in this way in the immediate post-war period; in 1947 the proportion was 58 per cent of the housing stock. In 1957 the Rent Act partly removed the control of rents which had remained in force since the war. In the early 1960s there was a real shortage of houses and flats, and rented accommodation was both scarce and expensive. At this time there was a scandal associated with the London landlord Rachman, with allegations of extortionate rents, forcible eviction and so on. The 1965 Rent Act gave more security to tenants, but the problem still remained of the large numbers of private tenants occupying inferior and sometimes decaying premises, and often sharing amenities. Although much new building took place in the fifties and sixties, older housing went on declining; in the early 1970s, over a third of the housing stock had been built before 1919 (as there was so little building during the First World War, this in effect meant before 1914). The figures are given in Table 4.10.

As for sharing amenities, or lacking them completely, this continued into the 1970s to a surprising degree, as Table 4.11 illustrates. Although the figures show improvement over the twenty years covered by this table, it is still remarkable that in 1971 8.7 per

Table 4.10 Age of Dwellings (estimated) in England and Wales, 1947–1971 (percentages)

Year	Pre-1919	1919–44	After 1944
1947	68.3	31.7	–
1967	38.4	27.1	34.5
1971	35.8	24.1	40.1

Source: Halsey (ed.), *British Social Trends since 1900* (1988).

Table 4.11 Proportion of Households Sharing or Lacking Amenities in England and Wales (percentages)

Type of amenity	1951		1961		1971	
	Share	Lack	Share	Lack	Share	Lack
Hot-water tap	–	–	1.8	21.9	2.0	6.4
Fixed bath	8	37	4.6	22.0	3.4	8.7
Water closet	13	8	5.8	6.9	4.0	1.1

Source: Halsey (ed.), *British Social Trends since 1900* (1988).

cent were still without a fixed bath and 4 per cent were still sharing a water closet. It is true, of course, that the proportion of households renting from private landlords went down noticeably from 52 per cent to only 22 per cent in 1971, mostly because renting out property became less and less attractive from the private landlord's point of view; in particular, he experienced increasing difficulty in obtaining the legal eviction of defaulting tenants. However, the reduction of the private sector did not help tenants who were not on a local authority waiting list (or very low down in priority), and who could not afford to buy, yet were desperately seeking accommodation. Meanwhile, slum clearance hardly kept pace with the provision of new housing.

In the mid-1950s local authorities calculated that about 850,000 houses fell into the slum category. The Housing Repairs and Rents Act 1954 provided subsidies for slum clearance, and clearance speeded up, but the rate of demolition in the late 1950s (20,000 to 35,000 a year) was not impressive. In 1963, the Housing Minister, Sir Keith Joseph, forecast the end of the slums within the next ten years, but was to be proved wildly wrong over the next decade. A new survey two years later provided a figure of 824,000 slum houses, while in 1967 a report by public health inspectors put the total as high as 1.8 million houses. Demolition speeded up in the 1960s to 60,000 to 70,000 premises a year. Over the whole period 1945–68, about 900,000 houses were demolished, but large pockets of slum property remained in most of the older towns, such as 92,000 unfit houses in Liverpool in 1965, and 42,000 in Birmingham in the same year. Under the Heath administration, 1970–4, slum clearance slowed down again. The estimated number of unfit dwellings in England and Wales in 1976 was still 1,262,000.

In summary form, it is clear that much new housing of a higher standard was erected by local councils and private builders between 1951 and 1974, the provision of central heating and of garages became universal, and many working-class tenants became owner-occupiers for the first time. In these respects it may be said that the home environment showed a distinct improvement (home furnishings and appliances will be discussed in the next chapter). Moreover, with the shortening of working hours and with longer holidays, more time was spent at home in do-it-yourself activities. But, having said all this, it is equally clear that as older properties fell into decline, and more rigorous standards were used to determine what constituted slum property, the national inheritance of slums showed little signs of diminishing. Their continued existence, even in a time of prosperity, was a reminder of the number of families still living at the bottom end of the income scale in wretched circumstances because they could afford no better. Poverty had not been totally abolished, even in times of full employment and the welfare state.

The Health of the Working Classes

During this period there were a number of beneficial influences bearing on the standard of health of working-class people. One of the most important undoubtedly was the availability of regular employment and the upward movement of real wages. These, together with the continued decline in the size of the family, meant that working people ate more regularly and fully, and improved their diets as their standard of living rose. At the same time there was an improvement in the home environment for many (if not for all), while conditions at work also improved in the form of shorter working hours and better working conditions. Better knowledge of hygiene and good dietary practices contributed to higher standards of health, while the services of the welfare state, and especially the better medical care available under the NHS, also played their part. The result of all this was the continued decline of the classic killer diseases of the nineteenth century such as tuberculosis and diphtheria. The major causes of death were now circulatory diseases (strokes and heart attacks), cancers and chronic lung diseases.

However, these general remarks require certain qualifications. In the first place, there does not seem to have been any lengthening of the natural life span during this period; it remained more or less what it had been in the mid-nineteenth century. What was happening was a reduction in the number of premature deaths, so that more people survived to old age. Then again, working-class health has always been of a lower standard than that of the middle and upper classes (though whether this is due to environmental or hereditary factors remains open to debate). Further the health of the working classes varies from one part of the country to another. For some time now death rates have been higher in the north and north-west than in other parts of the country. Crude death rates showed little change in the period 1951–74, the most marked signs of improvement being shown in the further decline of infant mortality figures, as Table 4.12 illustrates. Thus the most significant decline has been the cutting of the infant mortality figure of 1950 by very nearly a half by 1975. This is attributable to a variety of

Table 4.12   Infant Mortality and Death Rates, 1950–75

Infant mortality rates (England & Wales)		Death rates (England & Wales)	
1950	30	1951–5	11.7
1960	22	1956–60	11.6
1970	18	1961–5	11.8
1975	16	1966–70	11.7
		1971–5	11.9

Source: Halsey (ed.), *British Social Trends since 1900* (1988).

causes – better drugs, smaller family sizes which allow greater care and attention for the individual baby, more breast-feeding, better understanding of child care among mothers. Early deaths among infants fell more and more into the peri-natal category, that is, the period immediately before and after birth; some who survived till later died as a result of the 'sudden infant death' syndrome (though cot deaths were not specifically identified in this way till later on). On the whole, young children at school benefited from all the favourable influences mentioned above, though they suffered from a virulent outbreak of poliomyelitis in the late 1950s before an effective treatment (the Salk vaccine) became available.

No doubt there would have been an even greater improvement in working-class health had more attention been given to what constituted a healthy diet. Many working-class daily diets still contained too much fat, salt and sugar. The word 'cholesterol' and the existence of polyunsaturated fats had yet to become familiar to the general public. The consumption of dairy products was still thought to be entirely beneficial, and the drinking of milk was encouraged by advertising slogans such as 'Drinka Pinta Milka Day'. Above all, cigarette smoking was still widespread among men and women. In 1972, 57 per cent of skilled and semi-skilled men smoked, and 64 per cent of unskilled men. It was still a matter of controversy whether cigarette smoking caused lung cancer or not. Thus deaths caused by strokes, heart attacks and cancer were still common enough in the mid-1970s.

The Extent of Poverty

The subject of poverty between the wars was examined in some detail in Chapter One. During the Second World War and in the immediate post-war years, full employment meant an improvement in the standard of living for all, especially unskilled workers, and the welfare state provided a minimum standard for those who for one reason or another did not have a regular and adequate income. In theory, at least, poverty should have been reduced to very small dimensions in the 1950s and 1960s. A third survey of York, carried out in 1950 by Rowntree and Lavers, certainly seemed to show that unemployment was no longer a basic cause of poverty, but that old age and sickness had become the two greatest causes of impoverishment. The 1950 figures from York are given in Table 4.13.

Table 4.13   Poverty in York, 1950

Causes of poverty	Percentage of the poor
Unemployment	nil
Old age	68.1
Sickness	21.3
Low wages	1.0
Death of wage-earner	6.4
Miscellaneous (including large families)	3.2

Source: B. Seebohm Rowntree and G. R. Lavers, *Poverty and the Welfare State* (1951).

However, after this survey, social scientists became more and more dissatisfied with attempts of this kind to assess poverty on the basis of minimum dietary requirements, and turned increasingly to national assistance allowances (from 1966, supplementary benefit) as giving a better indication. Although variations in this approach have been employed to assess relative deprivation, the most common method recently employed has been to use these allowances plus 40 per cent, since in practice additional payments of this order above the basic scales have customarily been paid. The results of the adoption of this yardstick to measure the extent of poverty (or near poverty) have been striking. For obvious reasons, these scales permit only a most frugal existence. Yet a survey carried out on this basis in 1960 by Abel-Smith and Townsend estimated that whereas 7.8 per cent of the population in 1953 were in poverty, by 1960 the figure had risen to 14.2 per cent, that is, 7.5 million people in all.

Their important survey, *The Poor and the Poorest*, divided the 7.5 million into the categories set out in Table 4.14. On these figures it is apparent that poverty was actually increasing among certain

Table 4.14   Categories of the Poor, 1960

	Numbers (millions)	Percentage of total
Large families and/or low wage-earner as head	3.00	40
Pensioners	2.50	33
Fatherless families	0.75	10
Families with one parent disabled or sick	0.75	10
Unemployed head of family	0.50	7
Total	7.50	100

Source: B.Abel-Smith and P.Townsend, *The Poor and the Poorest* (1965).

sectors of society. The results were so striking that they prompted Coates and Silburn in 1966–8 to investigate conditions in a particularly run-down and impoverished slum district of Nottingham, St Ann's. Their conclusion was that the proportion of households in St Ann's in poverty was 37 per cent (as compared with Abel-Smith and Townsend's overall household figure of 17.9 per cent), this representing nearly 40 per cent of the local population. Moreover, a Ministry of Social Security investigation of families with two or more children, *The Circumstances of Families* (1967), revealed that by supplementary-benefit standards (*without* adding the 40 per cent), nearly half a million families, with up to 1.25 million children, were in poverty. Of these children, half a million were below the benefit line. In the same year, the Plowden Report on primary education emphasised the deprivation suffered by children living in slum areas. As for low wages, the emphasis given by investigators in the 1960s to this aspect was summed up by Coates and Silburn in their survey, published in 1970:

> At this point it suffices to say that the most important single cause of poverty is not indolence, nor fecundity, nor sickness, nor even unemployment, nor villainy of any kind, but is, quite simply, low wages.

A further important national investigation into poverty was carried out by Professor Townsend in 1968/9, the results being published in his *Poverty in the United Kingdom* (1979). These results are set out on the basis of three separate methods of measuring poverty. The figures for measurement by supplementary benefit, given in Table 4.15, are again striking. The division into the two categories 'In poverty' and 'On margins of poverty' makes it difficult to draw direct comparisons with Abel-Smith and Townsend, of course, and figures provided by Townsend in a more recent Fabian Society pamphlet, *Why Are the Many Poor?* (1984), allow a more direct comparison. Given in Table 4.16, they are based on national

Table 4.15   Poverty in the United Kingdom, 1968–9

	Percentage of households	Percentage of population	Estimated no. of households (millions)	Estimated no. of persons (millions)
In poverty	7.1	6.1	1.34	3.32
On margins of poverty	23.8	21.8	4.50	11.86

Source: Peter Townsend, *Poverty in the United Kingdom* (1979).

Table 4.16   Changes in Extent of Poverty 1960–1975 (000s)

	1960	1975
Below supplementary benefit	1,260	1,840
On supplementary benefit	2,670	3,710
At or up to 40 per cent above supplementary benefit	3,510	6,990
Total	7,440	12,540

Source: Peter Townsend, *Why are the Many Poor?* (1984).

assistance/supplementary benefit figures. The 1960 figures given here are those of Abel-Smith and Townsend. The 1975 figures come from Department of Health and Social Security sources.

It is obvious that there is plenty of room for discussion and indeed disagreement over all the survey figures given so far in this section. It should also be noted that the rates of unemployment rose sharply from 2.6 per cent in 1974 to 4.2 per cent in 1975, thus noticeably increasing the numbers on supplementary benefit in the latter year. Argument might well centre on the suitability not only of supplementary benefit but also of the 40 per cent addition as accurate indicators of real poverty. It would certainly be unwise for a number of reasons to take the figures as a completely reliable guide to the extent and increase of poverty in the period 1951–74. It is known, for example, that not all those entitled to benefit claimed it earlier on, while on the other hand the extent of fraudulent claims is always difficult to ascertain. Again, the use of the household unit presents difficulties, for it is well known that households vary widely in their needs according to the nature and age of the dependants. It is therefore necessary in any detailed examination to adjust for this fact.

Nevertheless, whatever qualifications are made, the conclusion seems inescapable that in spite of full employment and the welfare state a formidable amount of poverty continued to exist, and it is very likely that it grew larger over the two decades. The nature of this poverty is not difficult to identify; it was most commonly encountered among the elderly living alone or in couples, and among families with three or more children. More than half the retired were in households living in poverty, while families with children under fifteen constituted over half the population in poverty (most of the remainder was contributed by the elderly). In 1968–9, of the men in regular employment, as many as 1.45 million (14 per cent) out of the total male work force working regularly (10.4 million) were living in or on the margin of poverty. Thus old age and low wages were the basic causes, just as in 1960, though sickness and disability provided another large and often overlapping category of persons in need. One cause of this was an increase in the numbers of elderly folk earlier on, together with a disproportionate increase in the number of families with four or more children. Here the problem was that while child allowances between 1953 and 1960 went up by 25 per cent, money wages went up by over 50 per cent. In other words, in the 1950s numbers in need grew, yet benefits failed to keep pace with rising prices. In the 1960s, this situation failed to improve, and at the end of November 1971 there were 2,909,000 on supplementary benefit, that is, 5.4 per cent of the population.

In conclusion, it must be emphasised again that what constitutes true poverty is very difficult to judge. Clearly, standards vary from age to age. Rowntree used a much more generous standard of minimum comfort in 1936 than he had done in 1899. Then again, there is a political dimension. Some noted investigators in the field take a highly critical view of the economic system which permits such serious poverty (one eminent professor believes that poverty is 'a particular consequence of actions by the rich to preserve and enhance their wealth and so deny it to others'); others regard with suspicion the whole business of state support of the impoverished, and consider that too many are simply failing to help themselves. Hence there are varying interpretations of what figures are available. Yet it is surely undeniable that along with all the prosperity of the time, real poverty was still to be found among the aged, sick and disabled. The same may be said of many of those on low pay, though this is a more complex problem, usually involving unskilled and insecure work, and sometimes ill-health. Some efforts were made in 1971 to offset low pay by the introduction of family income supplement. This provides benefit when family income is less than certain prescribed levels, and also gives entitlement to other benefits such as free school dinners. However, as will be seen in Chapter Six, poverty among the low paid, the elderly, sick and disabled was to be increasingly overshadowed in the late seventies and eighties by the growth of unemployment on a massive scale.

Education

During the quarter-century after the end of the Second World War there was a considerable increase in population in England and Wales, from 43.7 million in 1951 to 48.7 million in 1971. In due course this was reflected in a growth of school population as Table 4.17 illustrates.

It can be seen that a large bulge occurred in the secondary school population in the 1950s, but this tapered off in the next decade, when a bulge appeared in the primary schools, only to disappear in its turn in the 1970s, as the national population declined (in fact, in 1977 the population fell in peacetime for the first time since the

Table 4.17 Changes in School-age Population, England and Wales

	5–9		10–14		15–19	
Year	No. of pupils (000s)	Change (%)	No. of pupils (000s)	Change (%)	No. of pupils (000s)	Change (%)
1951	3,162	−4.8	2,812	−14.0	2,705	−21.3
1961	3,262	+3.2	3,725	+32.5	3,200	+18.3
1971	4,044	+24.0	3,627	−2.6	3,314	+3.6
1981	3,200	−26.4	3,102	−14.5	4,071	+22.8

Source: Halsey: (ed.), *British Social Trends since 1900* (1988).

middle of the eighteenth century, and the decennial increase 1971–81 was the smallest since 1801). The general picture for the period covered by this chapter is of a growing school population with increasing numbers staying at school till eighteen or nineteen. Moreover, as education was considered an important part of the welfare state, increasing attention and money were devoted to it, and Professor Halsey has described the 1950s and 1960s as a 'period of remarkable expansion' in this respect. A much larger slice of the national output went to education, and real costs per pupil went up. More specifically, substantial changes took place in the secondary system; primary school education benefited from the Plowden Report of 1967; further education expanded; teacher training was broadened and also grew rapidly; new universities were founded, including new technological universities and polytechnics. All these developments were of great importance to the working classes, though here again evaluation of precisely how important is not easy.

To start with secondary schools: here the first major change was the increase in the numbers in these schools following the raising of the school-leaving age in 1947. This was followed later on by a large-scale reorganisation of these schools into comprehensive schools. This development was the result of the protracted political and educational controversy already mentioned in Chapter Two. Briefly, it was increasingly accepted that the tripartite system of secondary education adopted under the Education Act of 1944 left the secondary modern school as the poor relation of the grammar school; for the 11+ examination sorted out children very early (and probably too early) into the academically bright who went to the grammar school, and the grammar school 'failures' who went to the secondary modern schools. There was little opportunity thereafter for transfers between schools to remedy inaccurate selection. Moreover, it was argued that the system still favoured the middle-class child coming from a more cultured home as compared with the working-class child. Politically, as might be expected, the Labour Party favoured the abolition of the 11+, and the introduction of comprehensive schools as being both educationally and socially desirable. When Labour returned to office in 1964, following the Newsom Report, *Half Our Future* (1963), on the average and below-average child in secondary schools, they issued Circular 10/65 requiring local authorities to submit plans for comprehensive reorganisation. Already some authorities had been experimenting with comprehensive schools from as early as the 1950s, principally in Anglesea, Leicester, London and Coventry.

In 1970 the Conservative government withdrew Circular 10/65, but by then Conservative opinion had begun to view the comprehensive idea rather more favourably. At the local education authority level, the swing to these schools went on, until by the mid-1970s over half the secondary school population was in comprehensives. Further, more and more children were staying on beyond the school-leaving age of fifteen (sixteen, from 1972–3) at schools other than the grammar schools, which no longer had a monopoly in school of O and A Level GCE work (see Table 4.18). From these figures it will be seen not only that the bulk of the 15–18 age range was no longer in the grammar and technical sector in 1971, but that numbers staying on at school after the age of fifteen had more than trebled.

Table 4.18   LEA School Population for Ages 15–18

	1951		1971	
	No. of pupils (000s)	(%)	No. of pupils (000s)	(%)
Primary, all-age and special	4	1.5	9.7	1.0
Grammar and technical	176	63.7	248.5	28.0
Modern, comprehensive, and other secondary	24	8.6	506.9	57.0

Source: Halsey (ed.), *British Social Trends since 1900* (1988).

All these changes brought a good deal of upset in the schools themselves. Some comprehensive schools were purpose-built, but many were formed, sometimes on more than one site, either by the merger of a grammar school and local secondary modern schools, or by the enlargement of existing secondary modern schools. Some authorities set up sixth-form colleges in order to meet the problems of school sixth-form numbers which were too small for efficient A Level teaching. A minority of authorities such as Leeds and Worcestershire redivided their schools into three groups – first schools 5–9, middle schools 10–13, and upper or high schools 14–18. In all this reorganisation, the LEA grammar school gradually disappeared, in spite of the famous declaration by Harold Wilson that the grammar schools would be abolished 'over my dead body'. Meanwhile, controversy raged over the educational implications of these events. Opponents alleged that the old academic standards of the grammar school were being lost, and a series of 'Black Papers' by educational right-wingers in and after 1969 attacked the whole comprehensive idea. On the other hand, supporters argued that there was no deterioration in GCE results, and that the social gains of mixing all middle- and working-class pupils from a given area were great. Of course, some schools were in the middle of solidly working-class areas on large council estates, or sometimes served predominantly middle-class areas, so that this argument did not always apply. Teachers themselves faced problems when the customary practice of streaming children into academic and less academic streams became frowned upon as a species of elitism, and was replaced by mixed-ability teaching, that is, teaching a class of varying abilities ranging from those destined for university to those who would leave school with no paper qualifications whatever.

The question remains, how far did working-class education profit from all this ferment of change? The old tripartite system resulting from the 1944 Act was not without its virtues. Free grammar school places for all did enable more able working-class boys and girls to go to university and into professional and executive jobs, and in any case some grammar schools already drew on large working-class catchment areas. But this still left about three-quarters of the secondary school population in the secondary modern school, often in inferior buildings with inferior equipment, and with staff generally of lower academic quality. Until the mid-1960s and the arrival of the Certificate of Secondary Education (the CSE) there was not even a nationally recognised leaving qualification in these schools, though some began to enter pupils for the GCE. Further, the proportion of children admitted to grammar schools varied quite widely from one authority to another, so that the chances of an academic education depended very much on the number of grammar school places available locally, quite apart from the diagnostic skill of the 11+ examination. On balance, therefore, although the 1944 Act was a considerable advance for the working classes, it had its weaknesses, and the reorganisation of secondary education in the 1960s, in spite of all the attendant difficulties, probably widened quite significantly the educational opportunities of the average boy and girl. One interesting parallel development to which surprisingly little attention has been paid must also be mentioned: while comprehensive education was spreading, so was co-education at secondary level. By 1973, two out of every three secondary schools in England and Wales had become co-educational. There are arguments for single-sex schools, but in general this change has been well received, and indeed taken for granted.

The controversy over comprehensive education occupied the centre of the educational scene in the 1960s, and much less attention was paid to the primary schools, which were already comprehensive in their intake, of course. However, the Plowden Report (1967) was a valuable survey of modern approaches in the primary school, and it also suggested the setting up of educational priority areas in large cities into which extra resources could be directed. As for further and higher education, the most influential report here was the Robbins Report (1963), which stressed the existence of much untapped ability among working-class children, and suggested a massive increase in the provision of education beyond the school-leaving age. Even before this, numbers were rising in technical colleges (later mostly renamed colleges of further education), and in teacher-training colleges (where three-year courses instead of two-year had begun in 1960), and in the universities. There were already 31 British universities, 10 colleges of advanced technology, 150 teacher-training colleges and 600 technical colleges. Robbins set broad targets for the next ten years of 219,000 university students, 122,000 students in teacher training, and 51,000 in technical colleges on advanced courses. Sceptics viewed these proposals with some doubt. A popular novelist and former university teacher, Kingsley Amis, gave voice to their fears: 'More means worse.'

Whether it did or not, a massive expansion in higher education took place. Robbins' targets were reached by 1970, and in the case of technical colleges (or colleges of further education), the Robbins figure was exceeded by 51,000. Between 1963 and 1971, the total number of students in full-time higher education doubled to reach 457,000. In 1972, students in universities numbered nearly a quarter of a million (246,800) as compared with 85,421 in 1949. The colleges of advanced technology became technological universities, and seven new universities were founded in England. The teacher-training colleges, renamed colleges of education, doubled their student numbers in order to meet projected demand for teachers, and they also began Bachelor of Education degree courses (the B.Ed.). Their numbers amounted to over 150, and a further expansion of teacher training, with particular reference to the probationary year, was envisaged by the James Report (1972). The numbers of polytechnics increased, and their degrees were now validated by the Council for National Academic Awards (CNAA), established in 1964. By 1972 there were nearly half a million students in higher education, either in universities, or in colleges of education, or on advanced courses in polytechnics or in other colleges.

It would seem undeniable that opportunities for working-class education widened in the period 1951–74 as a result of the introduction of comprehensive education, and the rapid development of further and higher education. As a result, many working-class children acquired educational qualifications ranging from degrees in the universities, colleges of education and polytechnics to the humbler awards of Higher and Ordinary National Certificates, and the certificates of such bodies as the Royal Society of Arts and the City and Guilds Institute in the further education colleges. What is difficult to assess is how far working-class participation overall actually increased; obviously there was a substantial middle-class element in educational expansion as well, and Oxbridge was hardly swamped by working-class students. It would be reasonable to suppose that the greatest working-class participation would be at further education level, where the emphasis was on education in technological and commercial skills. Certainly a good many college of education students came from working-class homes, for teaching (especially for women in primary schools) remained a traditional route for self-betterment among the working classes. At the universities, however, the influx of working-class students was not on any massive scale. The figures for the proportion of working-class young people who entered university, as compared with the proportion of middle-class entrants of the same age, is not impressive: 3.1 per cent only of the 1943–52 working-class birth cohort (entering university for the most part in the 1960s), as compared with 26.4 per cent of the 1943–52 birth cohort of children from the homes of professional people, administrators, managers, proprietors and supervisors. Further, the 3.1 per cent figure quoted here is only a very modest increase on the figure for the earlier working-class cohort for 1932–42, entering university usually in the 1950s, of 2.3 per cent. This does not seem a very great increase. Indeed, it has been argued by some educationalists on the basis of a national survey in 1972 that not only did the chances of a working-class boy receiving selective (that is, grammar) education *diminish* in the 1950s and 1960s, but that the chances of his obtaining a university place actually declined because the expansion of universities failed to keep pace with the expansion of sixth forms. Thus some working-class boys and girls could have gained A Levels, but dropped out early on, while others obtained A Levels, but not the grades required for entry.

It follows that there is room for controversy over the extent to which working-class children actually benefited from changes in higher education, though it is accepted that an extra 2 per cent of working-class children as compared with the position before the war found their way to university in the 1960s (among the top two social classes the increase in university entry was 19 per cent and 6 per cent). In short, it is agreed that there was an increase in working-class entry in absolute terms, but not necessarily in direct or even increasing proportion to the increase in population numbers. Lastly, it is interesting to note that figures supplied by the Universities Central Council on Admissions (UCCA) show that the percentage of accepted university candidates from working-class homes in 1974 was 26 per cent (it had been 29 per cent in 1971). The percentage of acceptances from homes with professional or technical qualifications was 34 per cent, though this social group was roughly seven times smaller than the working-class groups. Further, different occupations among the working classes contributed different proportions of the total acceptances. For example, labourers were 7.2 per cent of the male adult work force aged forty-five to fifty-nine, but their children were only 1.4 per cent of the total entrants. Electrical and electronic workers, on the other hand, who were 2.4 per cent of the same work force, contributed almost that percentage to the total entrants, that is, 2.3 per cent. Perhaps this is only what one would expect.

Final Comments

The broad survey of the main aspects of working-class life in this chapter shows that material progress on an increasing scale was experienced in the period 1951–74. In simple terms, the working classes continued to rise; conditions improved at work and at home, real wages increased, standards of health rose and educational opportunities at least widened. Politically, the Labour Party was not in power for long, but the trade union movement was strengthened, reaching a peak of influence in the mid-1970s. However, though times were prosperous, the continued existence of poverty remained a blemish on the progress achieved, and not all the changes resulting from a period of unparalleled prosperity can be regarded as beneficial. The next chapter will discuss some of the remarkable changes in social attitudes of the 1950s and 1960s.

Chapter 5

The Permissive Society of the Fifties and Sixties

Changes in Attitudes

Whereas the last chapter was concerned very largely with the fundamentals of working-class life at work and at home, in this chapter it is proposed to deal for the most part with changes in social attitudes among the working classes. As we have seen, there is no doubt that economic conditions improved greatly during the thirty years or so after the end of the Second World War, but there were precedents for this in the recent past, of course. Between the wars, for those who stayed in work there was also an improvement in the standard of living, and, even before that, real wages had gone up in the last decades of the nineteenth century; but in neither period was there a noticeable relaxation of society's rules and conventions of the kind which took place in the fifties and sixties. What really makes this period unique in the history of the working classes was the combination of higher standards of living and of new permissive attitudes, especially in sexual relations. These changes in attitude, conveniently referred to as the growth of the permissive society, originated with the middle classes, but soon had a marked effect on working people, who along with everyone else found themselves exhorted to 'let it all hang out' (or, alternatively, 'hang down').

Just why prosperity should this time be accompanied by such a manifestation of permissiveness is not easy to explain; even in the sixties there were attempts to provide an explanation of the new mood in British society by suggesting that Britain had lost an Empire and was now seeking a new role. This hardly seems an adequate or satisfactory explanation for the change to more permissive attitudes. It is more likely that the seeds were sown between the wars (or even earlier) by the more liberated groups among the middle classes, and that after 1951 the economic prosperity of the time permitted further instalments of social reform as part of the general overhaul of society which seemed appropriate after the war. If the welfare state was essentially for the working classes, it could be argued that the permissive society was originally created by and for the middle classes. These social reforms were accompanied by changes in the nature of the family and in women's role in society, by a so-called cult of youth (made possible by teenage affluence), and by the growth of conspicuous consumption, not only in the home but in leisure activities outside the home. Inevitably, what amounted to an emphasis on self-fulfilment and personal gratification coloured social attitudes over a wide spectrum, and certainly affected attitudes to work.

The Importance of Work

During the Industrial Revolution, work gained an increasing significance for manual workers, to whom the expression 'working class' or 'working classes' was increasingly applied. Although it took time for the factory system to spread beyond the textile industry, it is still true to say that during the second half of the nineteenth century both the working day and the working week had assumed a new uniformity and regularity. St Monday (not working on Monday) faded away, Saturday half-day working became the rule, and by the end of the century the working day was usually of eleven to twelve hours' duration, inclusive of meal-times. At this period, work for many was still of a heavy physical nature, exhausting to the human body, and occupying most of the ordinary man or woman's waking hours during the week. Even for the skilled minority, who had the support and protection of their unions, the working day was still long, and work dominated their lives, too. However, as has been shown in previous chapters of this book, there was a substantial reduction in working hours after 1918, while after the Second World War, the five-day week became universal. Paid holiday entitlement increased, the working environment improved, trade unions provided additional protection, industrial tribunals came into existence and, above all perhaps, jobs remained plentiful for twenty-five years or so after the end of the Second World War. In these circumstances, the question arises, how far had attitudes to work changed by the early 1970s? How far was it still of central importance, the lynchpin of the worker's existence, as it had been a century earlier?

Naturally enough, the problem is to apply the right emphasis when attempting to generalise about such a broad subject. There can be no question of any very *drastic* change in attitude – few in the 1970s would deny that work was essential for human survival ('Them as don't work, don't eat') – but the fact remains that for most working people work occupied a substantially smaller proportion of their waking hours than it had done for their grandparents. Moreover, work was generally more readily available. The consequence seems to be that there was some tilting of the balance between work and leisure; work as part of one's normal existence was not quite as demanding as it had been. More attention was given to life in the home, especially to home decorating and maintenance, and also to family demands. More began to be expected of the family man at home, for the wife quite often had a full- or part-time job. As a consequence, a man's life at work became more and more of purely economic concern, and its primary function as a source of income was reaffirmed and emphasised. A well-known study of affluent workers in Luton, undertaken in the late 1960s, makes it clear that industrial workers there saw their work more and more in instrumental terms, that is, they saw it purely as a means of supporting themselves and families, with little intrinsic interest in itself.

Of course, this raises a number of interesting questions. For example, it could be asked whether most workers have not always viewed their work in this way, especially if unskilled. Presumably it was the craftsman, the skilled worker, who had always taken most pride in his work because it was the product of lengthy training and a hard-won expertise. For him, the pay packet was important, naturally enough, but so was the nature of the work on which he was employed. It was otherwise with the unskilled worker, often employed on boring and monotonous tasks. Yet, even here, job satisfaction depends on so many variable factors apart from the actual work processes – for example, the attitude of the employers, the work discipline applied by supervisors and foremen, the companionship of fellow workers, the support of the union and so on. A survey of workers' attitudes at a very large chemical complex on the north-east coast, published in 1972, suggests that the main features of what was considered by the workers to be a good job were (1) pay, (2) job security, (3) welfare benefits, (4) good working conditions. Of these elements, good pay was the most important, though security of employment was also highly valued – not surprisingly, as the area had a record of high unemployment in the 1930s. Significantly, interest in the job was not mentioned as a desirable feature of 'a good job' – other aspects were more important. Yet where workers could have a certain freedom to vary their work, to make their own decisions, to take breaks and move about the works fairly freely, some 72 per cent found their work interesting. Other workers, who were allocated to particular machines and whose efforts were controlled by the pace of the machines, experienced much less job satisfaction. Only 26 per cent of these workers thought their work interesting. However, the amount of interest generated by the work was not affected by the degree of automation. Indeed, workers in the first group (of whom nearly three-quarters found the work interesting) were in a highly automated part of the plant – in the words of the researchers, the work represented 'the paradigm of automation'; so that advanced technology in itself did not make for worker dissatisfaction, in this works at least. The same conclusion was reached by the researchers at Luton – namely, that mass-production technology did not necessarily lead to more antagonistic attitudes among the workers or (in the words of their report) to more 'conflict-laden work relationships'.

It may therefore be concluded that although work was seen in a somewhat altered perspective in the post-war decades, this was not the result of any major changes in work techniques, or of other changes in conditions of employment. In particular, automation and computerisation did not appear to have increased stress at work. If anything, they reduced the amount of hard physical labour formerly required. It was rather that steady employment, regular pay rises, improved working conditions and more time off all contributed to making work less burdensome as a necessary preliminary to the enjoyment of leisure, recreation and family life. Most workers at Luton had no great ambitions for personal promotion within the firm: pay was a primary consideration, but they expected more from regular pay increases than from personal, individual advancement. They were nearly all members of the union, but only a minority had joined as a matter of principle or duty. Few were members of social groups meeting away from work. Put at its simplest, most of them went to work to earn a living, and to enjoy weekends and holidays. The attitude of the younger workers was well described in a popular novel of the time (subsequently made into a film), Allan Sillitoe's *Saturday Night and Sunday Morning* (1958), the colourful story of a randy and somewhat bolshie young capstan-lathe operator who lived for his weekends of sex and booze. He thinks about the factory on his way in to work:

> The thousands who worked there took home good wages. No more short-time like before the war, or getting the sack if you stood ten minutes in the lavatory reading your *Football Post* – if the gaffer got on to you now you could always tell him where to put the job and go somewhere else ... With the wages you got you could save up for a motor-bike or even an old car, or you could go on a ten-day binge and get rid of all you'd saved.

The Family

During the three decades following the end of the Second World War, important changes took place in the family. In the first place, the rise in the birth rate which occurred in the 1950s reached a peak in the mid-1960s, but thereafter declined. The figures (rounded-off) are as follows:

Birth rates	1951	1961	1971	1972	1973
(live per 1,000 population)	16	18	16	15	14

The result of this was that the decline in the size of the family which had begun in the inter-war period meant that most young families in the 1970s had no more than two children. At the same time, it became increasingly likely that the mother would be going out to work, often part-time when the children were young, then later on full-time. The percentage of married women at work very nearly doubled from 22 per cent in 1951 to 42 per cent in 1971. The numbers of women (married and single) at work, either full-time or part-time, went up by 1.4 million between 1961 and 1971. The increasing numbers of married women at work had both social and economic consequences for the family. It is clear that many married women no longer regarded the bringing-up of children, together with household and cooking duties, as constituting a career in itself. They looked for a career outside the home, and a liberation from household chores, even though these had become progressively less of a burden with the use of labour-saving devices such as the washing machine and spin-dryer. In theory, their husbands were supposed to take a greater share in the housework, now that their wives had become wage-earners, often out all day. In practice, many men were still prepared to let their wives perform their traditional roles in the house once the women had returned from work. As for the economic consequences, more and more families had two wage-earners (though the wife's wages were rarely more than half the husband's), which certainly increased consumer purchasing power within the family, and also often helped to gain the wife a certain degree of financial independence.

The institution of marriage itself showed no signs of losing its popularity during this period. The numbers of marriages in Britain showed a steady increase over the period from 1951 to 1972 (it must be remembered, of course, that the population increased by about an eighth during these years).

Marriage totals	1951	1961	1966	1971	1972
(000s)	402	387	426	447	468

Prosperity led to a fall in the average age of marriage of both men and women. For women, the average dropped from 25.5 years in 1931 to 24.2 years in 1951, and then to 22.6 years in 1971. For men, the fall was from 27.4 years in 1931 to 26.6 years in 1951, and then to 24.6 years in 1971. The proportion of spinster brides who were under twenty years of age rose from one in five in 1951 to one in three between 1951 and 1971.

However, all this did not mean that marriage was still regarded as a sacred and solemn commitment to the same extent as before the war. For one thing, cohabitation either before marriage or as a substitute for marriage became much more common by the 1970s, however much it had been frowned upon earlier on as 'living in sin'. In the nature of things, figures are hard to come by, but some limited evidence shows that the percentage of young women under twenty-five who married for the first time in the 1960s, and who cohabited before marriage, was about 2 per cent, rising to 7 per cent in 1970–4 (and 14 per cent in 1975–8). For those under twenty-five marrying for the second time, the figures were much higher – 17 per cent in 1960–4, 28 per cent in 1965–9 and 39 per cent in 1970–4. Another and more striking indication that marriage was not what it used to be is that the divorce rates moved up sharply, as Table 5.1 illustrates.

Table 5.1 Divorces, England and Wales

	1961	1966	1969	1970	1971	1972
Decrees absolute granted (000s)	25.4	39.1	51.3	58.2	74.4	119.0
Rate per 1,000 married population	2.1	3.2	4.1	4.7	6.0	9.5

Source: *Social Trends*, No. 5 (1974).

To see these figures in perspective, it must be remembered that divorce rates actually declined in the 1930s and 1950s after peaks following each world war. Only 2 per cent of marriages in 1926 had ended in divorce twenty years later, only 6 per cent of marriages in 1936, and 7 per cent of marriages in 1951. Thus marriages appear to have been extremely stable in the thirties and fifties. This was certainly to change from the 1960s onwards. Previously, divorce was difficult and expensive to obtain for working-class people: it was necessary to show in court that a 'matrimonial offence' had been committed, usually adultery, cruelty or desertion, so there would be an 'innocent' party and a 'guilty' party to the case. Evidence was often contrived, of course, so as to permit the case to proceed, but in theory 'collusion' was not permitted and, if detected, the case would collapse. These antique procedures were swept away by the 1969 Divorce Reform Act which simply required evidence of irretrievable breakdown of the marriage after a period of two years (or five years if the breakdown was disputed). It is impossible to say whether easier divorce led disaffected couples to abandon their marriages too readily without trying hard enough to make them work, especially where there were children. It can certainly be argued that it permitted grossly unsuitable marriages to be ended relatively quickly without subjecting both parties (and the children, if any) to long years of unhappiness. For whatever reason, the fact is that the divorce rate rose strikingly in the 1960s even before the Divorce Reform Act took effect, and continued to rise thereafter.

Thus, though marriage was still very popular, it was no longer the indissoluble bond – 'till death us do part' – that it had been. The consequence was a noticeable increase in the number of single-parent families (commonly but not invariably the divorced mother and the children), with all the problems which can arise from the need for maintenance, and from the possible lack of a father-figure within the family. The numbers of these families were increased to some extent by the rise in the illegitimacy rates, though sometimes the children were born to cohabiting couples who were not married at the time, and did not legitimate their children by subsequent marriage. The illegitimacy rate, as a percentage of live births, rose from 5 per cent in 1951 to 6 per cent in 1961, and then to 8 per cent for each of the years 1971, 1972 and 1973.

It can be seen then that the working-class marriage underwent considerable changes in the period 1951–74. The old Victorian (and even Edwardian) picture of the working-class mother toiling away at the wash-tub surrounded by a numerous brood of small children had by now vanished completely, being replaced by a mother with usually not more than two children who spent much of her time outside the home in paid employment. Familial roles had changed. It is true that the wife and mother still occupied a sub-ordinate position in many traditionally minded working-class families, but she had more economic power, less physical labour to perform at home (thanks to labour-saving household appliances), more control over her pregnancies (to be discussed in the next section), and greater opportunities to end her marriage if she thought fit. As for the father, nominally head of the family, his role had changed, too; it had become more restricted. Admittedly at one extreme, traditional male attitudes might lead to wife-battering, and refuges for battered wives were first established at this time; but at the other extreme, and probably in most working-class marriages, there was far more of a working partnership than before the war. Marriage was no longer the simple union of a dominant male who went out to work and brought home the money and of a submissive female who stayed at home, did the housework and cooking and reared the children.

However, it was remarked earlier on in this chapter that the difficulty is to get the emphasis right, and it may be objected that to portray earlier marriages in this way could be misleading. Indeed, there are plenty of examples of strong-minded and sometimes dominant working-class women in earlier periods. This cannot be denied, but such women were severely restricted in their social roles in ways unthinkable by the 1970s, in particular by continual pregnancies, by the heavy demands of housework, and by the sheer lack of money. It may not be entirely fanciful in this context to consider the popularity at this time of a comic-strip figure, Andy Capp, in the *Daily Mirror*, a newspaper widely read by the working classes. Andy Capp is a dreadful fellow, highly sexist in attitude, who treats his long-suffering wife like dirt. It might well be that, for some men at least, he owed his popularity to the domestic folk memory of married men who (as they saw it) could no longer do as they pleased in their own homes.

Female Emancipation

If the married woman acquired an increase in freedom during the post-war period, the same may also be said of the single woman. One of the most important agents for change here was the increasing availability to women, both married and unmarried, of the oral contraceptive popularly known as 'the pill'. Invented in the late 1960s, by 1970 a survey showed that 18 per cent of married couples were already using this method of birth control, and most of the married women surveyed (in fact, 95 per cent of the actual users) were in favour of it. One typical comment was made by the 21-year-old wife of a plumber:

> A good idea. You can relax more. You are not worried about becoming pregnant. It isn't a worry all the time – you know – am I pregnant this month? Lots of people can't afford lots of children and the pill is perfect for planning your family.

One great benefit of the pill was that it was taken by the woman, who no longer had to rely on her husband's competence in the use of other birth control devices and methods. She had at last gained a more positive control over the workings of her own body; the only disadvantage was the possibility of adverse side-effects. All this produced some interesting comments in the 1970 survey, one or two of which betrayed traditional male attitudes to women – for example, a 39-year-old roof-tiler said of the pill: 'Bad thing; should be given to men; unbalances nature, making women more aggressive. Getting more like men, the women that have the pill.'

The advantages of the pill were obvious to single women, too, although there was some controversy at first over whether it should be available to them as well as to married women. An opinion poll on this subject in 1971, published in a London evening paper, found that 68 per cent of the men polled were in favour, and 51 per cent of the women (76 per cent of the women aged between fifteen and twenty-four). Later on, the use of the pill by single women became more commonly accepted, and controversy then centred on whether a doctor should be required to inform parents if he was prescribing the pill for their under-age daughter.

Another development of a different kind relating to feminine freedom was the reform of the law relating to abortion. Before the 1967 Abortion Act was passed, abortion was generally illegal, though the middle classes who could afford it could usually arrange for the operation to be performed on medical grounds in private (and expensive) clinics. For the working classes, it was either a matter of traditional home remedies (such as knitting needles or, as in *Saturday Night and Sunday Morning*, a very hot bath and a copious intake of gin), or a so-called 'back-street' abortion, an illegal operation carried out by some unqualified and unskilled person. All such attempts to get rid of an unwanted baby were accompanied by considerable risk to the physical and mental health of the woman concerned, and even to her life. The Abortion Bill was fiercely contested in the House of Commons, especially by Roman Catholics, though it was generally acknowledged that the unreformed law as it stood was grossly unsatisfactory. By the Act, abortion became legal, provided that it was certified to be necessary on medical grounds by two doctors; henceforth it became available under the National Health Service. Private clinics continued to provide abortion as before, though they were increasingly patronised by patients from abroad, from countries where abortion was still illegal. The figures for legal abortions in England and Wales from 1969 onwards are:

1969	49,800	1972	108,600
1970	75,400	1973	110,600
1971	94,600	1974	109,400

It should be mentioned also that a newer form of contraception which extended feminine freedom at this time was sterilisation; though it was undertaken by only 4 per cent of women in 1970, it was to become much more popular later on in the 1980s, especially among women over thirty years of age. Vasectomy also had a more ephemeral popularity among men in the early 1970s.

It should not be thought, however, that these more satisfactory and reliable means of contraception, and the legislation of abortion, signalled a great increase in sexual activity among all classes. Once more, it is necessary to see things in perspective. Undoubtedly there was more sexual freedom, but a misleading impression can easily be gained from the contemporary popular press and the media generally of a great wave of sexual licence. In fact, the author of the 1970 survey just quoted, the social anthropologist Geoffrey Gorer, remarked at the time that 'England still appears to be a very chaste society, according to the replies of our informants.' These replies showed that 26 per cent of the married male informants and 63 per cent of the married female informants were virgin at marriage. A further 20 per cent of the men, and 25 per cent of the women, married the person with whom they first had intercourse. For these men and women, intercourse often started at betrothal, and if this is taken as the point of reference, rather than marriage itself, then it seems that just under half the men (46 per cent) and nearly nine-tenths of the women (88 per cent) were virgins up to that point. As for the unmarried, half of Gorer's informants with a current girl- or boy-friend said that they were on terms of 'real physical intimacy' with their partner, but a quarter of these excluded complete intercourse. Gorer calculated that 11 per cent of his sample might be considered relatively promiscuous, since they had had three or more partners. They were nearly all male, and more than half under twenty years of age. They occurred almost equally in all social classes, including, of course, the working classes. Among them was a 25-year-old engineer, who certainly believed in male sexual freedom:

> It is good for your ego; it is a natural thing to lead to lovemaking if your feelings are mutual; one has not got to be in love to make love; physical attraction is all that is wanted.

On the other hand, there were those who were opposed on religious grounds to extramarital intercourse, and also those who took a traditional view of 'saving yourself for marriage'. Thus the 21-year-old daughter of a railway worker, a virgin without a steady boy-friend at the time, said: 'I have been brought up to believe that you should wait until you are married; and I think if you love someone enough you can be prepared to wait until marriage.'

Other surveys about 1970 appear to confirm that Gorer's findings were typical, and to show that though there was a considerable extension of female sexual freedom, this did not necessarily lead to much greater promiscuity. One major difficulty in trying to assess just how much greater freedom was gained is the lack of earlier enquiries into sexual behaviour which would allow comparisons to be made. Thus it is impossible to say how far Gorer's 1970 findings represent a marked change in attitudes since, say, 1951. It is true that Gorer conducted an earlier investigation into attitudes to marriage in 1951, but his sample was not altogether satisfactory (or so he thought), and it also lacked a detailed enquiry into sexual practices. A common-sense historical guess might be that views and practices had changed (this seems undeniable), but that it is easy to exaggerate the extent of change and that, for many, traditional beliefs still prevailed.

Another difficulty already touched upon in assessing the magnitude of change is the prominence given by the media to aspects of the permissive society. The sixties were the decade when the movement for the social liberation of women (women's lib) attracted much attention in the press, and liberated women were supposed to celebrate their new freedom by burning their bras (though why this sacrifice of a helpful article of clothing should be thought liberating is not entirely clear). Naturally, the abandoning of bras by some younger women stimulated male attention at the time, together with the ubiquitous wearing of the mini-skirt (which became extraordinarily short), combined with nylon pantihose or tights instead of stockings. There was even an attempt to introduce topless dresses for evening wear, though this failed to catch on. As for men, they attracted a new derisive nickname employed by the emancipated female – MCP (Male Chauvinist Pig); it is unlikely that many using the term knew the meaning of 'chauvinist', though all were happy with 'male' and 'pig'. The woman priding herself on her newly emphasised independence began to drop the title 'Miss' or 'Mrs' in favour of 'Ms' (defined by the Concise Oxford Dictionary as 'title of woman without higher title, used like "Mr" without distinction between married and unmarried'). The emphasis given to these developments owed much not only to the popular press but also to the films and TV programmes of the time which, when shown again on TV today, are a reminder of the abbreviated feminine fashions of those days. Whatever the underlying reality, it undoubtedly appeared that women were taking a far more independent (and, some would say, more aggressive) role in society.

Yet in fact there were limits to all this. By no means all working-class women, married or single, were affected by the changes set out so far. Although many benefited from them, the social status of working women in England in the early 1970s was based upon many centuries of subordination to men, itself the product fundamentally of biological limitations stemming from the role of woman-as-mother. Enforced gender inferiority of this kind was not likely to be overthrown within the space of a few years. The economic facts were still against working-class women. Although the Equal Pay Act was passed in 1970, it did not come fully into effect until 1976. In April 1973 the earnings of full-time women workers aged twenty-one and over in manual occupations were only 64 per cent of those of men, and in non-manual occupations only 56 per cent of men's earnings. Then again, even when in work, women continued to be subjected to the sexual harassment which was still traditional in many workplaces. In higher education, fewer girls went to university; in some families, it was still considered that sons needed more education than daughters, and that higher education was wasted on girls who might soon get married and settle down to domestic life. So inequalities in society of many different kinds remained as a handicap to women in spite of the advances of the time. These advances certainly did not go far enough for ardent feminists, including Dr Germaine Greer, who published the best-selling *The Female Eunuch* in 1970, a bitter denunciation of male discrimination and prejudice against women. Early on in the book, in her introductory summary, Dr Greer makes clear her view of the basic male–female relationship:

> The castration of women has been carried out in terms of a masculine–feminine polarity, in which men have commandeered all the energy and streamlined it into an aggressive conquistatorial power, reducing all heterosexual contact to a sado-masochistic pattern.

Not all feminists, of course, took such an extreme view as this, which was intended to be provocative.

The Cult of Youth

To turn to another remarkable social phenomenon of the time: the 'cult of youth' is not a very helpful or precise description of the transformation of youthful activities and attitudes which occurred, since it could be taken to mean that youth in itself became increasingly admired and encouraged. 'Teenage Revolution' might be more appropriate, except that the important changes which took place were not confined to those under twenty. At the heart of the matter was the boom in the national economy and the ready availability of jobs which gave young people greatly increased spending power. As a consequence, they gained a new independence which had striking consequences for styles of dress, for spending habits, and (to a spectacular degree) for the entertainment industry. These changes affected working-class and middle-class youth alike. Indeed, so far as dress, speech and leisure interests were concerned, there was some assimilation of the younger members of these classes. It did not last for long, but for some time it was difficult to tell them apart (as they all wore the same leisure clothes) or indeed to distinguish between young men and young girls from the length of the hair.

The first sign of things to come was in the early fifties when the teddy boy first appeared. The name came from the wearing of a kind of Edwardian suit with a close-fitting jacket, short lapels, sometimes a velvet collar, and tight trousers. Along with this suit went a thick mop of hair, heavily greased, curling at the back but off the collar (the DA or 'duck's arse'), sideburns, a string or bootlace tie, and heavy, crepe-soled shoes (known popularly as 'brothel creepers'). This outfit was by no means cheap, and was at first regarded by the older generation as a harmless affectation, but later teddy boys met with some hostility and even fear when gangs of them were involved in brawls in public houses and dance halls. Their style of dress persisted until fashions changed, and they were succeeded by the rival groups of mods and rockers. The mods still went in for a more or less conventional style of dressing based on a suit, while the rockers dressed more casually with the emphasis on leather jackets. A further group favoured studded and fringed leather jackets (often with emblazoned skull and crossbones), calf-length boots, helmets and powerful motorcycles; they were the Hell's Angels, who unlike the other groups, were loosely organised nationally into chapters. To some extent their dedication to the open road and to roaming the country on their bikes was inspired by the American cult movie *Easy Rider*. Motor scooters were also popular, and led to the mass invasion during Bank Holiday week-ends in 1964 of seaside resorts such as Clacton and Brighton by gangs of youths and their girl-friends on scooters. These visitations were alarming to local residents and caused problems for the police, who had to deal with the fighting and brawling which took place, but it proved only a passing fad. Hell's Angels were still to be seen in the early 1970s, but by then the new groups were the skinheads and punks. Skinheads was an appropriate name, since they were distinguished by shaven heads at one end and heavy Dr Marten boots at the other end (in theory, very useful for kicking). Punks, by way of contrast, cut their hair into odd shapes (some-times with a central coxscomb from front to back, the 'Mohican'), dyed it with a variety of colours but often orange or green, used heavy eye shadow, and pierced their noses and ears with safety pins and the like.

Of course, these eccentricities were adopted by only a small minority of working-class young people, and were most often seen at the weekend. In the earlier part of the period, one kind of uniform – that of the armed forces – was compulsory for all young men when they became eighteen, but national service was abol-ished in 1960. Then in the early 1960s casual wear began to change for the vast majority who had never joined any of the groups de-scribed so far. This was due to the introduction of jeans – the new casual wear from the United States. They were not entirely unknown here at the time, being used as working gear by butchers, stevedores and others. Now under a variety of cherished trade names – for example, Levi's – they became the wear for leisure activities, often washed before use so that they were pre-shrunk and then worn very tight by both sexes, purposely faded, patched and frayed at the trouser bottoms; they were the new standard wear for the young. Above the jeans there might be a battle-dress top of the same denim material, with a shirt (preferably collarless), tee-shirt or blouse beneath. Tee-shirts became very popular, with a variety of slogans and/or jokes printed on them. Hair was worn long by the men, over the collar, and sometimes down the back. Beards reappeared – they had gone almost completely out of fashion (save in the navy) between the wars. Earrings were affected by some young men, and sunglasses were often worn – presumably a fashion imported from America (especially from the San Francisco scene), where hostility to the Vietnam war encouraged slogans such as 'Make love, not war', and the wearing of badges which read 'Free Angela Davis' (she was a leading American activist). Flower-power also flourished in the States, and enjoyed a brief popularity here; its advocates carried flowers, wore headbands and beads, and dispensed with shoes (somewhat impractical in the English climate, but persevered with by some over here, not necessarily flower people). A small minority not only adopted the new mode of attire, but took up an itinerant lifestyle, supporting themselves by casual labour or simply begging. They became known as hippies.

All these changes were understandably greeted with some reserve by the middle-aged, some of whom nevertheless began to grow their hair longer, and cautiously adopted jeans for casual wear. Meanwhile, an enormous expansion of the entertainment industry occurred, based largely upon teenage spending. In the 1950s, the modern era of pop music really began; swing music and big bands went out of fashion, being replaced by small groups playing rock and roll. When the first American group of this kind – Bill Haley and his Comets – visited England in 1957, featuring his smash hit, 'Rock Around the Clock', it had an immediate impact. Haley's film of the same title caused riots in some of the cinemas where it was shown. Rock and roll's only rival for a time was 'skiffle', played partly on cheap, improvised instruments. By the early sixties, rock was well established, and there emerged the phenomenon of the Beatles, four young working-class Liverpudlians who achieved an extraordinary success on their American tour in 1964. Their great international popularity was not simply the result of their performance as a group – they had no special instrumental talent – but was based rather on a remarkable outflow of songs written by two of them, Paul McCartney and John Lennon; they wrote no less than 105 songs together, all recorded by the group, up to April 1968. Their total sales in singles up to January 1968 amounted to 225 million, and their gross receipts from records over the years 1963 to 1968 were about £70 million.

It is fair to say that a kind of 'Beatlemania' descended on the country in the mix-sixties; the Beatles became popular heroes. They made two very successful films, and they were awarded the MBE by Harold Wilson's Labour government, presumably for their services to the music industry and the export drive. Their music received glowing notices from the music critic of *The Times*, William Mann. In fact, it made a great impact on listeners of all ages, not merely the young. Some songs have conventional enough love lyrics: 'Love Me Do' (1962) – the first Beatle song to be recorded; 'I Want to Hold Your Hand' (1963); 'All My Loving' (1963); 'Michelle' (1965). One or two need a knowledge of Liverpool to acquire the full flavour: 'Penny Lane' (1967) and 'Strawberry Fields For Ever' (1967). Still others have more than a touch of melancholy – 'Eleanor Rigby' (1966) and 'She's Leaving Home' (1967). Perhaps the most popular even in the late sixties was 'Yesterday' (1965). Paul McCartney's handwritten script, to accompany a simple and haunting melody by Lennon, reads:

> Yesterday, all my troubles seemed so far away,
> Now it looks as though they're here to stay
>   oh I believe in yesterday.
> Suddenly, I'm not half the man I used to be
> There's a shadow hanging over me
> Yesterday came suddenly.

middle

> Why she had to go, I don't know
>   she wouldn't say
> I said something wrong, now I long
>   for yesterday . . .

> Yesterday, love was such an easy game to play
> Now I need a place to hide away
>   oh I believe in yesterday.

Later on, after a brief flirtation with Indian mysticism, the group split up, all of them having become immensely rich. George Harrison and Ringo Starr moved out of the public eye, John Lennon lived a bizarre life with his Japanese wife in New York where he was gunned down and murdered in 1981, while Paul McCartney went on composing and has become the most successful writer of popular songs ever. The Beatles remain the most remarkable example of a working-class pop group becoming world-famous and millionaires by their mid-twenties.

Other aspects of the pop scene may be summed up briefly: some groups besides the Beatles achieved international success in the 1960s – the Rolling Stones led by Mick Jagger, purveying a rather more violent and aggressive kind of music, were also very popular. Still other groups came and went, few lasting any length of time, though more traditional groups like the Bachelors and the Shadows lasted longer than most, and one member of the Shadows, Cliff Richard, went solo and appeared to be able to keep going indefinitely. Stage performances of pop groups became ever more frenetic for a time, with elaborate stage lighting, immensely amplified sound, much swirling dry ice or stage smoke, and crude effects such as the smashing of guitars. Pop festivals and concerts, often held on rural sites, might last several days and attracted crowds of many thousands. Conventional dance halls declined in popularity, being replaced by discotheques where couples danced facing each other rather than in each other's arms. Ballroom dancing fell out of fashion, though it was kept going by limited numbers of enthusiasts, not all of them middle-aged; it continued to receive support from the veteran BBC TV programme *Come Dancing*. Younger viewers preferred to watch *Top of the Pops* and *Juke Box Jury*. Pop music was *the* music for most of the young, as dance music had been in the thirties, and for a time swinging Britain was the pop capital of the world. In his amusing and perceptive account of the sixties, *The Pendulum Years* (1970), Bernard Levin sums it all up:

> The growth of pop music groups – many, no doubt, inspired by the gigantic commercial success of the Beatles to believe that the lightning might strike them too, if they only formed fours and began to perform, but many also, clearly in the business of self-expression – was the most extraordinary phenomenon in the world of entertainment of the whole decade . . .

He goes on to name ninety-eight groups in all, many with the most fanciful and remarkable names. None of the American groups could rival the Beatles, though Elvis Presley was still the singing idol of the young both in the USA and here, while Frank Sinatra continued to appeal to the older generation.

One ugly side to pop festivals was the police searches for drugs. In the immediate post-war years there was hardly a drug problem in this country. Users of hard drugs were registered with their local NHS doctors and were supplied quite legally with their drugs. In this way it was thought that the problem could be monitored and kept under control, and indeed it was believed that drug addiction was handled much more sensibly here than in other countries, such as the United States, where it was out of control. Unfortunately, over-prescription by GPs led to the illegal sale of drugs, and a growing problem of drug abuse in this country. By the 1960s it was clear that the existing policy was increasingly inadequate, and the 1964 Drugs (Prevention of Misuse) Act made the possession of certain drugs without lawful excuse a criminal offence. This did little to stem the rising tide of the use of soft drugs such as 'purple hearts' (amphetamine pills) and cannabis (also known as 'pot' or 'hashish'). Cannabis in particular became popular among the young, especially as it appeared to be relatively harmless and non-addictive. Joints (cannabis rolled for smoking) would be passed around at parties, and the smoking of pot spread even among the respectable professional classes, who wished to show that (in the idiom of the day) they were 'with it'. A full-page advertisement appeared in *The Times* bearing the names of many distinguished men and women in public life, mostly with well-known liberal views, advocating the legalisation of cannabis. The Wootton Committee (1968), calculated that there might be up to 300,000 users. Other estimates were far higher – one was up to two million. What was unknown at the time, of course – and is still a matter of controversy – is how far cannabis use can lead on to hard drugs such as cocaine or heroin. These two latter drugs were not widely used before the mid-seventies, though the drug LSD had a brief popularity at this time. The figures in Table 5.2 for persons in Britain found guilty of drug offences in the early 1970s tell their own story.

Table 5.2 Drug Offences, 1971–3

	1971	1972	1973
Cannabis	9,219	12,611	13,827
Amphetamines	2,387	1,971	2,173
LSD	1,601	1,457	1,496
Heroin	580	665	628
Cocaine	126	245	293
Opium	55	98	244

Source: *Social Trends*, No. 5 (1974).

A good deal of space has been given here to what has been loosely termed the 'cult of youth' simply because it affected such a large proportion of the working population, and of society as a whole. Undoubtedly it influenced the relationships between parents and their older children, who were reaching puberty at a younger age, were more conscious of the need for independence, and were generally more demanding, even when still at school. In 1969 the age of attaining majority and of having the vote was lowered from twenty-one to eighteen years of age. One interesting aspect of all this change is that it was not confined to the working classes. The characteristic form of middle-class protest was that of student demonstrations and 'sit-ins' in the universities, especially at Essex, Sussex and the London School of Economics, mostly in the late sixties (middle-class students still predominated in the universities at this time). These demos did not receive very widespread support, or have very clear objectives, though they may have been instrumental in clearing away some of the more out-of-date rules and regulations in some places. Being mostly peaceful enough in nature, they were very different from the violent *événements* in Paris in 1968, where the barricades went up, and there were many casualties resulting from clashes between students and the police.

One other oddity of the changes in youth culture deserves to be mentioned: whether it was the influence of the Beatles or not, regional accents and especially Liverpool accents became increasingly popular. They were heard more and more on radio and TV, and two long-running TV series helped to make them more familiar in the south – *Coronation Street*, and the first series to show the police in a rather more realistic light, *Z Cars*. It was even said (probably with little foundation in fact) that some middle-class young men and women were attempting to adopt working-class accents, presumably so as to demonstrate their classlessness. However, the mere fact that this sort of thing could be said gives some indication of the anti-establishment spirit which characterised the age of the permissive society. Many of the older conventions and beliefs were regarded as out of date, stuffy and old-fashioned. The more modern outlook was (in the argot of the time) to do your own thing, let it all hang out, and right on, man ...

So it appeared that the permissive society and the new youth culture had apparently produced a new generation of young men and women, the men very hirsute and bejeaned, the women in mini-skirts or also in jeans, both sexes more self-assured than ever before, and both sexes more sexually liberated. Needless to say, older people gained exaggerated ideas of how far sexual liberation and pot-smoking really went. It did not last. Attitudes changed and so did the fashions in the second half of the seventies; but it is fair to say that significant changes had taken place in young people's attitudes and activities, and the world of the teenager would never be the same again.

The Forms of Affluence and Leisure Pursuits

Greater affluence among the working classes certainly meant changes in lifestyle. For many, this took the form of spending on the home, and in the previous chapter something was said about this, in particular, the installation of central heating and the possession of a motor car. Homes themselves were certainly more comfortable, not only because they were warmer, but also because the furnishing included more carpets. Relatively inexpensive fitted carpets were now available, made from synthetic fibre such as nylon. Working-class homes also tended to be lighter, as the favourite colour for woodwork was now white. Bathroom and kitchen underwent noticeable changes. Both were now likely to be half-tiled, the bath itself would have enclosed sides, and the water closet would be in the form of a low-level suite – that is, the cistern would be set low down on the wall rather than above head-level with a chain to pull. In the kitchen, wall cabinets at eye level had become fashionable, sinks were of stainless steel, and the possession of an electric kettle, toaster, washing machine and refrigerator had become commonplace. In 1973, 66.6 per cent of all households had a washing machine, and 77.6 per cent had a refrigerator. Housekeeping itself had long been influenced by TV advertising (Independent Television began in 1954), especially by persuasive advertisements for washing powders, detergents of various kinds and convenience foods. In the living room, 93.4 per cent of households had a television set, and 43.4 per cent a telephone. Radio sets were relatively inexpensive, and by now were much smaller, having been transistorised. Much of the decorating, and even some of the fittings and the plumbing in a well-maintained house were the result of do-it-yourself – a form of self-help which owed its popularity partly to householders having more time on their hands, and partly to the high cost of professional decorating and repair work.

Outside the home, increasing numbers of the working classes could afford a car – 42 per cent of all households in 1972 had one, and just over 30 per cent of those in council accommodation. This made it easier to get out and about, and to do a weekly shop at the new supermarkets. It also encouraged a trend towards eating out. Hitherto, food cooked outside the house had been supplied largely by fish-and-chip shops. They continued to flourish, but public houses began to supply first bar snacks and then larger meals in their own restaurants – a remarkable expansion of the somewhat crude facilities, not going far beyond the odd packet of potato crisps, which had been provided previously. At the same time, breweries began to refurbish their public house premises so as to offer more modern and luxurious surroundings (not all customers welcomed this; and the introduction by some brewers of gassy types of beer led to the founding of the Campaign for Real Ale). For those who still liked to eat at home without the bother of cooking a meal, first Chinese and then Indian take-aways appeared, the Chinese being the first in the field with their own restaurants serving both Chinese and English food at moderate prices.

When a survey was carried out of leisure activities in London in 1970, based on the leisure interests of married men in full-time work, watching television was easily the most popular activity at home, followed by playing with the children, home decorating and repairs, and cleaning the car. Sporting activities included swimming and (much less popular) fishing. Other outdoor leisure activities were (in order of priority) going for a drive, going to a pub, going for a walk, going out for a meal and attending church. This survey broke down activities by class, and showed that going to a pub (as one might expect) was more popular with working-class men than with the professional and managerial classes; while for the latter classes going out for a meal was over twice as popular as with the working classes, and going to church was just over three times as popular.

Another survey made in 1973 of all ages, and broken down by age groups, supplies some interesting contrasts. Of home-based activities, watching television was again easily the most popular of all, but followed this time by reading papers, resting and relaxing, listening to music, reading books and gardening. Activities not at home, again in order of priorty, were: visiting friends and family, going to the pub, car rides, going out for a meal, going to clubs and societies, taking part in or watching sport, going to the cinema or theatre, and going to bingo (a revived form of the services game of tombola, very popular with older ladies; sums of money could be won).

Two leisure pursuits in particular deserve further comment:

watching television and church-going. As for television, this clearly was *the* new leisure activity (if activity is the right word) of the age, replacing cinema-going to a very large extent. Not only did it provide entertainment and news over three channels by 1974 (BBC2 had begun in 1964), but the commercials on ITV exercised a powerful influence on popular taste in consumer goods. Licences for black and white reception numbered 15.6 million in 1970, falling to 11.8 million by 1974 as more colour licences were issued: 0.3 million in 1970, and 5.6 million in 1974. As for viewing hours, the average number of weekly viewing hours for all persons aged five and over was 19.3 hours in February 1973, and 15.3 hours in August 1973 (lower hours were to be expected, of course, in summer). The heaviest viewing was by the five-to-fourteen years age-group – 24.5 hours per week in February 1973, and 22.7 hours in August 1973. The working classes spent three to four hours more per week at the box than the upper classes. There was already considerable concern (principally among the middle and upper classes) at the amount of violence and sexual activity shown on TV, and in 1964 a Mrs Mary Whitehouse, a middle-aged school teacher, began her campaign to set limits to the permissiveness of the age, at least as exhibited on the TV screen.

As for church-going, the total Sunday attendances at all services of the Church of England slipped from 1.606 million in 1968 to 1.542 million in 1970. The total confirmed membership, however, remained fairly steady at 9.7 million in 1956 and 9.5 million in 1970. There was still a decline in the numbers on the electoral roll of the Church of England, however, from 2.95 million in 1950 to 2.56 million in 1970. Other major churches similarly experienced a fall in numbers of members, as Table 5.3 illustrates. The one exception in the general decline of membership is the Roman Catholic Church, which increased membership from 3.56 million in 1950 to 4.99 million in 1975. The various Orthodox churches also had a not insignificant following in 1970, as did the Pentecostal churches, the Salvation Army, the Quakers and other independent churches such as the Christian Brethren. All in all, the general picture is certainly of a decline in both church membership and attendance in the period 1951 to 1974, and of an increasingly secular society. Nevertheless, more than one in ten of the adult population still went to church at least once a month, and probably a majority still believed in some kind of supernatural deity.

Other forms of leisure activity not mentioned so far are various.

Table 5.3   Church Membership, 1950 and 1975

	1950	1975
United Reform (Presbyterians and Congregationalists)	2,053,059	1,716,543
Methodists	744,815	541,518
Baptists	337,203	181,798

Source: Halsey (ed.), *British Social Trends since 1900* (1988).

They include: needlework and knitting; attending evening classes; social and voluntary work; visits to stately homes, museums, art galleries and theatres; hobbies of many different kinds; watching football; and playing darts. Betting continued to be a working-class interest, and since the 1960 Betting and Gaming Act, betting shops could operate legally and freely, so that the street bookie and his runner became figures of the past. The television sports programmes and sports news now supplied the odds at the leading race meetings.

Another significant change was to be found in the taking of holidays. As already noted, by 1974 38 per cent of full-time workers had an entitlement to three weeks' paid holiday, and 52 per cent to between three and four weeks. If a holiday is defined as a period of four or more nights away from home regarded by the person concerned as a holiday, then the number of holidays taken went up from 36.5 million in 1966 to 40.25 million in 1970, with a further rise to 48.75 million in 1973. Moreover, whereas the figure for holidays abroad in 1966 was 5.5 million, in 1973 it had shot up to 8.25 million, by far the greatest number being taken in Spain. Here then was the beginning of the decline of the traditional working-class holiday taken in Blackpool, Morecambe, Skegness, Southend, Margate and similar seaside resorts. Package holidays abroad for the working classes were becoming popular – something which very few if any working-class men and women could have contemplated between the wars, when holidays abroad were very much for the middle classes, not the working classes. At the same time, another form of holiday which had enjoyed some popularity with the working classes in the fifties and sixties became less attractive – the week or fortnight at the holiday camp. Holiday camps had provided a convenient (but not particularly cheap) form of holiday for young families in the years after the war when a kind of cheerful regimentation was more acceptable than it became later. Curiously enough, their memory was preserved in the late eighties by an immensely popular TV comedy series set in the post-war years and entitled *Hi-di-hi* (a greeting to be answered by 'Ho-de-ho').

Attitudes to Immigrants

Immediately after the Second World War the English work force was augmented by successive waves of Commonwealth immigrants, at first from the West Indies, and then later from Asia. In itself, there was nothing new about immigration, particularly from the Empire. Asians have lived in England from as early as the seventeenth century, while communities of lascars (Indian sailors) were to be found in seaports, especially London, where in 1814 the East India Company fed and housed over 1,000 of them. In the nineteenth century, there was a steady flow of immigrants from Ireland, which became a flood for a time after the Famine in the 1840s, while towards the end of the century there was an influx of Jews, many of them into the East End of London, fleeing from persecution in Central and Eastern Europe. What was distinctive about Commonwealth immigration after 1945 was that the immigrants were immediately recognisable by their colour, especially the West Indians.

These immigrants arrived from the late 1940s onwards, and came at the invitation of London Transport, British Rail and the National Health Service. Immigration was at first in the region of 1,000 a year, rising to a peak of 75,000 in 1961. Thereafter the figures declined as immigration controls were imposed and there were fewer jobs available; by 1971 there was actually a negative net immigration figure – that is, 1,163 more West Indians left Britain than entered it. However, by 1974 there was again a positive figure of 5,845. As for Asians, they began to arrive mostly from India and Pakistan in annual numbers of between 8,000 and 10,000 from 1955 onwards, like the West Indians coming in search of better economic opportunities; the early arrivals were guaranteed free accommodation and help in getting jobs. By 1971 they numbered 546,000 (including East African Indians), representing 40 per cent of the coloured population in the country.

At first, no efforts were made by the government to ensure that immigrants settled peacefully in their new surroundings. It was simply assumed that they would adjust as time went on. In government circles, on the whole, immigration was thought to be a good thing; the West Indians were a valuable source of additional labour, and in any case it was thought only right and proper to offer work to those who had been born in what was formerly the Empire and was now the New Commonwealth. So the West Indians settled down, mostly in London and in the West Midlands. Some had been here before, having served in the armed forces during the war. The reaction of the working classes in the early days was somewhat mixed. On the one hand, it was clear that the West Indians were good workers, and were prepared to take what were often unskilled jobs which were unattractive to the British worker. West Indian men were to be found in transport, communications and the metal and engineering industries. As mentioned previously, West Indian women proved extremely helpful in the NHS. On the other hand, West Indian immigrants were noticeably different in appearance from the indigenous population, and often had a different and more exuberant lifestyle. The British working man is notoriously xenophobic – there are geographial and historical reasons for this, of course – and is often suspicious of strangers. Here then was a potentially inflammable situation.

The first proof of this came in August 1958 with the Notting Hill riots in west London. These seem to have been caused by antagonism between the native white population and the local West Indian community. Racism, which had been simmering below the surface, had at last manifested itself on an alarming scale. Exemplary sentences were imposed on those convicted of taking part in the rioting; fortunately there were no fatalities. This appeared to be the right policy, for there was no reoccurrence of the riots. At the same time, the Institute of Race Relations was set up, and as the immigration figures for the early 1960s showed an actual increase, the 1962 Immigration Act placed restrictions on the numbers immigrating into this country. Further restrictions followed early in 1965, and later in that year the Race Relations Act established the Race Relations Board. The Labour government followed this up by passing the Commonwealth Immigrants Act 1968, and also an extended Race Relations Act in the same year. It was during the discussion of this Bill that Enoch Powell, MP for Wolverhampton, a town in the West Midlands with a substantial coloured population, made his notorious speech predicting a frightening increase in the numbers of immigrants, and prophesying social disorder and bloodshed. He was immediately dismissed as a member of the

Conservative shadow cabinet, but he received much popular support. Liberal middle-class sentiment, of course, was strongly against Powell's views, but then the vast majority of the middle classes did not live in the same neighbourhoods as the immigrants, whereas many working-class people did, and often in dreary, run-down inner-city areas. Some London dockers actually staged a march in support of Powell.

The remaining years of the period up to 1974 saw the passing of a further Commonwealth Immigrants Act in 1971, but no further riots for the time being. Meanwhile, Asian immigration was growing and outstripping that of the West Indians. Indian and Pakistani newcomers often arrived individually and without their families, who came over later (thereby raising problems as to who could be considered legitimate family members and who could not). Some illegal immigration also took place, though it is impossible to say on what scale. Most of the Asian immigrants had a higher standard of education than the West Indians, and more had professional qualifications. Clearly they were prepared to work hard, and to show enterprise, for example, in running their own businesses in light engineering and in clothing manufacture, and (perhaps above all) in retail grocery, where their corner shops remained open in the evenings, and sometimes seven days a week. Thus Asian immigrants soon acquired a somewhat different image from West Indians, being quieter, more self-effacing, yet at the same time very hard-working, and aiming at economic independence. Many started in privately rented accommodation, later moving into cheap owner-occupied housing. In contrast, many West Indians occupied council-rented houses or flats.

In surveying the attitudes of the English working classes to coloured immigration in the post-war period up to 1974, it seems that most of them were tolerant of the individual immigrant whom they knew personally while reserving a vague hostility to immigration as a whole. Where this existed, it may be conjectured that its roots lay deep in the ancient fear of 'strangers within the gates', and of being increasingly disadvantaged by the presence of whole communities with different cultural patterns, different religions (in the case of the Asians), different ways of dressing, different diets and cooking habits, and so on. Such communities were the result of the natural concentration of immigrants – for example, in Bradford, Blackburn, Leicester, Notting Hill and Handsworth in Birmingham – natural, because it permitted mutual support in times of need, protection against possible racial attacks, and the provision of community services such as mosques and temples, ethnic food stores and other specialist services. It is understandable that immigrants should wish to preserve their own cultural identity (though small, white immigrant groups from Europe such as the Poles were able to do this more easily without exciting adverse comment). Since, as mentioned earlier, many of the West Indians settled in decaying inner-city areas, these tended to turn into immigrant ghettos, at times much resented by impoverished local white inhabitants who lacked the resources to move out.

Another problem presented by the second wave of immigrants – the Asians – was one of language. A surprising proportion of Asian men were at first unable to speak English, and this applied even more to their womenfolk, many of whom were kept in virtual seclusion. Young daughters had to attend school, of course, and so learned some English, though later on they might have to submit to arranged marriages. So far as West Indians were concerned, there were increasing complaints of police harassment and discrimination, though these were less noticeable before 1974 than afterwards in the eighties. Similarly there were fewer complaints about discrimination against immigrants in appointment to jobs before 1974, when unemployment was still relatively low, than in the following decade. Lastly, though only a very small minority of white young people supported the National Front (founded 1966), a larger number probably sympathised secretly with their hostility to coloured immigrants, as expressed by a member of the Front in 1978:

> I don't want parts of my country to become no-go areas, where I feel I can't walk without the risk of being knifed or mugged. I don't want to be with black people, I don't want a multi-racial country. Why should I? I've got nothing in common with them, they don't want to mix with me any more than I do with them. Why should I be forced to live with them?

A middle-class liberal would find rational argument difficult with a young man like this. Certainly the middle classes were far more sympathetic to the coloured population than some members of the working classes who, as pointed out earlier, lived in the same areas. On the whole, TV and the media generally did well in excluding racial comments, though, curiously enough, racial jokes of a traditional kind were still permitted at the expense of one white immigrant group – the Irish, who were still depicted as ignorant but amiable simpletons. Such jokes were probably inoffensive enough, especially when compared with the crudity of the racial comments by some comedians in working men's clubs.

Crime and the Permissive Society

It might perhaps be imagined that the relaxing of social conventions and the instituting of permissive social reforms could lead to an increase in criminal activities as social controls were loosened. In fact, there was an increase in crime, but to suppose that it was due simply to permissiveness is to over-simplify. To start with some basic facts: as we have already seen, the criminal law was reformed in a number of directions in the post-war period. Capital punishment was abolished, male homosexual acts between adults became legal, and abortion (on medical grounds) was also legalised. In addition, by the 1961 Suicide Act, it was no longer a criminal offence to try to commit suicide (it is worth recording that in 1952 there were more than 500 prosecutions for this offence, and still as many as 60 prosecutions in 1960). In all these directions, the law was humanised. As for sentencing, the courts could no longer order flogging and birching after the passing of the Criminal Justice Act 1948. The parole system was begun in 1967, and community service was introduced as an alternative to prison in 1972. In 1963 the Children and Young Persons Act raised the age for criminal responsibility from eight to ten years.

However, all these reforms were carried out against a background of rising crime statistics. To see these in perspective, it must be remembered that the number of criminal offences rose between the wars at an average rate of about 5 per cent per annum. The trend continued during the Second World War, and then after a period of some fluctuations was resumed at the higher rate of about 10 per cent after 1955. The other matter to bear in mind is that official criminal statistics cannot possibly give an exact picture of the extent of crime at any one time: there are numerous reasons for this, perhaps the most important being the failure of the public to notify the police of an offence, either because they think the crime is too trivial, or because they think that the police could not (or would not) do anything about it. Again, from time to time the police have altered their ways of recording crime, while crimes themselves have sometimes been reclassified or redefined by a new Act of Parliament, thus making comparisons difficult.

These caveats having been uttered, there is no doubt that there was a substantial rise in recorded indictable crime from 1955 onwards. In the period 1955 to 1965 alone, the rate rose 159 per cent. The increase in real terms in the value of property stolen in the same period was 261 per cent. The key year is 1960, when there was a rise in serious crime of roughly 70 per cent over 1955 (about the same as in the Second World War). Table 5.4 gives the figures for indictable offences known to the police. In more detail, *crimes of violence* against the person rose 100 per cent, 1955–60 (from 7,884 to 15,759); *offences against property* also shot up, from 399,924 in 1955 to 688,381 in 1960; but *sexual offences* rose much more moderately, from 17,078 in 1955 to 19,937 in 1960.

Table 5.4   Indictable Offences, 1945–75

Year	Total offences	Percentage change over preceding five years	Rate per million of population	Percentage change over preceding five years
1945	478,394	+65.8	12,705.3	+30.7
1950	461,435	−3.6	12,097.2	−4.8
1955	438,085	−5.1	11,234.7	−4.8
1960	743,713	+69.8	18,474.1	+64.8
1965	1,133,882	+52.5	28,258.7	+53.0
1970	1,555,995	+37.2	38,030.9	+34.6
1975	2,105,031	+35.3	50,350.1	+32.4

Source: Terence Morris, *Crime and Criminal Justice since 1945* (1989).

What could have been the cause of these substantial increases? One group of investigators has suggested that it is impossible to separate what were probably the two major causes, the growth of affluence and an increase in organised crime. One might remark that if the latter were a principal factor, the police would soon have pinpointed it. In fact, most commentators concentrate on the growth of affluence, Professor Terence Morris pointing out that 'by the 1960s, ordinary people simply owned more property than they had ever done before'. There were more cars about, often left unlocked, with contents freely displayed. There were more desirable (and portable) goods available, such as transistor radios and record players. Supermarkets displayed their goods on open shelves freely accessible to the shoplifter, and so did the great multiples such as Marks & Spencer, Littlewoods, British Home Stores and Woolworths. There was simply more of everything to steal.

All this certainly helps to explain why there should have been such a boom in crime from 1955 onwards, though as an explanation it hardly penetrates to the heart of the matter. Does it follow automatically that the richer a society becomes, the more crimes are committed? Fortunately this is not our business here. Rather more relevant is the question of how far the increase in crime affected the working classes of the period. So far as that portion of the criminal fraternity recruited from the working classes is concerned, obviously they were busily and gainfully employed during these years. One commentator has suggested that part of the rise in the figures might be accounted for by an increase in productivity among criminals, for example, burglars might have been carrying out more burglaries per week or month than previously. This seems somewhat fanciful, and something which the police would have detected quite quickly. As for the law-abiding, vast majority of the working classes, their contact with the criminal law was very limited, and confined principally to the increasing number of motoring offences, and to the occasional fracas either after closing time at the pub, or on the football terraces. For obvious reasons, burglary of middle-class homes was more common than of working-class homes. Domestic disputes were still largely ignored by the police, though many murders arose out of domestic relationships, with the murderer known to the victim. For some members of the working classes, of course, the police were always to be regarded with suspicion, being representatives of the establishment and of officialdom; but in the period up to 1974 the number of large-scale clashes at public demonstrations was limited, though growing after the 1968 student protests, and the great protest meeting outside the American Embassy in Grosvenor Square against the war in Vietnam in the same year. Lastly, it must be remarked that as always the great majority of criminal actions were the work of younger people, especially of young men and juveniles; in 1965, young male offenders in the age group fourteen to twenty-five outnumbered those aged twenty-five and over by more than five to one – another worry for the parents of teenage boys who were trying their wings. Whatever increase in crime took place – and again it must be emphasised that the official figures are subject to different interpretations – there seems no doubt that much of it was the work of the young, some of whom later became respectable citizens, while others lapsed into recidivism.

The Permissive Society Reassessed

At the beginning of this chapter it was asserted somewhat boldly that the permissive society was essentially the creation of the middle classes. If this is true, it follows that some aspects of the change to a less inhibited form of society might well have affected the middle classes rather more at first than the working classes. An obvious example here is the abolition of stage censorship in 1968. As Professor Marwick has remarked, 'Theatre-going (like divorce) is a minority activity' (he is right about going to the theatre, but the passing of time may prove him wrong about divorce). Certainly the working classes were not greatly moved by the Lord Chamberlain's loss of his powers of censorship; and so they were spared the excitement generated by what Bernard Levin calls the first 'tribal love-rock musical' *Hair* (much nudity and hair, some of it pubic), and by the equally revealing *Oh Calcutta!*, devised by the theatre critic Kenneth Tynan.

The same reasoning applies to the most celebrated literary event of the 1960s, the prosecution of Penguin Books in 1960 for publishing the hitherto banned novel by D. H. Lawrence, *Lady Chatterley's Lover*, following the passing of the Obscene Publications Act 1959, an Act actually intended to free certain serious works of literary merit from the threat of prosecution. The trial itself provided middle-class observers with a good deal of entertainment, not only because of the absurdly old-fashioned and prudish approach of the prosecution – at one point the jury was asked whether it was a book which they would wish their wives or servants to read – but also because of the frequent reference to the four-letter words used by the author. Penguin Books were found not guilty, and thereafter a number of novels were published which could scarcely have been printed before 1960. As for the most offensive (to most people) of all the four-letter words, this was used for the first time on BBC TV in 1965 by Kenneth Tynan on a live, late-evening discussion. It caused some outrage at the time, though it was unlikely to have been very shocking (as opposed to merely surprising) to many working-class viewers, large numbers of whom habitually used the word among their mates every day at work (but not usually in front of the ladies). In his *English History 1914–1945* published in the same year, the historian A. J. P. Taylor recorded that the word seemed to be approaching literary, though not conversational, respectability. Clearly, middle-class proprieties were being mocked by Tynan, as indeed they were in satirical TV programmes like *That Was the Week That Was*, but the liberating effect on working-class viewers was likely to have been limited. Many would have felt more at home with the TV serial, *Coronation Street*, first shown in 1960, where most of the characters, at least, were recognisably working class.

What then were the most important aspects of the so-called permissive society for ordinary working-class people? More important, perhaps, than any of the legislative changes, significant as they undoubtedly were, was the simple fact of full employment, which enabled the majority to practice freedom of choice, to buy their TVs and fitted carpets, to take regular holidays, to pay for teenagers staying on in sixth forms and at college, and (when young) to buy their jeans and to go to pop concerts. This was the most important form of liberation for them. Marx and Engels may have got a good deal wildly wrong about the development of capitalist society, but they were certainly right about the importance of the economic factor:

> We make our own history, but in the first place under very definite presuppositions and conditions. Among these, the economic ones are finally decisive.

At the same time, it is abundantly clear that working-class women were increasingly liberated from the traditional routine of child-bearing, bringing up children, cooking and housework. The development of better contraceptive methods (by 1975, 41 per cent of mothers in unskilled manual workers' households were using the pill), the greater availability of divorce and abortion, and the increasing emphasis on women's rights as individuals, all contributed to this end. It is tempting to describe all this as a 'quiet revolution' or to use some similar term denoting the extent of change, but for the fact noted earlier, that many men still adopted traditional attitudes, and many women, too, so that the amount of change which actually occurred must not be exaggerated.

Jerusalem was not yet built in England's green and pleasant land, not as long as (for understandable reasons, of course) the police were still reluctant to interfere in domestic disputes, and refuges for battered wives were still necessary, and indeed too few in number.

The other obvious beneficiaries of the permissive society were male adults, and the young. As for the former, it must not be forgotten that they, too, benefited from safer and more reliable contraception, from easier divorce and from the reform of the law relating to adult homosexuality. This last is a tricky subject: although it was said at the time that one in twenty males was likely to be orientated towards homosexuality, there are no reliable figures to show this in terms of class. The Wolfenden Report (1957) on homosexuality and prostitution does not discuss this in any detail, simply dismissing the idea that homosexuality was peculiar to the intelligentsia, and stating baldly that it existed in all callings and at all levels of society; it was to be found not only among those possessing a high degree of intelligence, but also among 'the dullest oafs'. Of course, the alleged prevalence of homosexuality among middle- and upper-class men educated at public school is well known, while the sexual preferences of middle-class literary figures of the time like E.M.Forster, or of political figures like Tom Driberg, were common knowledge, together with the fact that these gentlemen had a liking for working-class partners (known usually as 'rough trade'). Presumably working men as much as middle-class men could now 'come out', that is, make known their true sexual natures, if they wished to do so. Some, indeed, were quite aggressive about this, both in dress and behaviour. The older, derisive nicknames, such as 'nancy boys', 'pansies' and the post-war 'poofs' and 'queers', fell out of fashion, though 'straight' and 'bent', 'butch' and 'queen' were all retained as useful terms, while 'gay' became the customary word for homosexual. *Gay News* actually dates from 1962, while later on the adult students of the Open University formed their own university Gay Society. Curiously enough, there was no specific mention of lesbianism in the Wolfenden Report, or in the subsequent legislation, possibly because female homosexuality has always drawn less attention than male homosexuality, with its associated problems of soliciting, corruption of young boys and blackmailing of public figures.

As for the young, they achieved greater spending power just at a time when social conventions were changing, so that all the natural rebelliousness of youth could express itself more freely than before. Once more, it is necessary to try to see things in perspective. Change had begun in middle-class circles even in the 1930s. A Shell petrol advertisement of the time shows a 'then' picture of an old-fashioned schoolmaster roaring at a small boy, 'No, Smith Minor!' The 'now' picture alongside shows a teacher in casual clothes with an open-necked skirt and sandals saying to a boy similarly attired, 'Certainly, Gerald!' The slogan in the advertisement is that times change, so does Shell. Times did change for working-class young people in the sixties. For the first time, teenage bedrooms acquired an appearance characteristic of the new, teenage affluence, with photos of pop stars, posters for pop concerts, a record player and radio, often a guitar, and the inevitable tee-shirts and jeans. No doubt all this had much to recommend it as representing gains in individual freedom and the opportunity to 'do one's own thing'; but for many parents it meant increased fears of underaged sexual activity, teenage alcoholism and the danger of drugs. Responsible parenthood had become more worrying than ever before.

Obviously enough, the permissive society brought positive gains to the working classes in England in a number of directions. These benefits operated at different levels and within the framework established by the continuance of full employment, and the rise in the standard of living. Most of the advances were to become permanent features of society in the years which followed. Nevertheless, one disturbing exception to it all was provided by the ranks of the poor, still alarmingly numerous in spite of the welfare state. They seemed to be a survival from a previous period of history. Yet from the mid-1970s onwards, the permissive society (and the affluent society even more so) also began to look a little dated, as unemployment bit more deeply and increasing numbers found themselves on the dole. A new era had begun.

Chapter 6

Darkening Horizons 1974–1990: Part I

Changes in the Economy: An Overview

Throughout this book emphasis has been placed on changes in the economy which have affected the working classes and, as we have seen, the golden years of the fifties and sixties brought a doubling of the standard of living for them. From the mid-seventies on, however, the OPEC oil-price rises of 1973 drove up prices all round, leading eventually to a global recession. The existing trends of change in the British economy continued and were accentuated: manufacturing industry went on declining, and in 1978–9 prices were forced up again when oil prices rose by a further 45 per cent, and by a further 68 per cent in the following year. World trade slowed down, and this country entered into a severe depression lasting from 1979 to 1981, not really bottoming out until some time in 1982. Home industry continued on its downward path, the service industry still expanded and, ominously enough, manufactured imports continued to grow in volume year by year. Only the availability of North Sea oil and its profitable export saved the economy from real disaster.

In and after 1982 a slow recovery took place as inflation was brought under control, and the decline in manufacturing was checked, but by no means completely arrested. It was not until late in 1988 that manufacturing industry was back to the 1979 level. Only two major industries expanded to any significant degree in the 1980s – chemicals and electrical engineering, while the output of the British car industry actually fell by 25 per cent in the period 1981–5. Yet the service sector continued to grow, particularly banking, retailing and oil production. Meanwhile, manufactured goods were imported on an ever-increasing scale, until in the mid-eighties they exceeded exports of British manufactured goods in value – something without precedent in Britain's economic history. Surprisingly enough, the demand at home for such goods remained buoyant, and even expanded, much of it financed by credit trans-actions. As one economist, Dr Keith Smith, has commented re-cently, 'British people wished to consume more, and were pre-pared to go into debt.' Denis Healey has put it even more simply, 'Britain was living on tick, as never before in its history.' So the plastic credit card came into its own. Smith points out that the demand for consumer durables grew at an average rate of 14 per cent in the period 1981–7, while consumer expenditure increased by 17 per cent in the same period; but the savings rate fell from 14.2 per cent in 1980 to 3.6 per cent in 1988. At the same time, annual borrowings from the banks rose over 100 per cent, and from building societies 230 per cent.

So a remarkable transformation overtook the British economy in the 1980s. Deindustrialisation intensified; Britain was no longer the workshop of the world as she had been a hundred or so years earlier. The home market was flooded with foreign goods, many of them Japanese in origin. Only one British car manufacturer sur-vived. The substitute for a booming export of manufactured goods turned out to be North Sea oil (even though it was known to be a wasting asset unless other oil fields could be opened up). Between 1980 and 1987, exports other than oil went up 15.2 per cent, but imports were up 40 per cent in value over the same period. The rise of manufactured imports can be seen clearly in the figures set out in Table 6.1. In 1987, the trade deficit in manufactures was £7.4 bil-lion, and in 1988 about £15 billion. Although British productivity had increased, and industrial growth had taken place, the long-term prospects for British industry were hardly encouraging.

What effect had all this on the working classes? The most dis-quieting effect was the return of unemployment on a scale which in the early 1980s matched and even exceeded that of the depression of the 1930s. This subject will be considered later in this chapter. It is enough to say here that employment itself fell by nearly two million in the years 1966–79, and then by another two million in 1979–87. Unemployment in the mid-eighties was well over three

Table 6.1 UK Trade in Manufactures 1978–1986 (at 1980 prices, £ million)

	1978	1980	1982	1984	1986
Exports	31,695	34,880	34,898	40,411	45,625
Imports	25,478	29,432	32,803	43,146	49,736

Source: Keith Smith, *The British Economic Crisis* (1989).

million officially (in spite of various downward adjustments of the figures). Another serious result of industrial depression was the effect on real wages and on the standard of living of the working classes (again a topic to be discussed later). Given the severe reduction in working-class bargaining power as unemployment grew, pay increases were only limited, and real wages rose only marginally throughout the eighties. Although the earlier gains of the fifties and sixties were not lost, further progress was necessarily limited. Another aspect of diminished bargaining power over wages was that trade union membership also fell, while government legislation limited trade union authority and influence even further. All in all, there were considerable setbacks for the working classes and the Labour movement from 1979 onwards, though paradoxically, for the most part, the working man or woman who stayed in employment experienced no fall in living standards. The better paid continued to enjoy a lifestyle very little different from that of the lower middle classes.

At this point, a word or so might be appropriate regarding the role of governments in the economic changes just described. The economic policy of the Labour government and of the Labour Party will be dealt with in the next section of this chapter. As for the Conservative Party, who dominated the scene throughout the eighties, their policy took the form initially of attempts to implement monetarist theories such as those of Professor Milton Friedman, which held that, by restricting the money supply, inflation could be brought under control. To this end, interest rates were raised to 14 per cent, then in the autumn of 1979, to 17 per cent. This early period of the attempted manipulation of the money supply coincided with the very severe recession mentioned earlier. In May 1980, inflation still stood at 21.9 per cent; during the same year, another 645,000 became unemployed, and more than 27,000 companies went out of business (the comparable figure in 1978 was about 5,000). Interest rates were cut in 1980, and the situation eased distinctly from 1982 onwards. The country's economic difficulties were blamed by the Conservative Prime Minister, Mrs Thatcher, on the world depression, though critics have not been slow to point out that world trade in manufactures was still growing during these years, employment actually increased in the European Economic Community, and Britain's recession began before the world recession. At all events, inflation was down to 4.6 per cent by March 1983, though unemployment was still high, averaging more than three million for the year as a whole. Great stress was laid by the government on the need to keep down wages, to limit public expenditure and to allow full play to market forces and free competition. This led to attempts to cut both central and local government spending, to reduce trade union power and to bring all forms of nationalisation of industry to an end, including assistance to individual firms, by a policy of privatisation.

The policies pursued by the Conservative governments of the eighties were thus directly opposed to Labour Party policies of the later seventies. By now, consensus had disappeared completely. Mrs Thatcher remained true to views expressed earlier in her career:

> To me, consensus seems to be the process of abandoning all beliefs, principles, values and policies. So it is something in which no one believes and to which no one objects.

More than that, she was ready to proclaim that people who believed in consensus were 'quislings and traitors' – a far cry from the Butskellism of the 1950s. To what extent the policy of either party had any deep-seated effect on long-term trends in the economy is a matter for argument. The decline of British manufacturing industry continued inexorably under both parties throughout the seventies and eighties, in spite of efforts to make industry more competitive. However, the electorate, including substantial numbers of working-class voters, of course, were clearly unmoved to any marked extent by this decline, and most thought that the Conservatives were making a better job of managing the economy than Labour, for after their return to power in 1979, the Conservatives went on to win two further general elections in 1983 and 1987.

Arguments raged, naturally enough, over the fundamental causes of the loss of Britain's economic supremacy – was it due to entrepreneurial failure? To lack of investment? Trade union influence over wages and work processes? Overspending abroad, especially on the armed forces? And so on. For the social historian, whatever the causes of British economic decline, the major social consequences were plain enough: the return of mass unemployment, and a distinct slowing up in the improvement of the standard of living of the working classes. They also resulted in a widening of the gulf between the employed and the unemployed, and between those still earning good wages and the poor, the elderly and the handicapped – a growing underclass in society. The welfare state itself became a subject for hot dispute, being part of what was derisively called 'the dependency culture'. All this was very different from what the Labour Party had promised the electorate in the general election of February 1974 – 'an irretrievable transfer of wealth and power to working people and their families'. This socialist aim was certainly not achieved under Labour, and became increasingly distant and remote during the 1980s.

Labour In and Out of Power

The result of the election of 1974 was that Labour secured only four more seats than the Conservatives, with a marginally smaller percentage of the total vote. However, with the voting support of the Liberals, they formed a minority government (the first since 1929) under Harold Wilson. According to Denis Healey, the Chancellor of the Exchequer, the economic situation was alarming: the miners' strike was still on, retail prices were rising at the rate of 13 per cent, the balance of payments figure was in deficit by over a billion pounds, and the Public Sector Borrowing Requirement was well over £4 billion for 1973. Remedial action was urgently required. The miners' strike was soon settled, and the three-day week and state of emergency brought to an end. The Pay Board was abolished, and compulsory wages restraint was also ended, but rents were frozen, and price controls were retained. As for future wages policy, a so-called Social Contract was drawn up, whereby in return for the repeal of the Industrial Relations Act 1971, the TUC agreed on a voluntary wage restraint. There was to be a year's interval between wage increases, and increases were to compensate either for rises in prices or for anticipated price increases before the next settlement. By September, Wilson had decided on another general election (held in October 1974) in an attempt to increase his majority. The results were disappointing for Labour. True,

Table 6.2   The General Election, October 1974

Party	Votes	Percentage of votes	No. of MPs
Labour	11,457,079	39.2	319
Conservative	10,464,817	35.9	277
Liberal	5,346,754	18.3	13
Plaid Cymru	166,321	0.6	3
SNP	839,617	2.9	11
Others	914,590	3.1	12

Labour was no longer in a minority, but the Party's clear majority was limited to only three – a majority which could soon disappear if the government lost by-elections.

In these circumstances it could hardly be expected that Labour would produce a very ambitious programme of reforms. The list of proposals was mostly of a familiar kind: private practices in the NHS were to be abolished, comprehensive secondary education to become compulsory in state schools, and there was to be devolution in Scotland and Wales, subject to the holding of referendums (the Scottish Nationalist Party had gained another four seats in the election, and were beginning to claim the right to control what they called the 'Scotch Oil' in the North Sea). Undoubtedly, the most urgent problem was the state of the economy, in particular inflation and the level of wages. Harold Wilson did not stay in office long enough to see this problem solved. In March 1976, at the age of sixty, he announced his retirement, having formed his intention of retiring some two years previously, and having informed the Queen of this in December 1975. His resignation Honours List attracted much criticism, as it included an odd mixture of names from the world of show business and of City finance (one of the businessmen honoured was subsequently sent to prison while another committed suicide to avoid disgrace). Wilson was replaced by James Callaghan, with Michael Foot running second in the party ballot for the leadership. Harold Wilson had a sharp mind, and served his party well as a political leader, an organiser and a manager of men, but the achievements of his time in office are hardly outstanding; and the circumstances of his resignation remain somewhat puzzling.

Since the major task of the Labour administrations of 1974–9 was to bring the economy under control, a great burden of responsibility was carried by Denis Healey, the Chancellor of the Exchequer. He was well aware of the difficulty of gaining the co-operation of the trade unions in stabilising the economy, and he has quoted approvingly the Harvard economist Joseph Schumpeter on this subject:

> ... the real problem is labor. Unless socialisation is to spell economic breakdown, a socialising government cannot possibly tolerate present trade union practice ... As things actually are, labor is of all things the most difficult to socialise.

In fact, these words were published many years previously in 1946. Over forty years later, Healey commented that he spent five years as Chancellor discovering how right Schumpeter was. In brief, in mid-June 1975 inflation was at 26 per cent. Some wage claims were up to 30 per cent. Healey limited increases in wages, salaries and dividends to 10 per cent in the next pay round, and then accepted a TUC proposal for a £6 a week increase for all earning up to £8,500 a year. In the same year, an Enterprise Board was set up to extend public ownership (in full or in part) to selected firms. The British National Oil Corporation was also established to manage North Sea oil. A national referendum on continued membership of the European Community confirmed that a majority wished Britain to stay in the Common Market (the cabinet itself was divided on the issue). By July 1976 inflation had been halved, and was down to 12.9 per cent.

Unfortunately, this improvement was accompanied by a crisis in the value of sterling which forced the Chancellor to approach the International Monetary Fund for a loan. At the same time the Social Contract showed signs of breaking down, though an agreement was made in May 1976 for a 4.5 per cent ceiling on pay increases. The year 1977 and the first part of 1978 proved more satisfactory, with inflation down to 8 per cent by mid-1978, while the government's finances were assisted by an increasing income from North Sea oil. There were still problems with excessive wage claims, and Callaghan admitted privately that he was thinking of introducing legislation to control the trade unions, this being somewhat ironic in view of his earlier opposition to *In Place of Strife*. He has been criticised for failing to call an election at this point when the economy had at last improved. A favourable result for Labour would have freed them from dependence on Liberal votes in the Commons – it had become necessary to enter into a pact with the Liberals in March 1977 when the Labour majority had fallen to one at the beginning of the year. Later on, the Liberals withdrew from the pact, which left Labour dependent in turn on the Scottish Nationalists. They were anxious to see their referendum carried out under the terms of the devolution Bills passed in 1978, and so were prepared to continue to back the government.

Undoubtedly Callaghan paid the penalty for postponing the general election till 1979, for in and after December 1978 troubles piled up for him. This was the beginning of the so-called Winter of Discontent, 1978–9, when, having rashly fixed a 5 per cent maximum for pay rises, the government was overwhelmed by a flood of far higher pay claims. In December, local authority manual workers claimed a 40 per cent pay rise. Ford workers settled for a rather more moderate 17 per cent. In January 1979 lorry drivers and tanker drivers went on strike for 25 to 30 per cent. On 22 January, one and a half million public service workers went on twenty-four hour strikes. Water workers, ambulance drivers, sewerage workers and dustmen all came out. In Liverpool, grave diggers refused to bury the dead, so that bodies had to be stockpiled, thereby causing much offence. Three of the public service unions settled for a modest 9 per cent plus £1 per week, but it was only too clear that pay claims were now quite out of control. The 5 per cent government norm was utterly disregarded. Further discomfort was suffered by the government when devolution was rejected early in March by the referendums in both Wales and Scotland. The votes in Wales were: for, 11.9 per cent; against, 46.9 per cent. In Scotland, the votes were: for, 32.85 per cent; against, 30.78 per cent. But the vote in favour failed to reach the 40 per cent of the electorate necessary for devolution. On 28 March, the government was defeated by one vote on a vote of confidence. Callaghan had had enough. Parliament was dissolved, and a general election held on 3 May. The Conservatives were back with an overall majority of forty-three seats. Margaret Thatcher became Britain's first woman Prime Minister. At the time of writing, Labour have not been in office since.

Certainly Labour had a most unhappy time in office in the period 1974–9. One reason for their winning the election of 1974 was that voters expected they would do better than Heath in sorting out labour disputes. In fact, at the end of the day, they did no better

Table 6.3   The General Election, May 1979

Party	Votes	Percentage	No. of MPs
Conservative	13,697,000	43.9	339
Labour	11,509,000	36.9	268
Liberal	4,313,000	13.8	11
SNP	504,000	1.6	2
Plaid Cymru	132,000	0.4	2
Others	887,000	2.8	13

than Heath, and the collapse of their government was equally igno-
minious. However, it would be unfair to put the whole blame on
the unions for what had happened – the government must take part
of the blame for fixing a 5 per cent wage limit without securing the
firm agreement of the TUC. Further, much of the union discontent seemed to have been caused by local union activists frustrated
by three years of having incomes policy decided above their heads
by national leaders. It must also be said that the Labour Party
leadership had little that was new or attractive to offer the electorate
by 1979 – an apparently half-hearted commitment to the EEC, the
reform of the House of Lords, a kind of creeping nationalisation
through the National Enterprise Board, more reform in the health
service and in education, and an ambivalent attitude to nuclear
disarmament – all this scarcely set the pulses racing. Margaret
Thatcher's promise of a return to free-market enterprise and cuts
in government expenditure made a greater appeal to many.

However, the economic and social policies of the Labour
government were not entirely unsuccessful. In fact, something had
been done to bring down inflation and to moderate wage demands
earlier on, while useful domestic reforms were passed such as the
Police Act, by which the Police Complaints Board was established,
the Education Act 1976, requiring LEAs to proceed further with
comprehensive education, and the Race Relations Act 1976, which
set up the Commission for Racial Equality. Then again, some
credit is due for at least putting the notion of devolution for Scotland and Wales to the test. Nevertheless, the fact that minority
governments cannot be expected to produce sweeping and controversial reforms cannot conceal the barrenness of much of
Labour's thinking. They had little that was new to offer, and, even
if the left had had its way, more radical ideas would have probably

lost votes rather than gained them. The word 'socialist' was still bandied about, with no clear agreement as to its modern meaning or implications (other than Herbert Morrison's neat cop-out – 'socialism is what the Labour Party does'). It gave little help in determining what should be the future direction of the party. Keir Hardie was wise in 1900, when the Labour Representation Committee was set up, in excluding the word from the aims of the new body: 'promoting legislation in the direct interest of Labour' was good enough for him. How far the Labour administrations of the 1970s kept in mind this precept from the past is a nice question for discussion.

What is certain is that most of the 1980s proved an exhausting and nerve-wracking experience for the Labour Party. True to form, recriminations broke out within the party following the 1979 electoral defeat. Left-wing groups such as the Campaign for Labour Democracy and the Labour Co-ordinating Committee became prominent, all seeking to move the party to the left. The Militant Tendency, a Trotskyite splinter group, established a power base in Liverpool and pursued a policy of 'entryism', that is, infiltrating the Labour Party – the old tactic of the Communist Party between the wars. Tony Benn became the leader of the left movement within the party. The 1979 party Conference gave the constituency parties power to deselect their MPs, and the National Executive was instructed to draw up proposals whereby it could make final decisions regarding the party manifesto – both moves intended to reduce the influence of the Parliamentary Labour Party. In June 1980 a Committee of Enquiry recommended the setting up of an Electoral College to choose the party leader and to approve the party manifesto. These proposals were finally agreed at a special conference of the party at Wembley in February 1981. Again, the College was deliberately designed to cut down further the powers of Labour MPs: its constitution gave the unions 40 per cent of the votes, the constituency parties 30 per cent, and the Parliamentary Labour Party 30 per cent. Meanwhile, the 1980 party Conference was so divided that it managed to pass resolutions in favour of both unilateral and multilateral disarmament; it also voted in favour of withdrawal from the Common Market. Callaghan retired in November 1980, to be replaced by Michael Foot, a brilliant speaker and intellectual of the left, prominent in the Campaign for Nuclear Disarmament and at this time usually to be seen wearing its badge on his donkey jacket. At the same time, the right-winger Denis Healey became deputy leader. It was not long before Benn challenged Healey for the deputy leadership in the new Electoral College; and at Brighton in September 1981 Healey defeated Benn by a mere hairsbreadth. So here at least the right had succeeded in holding off the challenge from the left.

This internecine warfare naturally took its toll on the party. After the Wembley Conference, some leading members on the right of the party broke away to form the Social Democratic Party in March 1981. They were nicknamed the 'Gang of Four' – David Owen, William Rodgers, Shirley Williams and Roy Jenkins. Initially the new party consisted of fourteen MPs – thirteen Labour and one Conservative – and they were soon contesting by-elections, having formed an electoral alliance with the Liberals. By December 1981 a Gallup Poll of the electorate produced an extraordinary result – for the Alliance of the SDP and the Liberals, 50.5 per cent; for Labour, 23.5 per cent; and for the Conservatives, 23.0 per cent. This was really something of a freak result, and the Alliance's lead did not last long. The beginnings of the Falklands War in April 1982 and Margaret Thatcher's resolute prosecution of the war brought a great revival in the fortunes of the Conservative government. By May in the following year, Gallup gave the Conservatives 49 per cent, Labour 31.5 per cent and the Alliance only 17.5 per cent. All the same, Healey considers that the founding of the SDP delayed the Labour Party's recovery by nearly ten years, and guaranteed Mrs Thatcher two more terms of office. This sidesteps adroitly the basic disruption already existing in the Labour Party at the time (which Healey freely acknowledges, of course) which led to the breakaway movement of the Gang of Four in the first place. Certainly Margaret Thatcher profited greatly not only from the Falklands War, but also from the divisions within the opposition party. With the opinion polls strongly in her favour, she called a general election in June 1983.

The election campaign proved a greater disaster for Labour than the campaign in 1979. Their election manifesto, *New Hope For Britain*, was a lengthy statement which included familiar pledges to withdraw from the Common Market, to abolish the House of Lords and to renationalise the shipbuilding and aerospace industries; on defence, there was an attempt to satisfy both unilateralists and multilateralists. Gerald Kaufman, a senior member of the shadow cabinet, described this manifesto in a classic phrase as 'the longest suicide note in history'. So it proved to be. Labour polled three million votes less than in 1979, and came third or lower in 292 constituencies. The Conservatives won 397 seats, and an overall majority of 144. Labour's share of the vote was 27.6 per cent, while the Alliance was close behind with 25.4 per cent. Labour had paid the penalty for the years of in-fighting and divisions on policy. Later in the year, Neil Kinnock was elected leader in place of Michael Foot, with Roy Hattersley as deputy leader. At the same time in October 1983 the party at last committed itself unequivocally to unilateral disarmament, a policy generally unpopular with the electorate. Although the party clearly benefited from having a younger leader, it was obvious that he had an immense task ahead of him.

Indeed, there was little to show any real revival in Labour Party fortunes over the next few years, except that Kinnock had some success in expelling Liverpool Militant supporters, and in achieving co-operation between the soft left (his own group) and the centre and right elements of the party, thus isolating the hard left. But this was not enough to change very markedly the public image of the party by the time of the next general election in 1987. This image had not been improved by the miners' strike, nor by the party's unconvincing pledge to reduce unemployment by one million in two years (April 1985); nor, above all, by the party's unilateralist stance. So although the Labour Party's general election campaign in 1987 was generally considered to have been very well presented – far better than that of its rivals – the Conservatives were returned to power again, though with a reduced majority of 102. Kinnock privately blamed Labour's defeat on the confusion during the campaign over exactly how much Labour's tax reforms would cost; but, significantly, one of the most effective Tory posters showed a British soldier surrendering with his arms up, the wording being 'Labour's Defence Policy'. The one positive gain for Labour was that the Alliance had been pushed back firmly into third place by the electorate.

Obviously enough, it was vital for Labour's future as a party to reassess their policies as a whole, cutting out the dead wood, and updating their basic principles. Seven Policy Review Groups were appointed, and a new campaign was launched, 'Labour Listens', the public being assured that Labour was prepared to listen to all new suggestions (opponents naturally claimed that the party seemed prepared to accept *any* policy that was popular and would gain votes, regardless of principle). Meanwhile, Kinnock made it clear that Labour accepted the need for a mixed economy, and had no intention of renationalising everything privatised by the Conservatives; but at the same time he rejected totally Mrs Thatcher's extreme emphasis on individual enterprise and the freedom of the market. At the 1988 Labour Conference, he made one of his best speeches, fiercely attacking Thatcherite views:

> 'There is no such thing as society,' she says. No sister, no brotherhood. No neighbourhood. No honouring other people's little children. 'No such thing as society.' No number other than one. No person other than me. No time other than now. No such thing as society, just 'me' and 'now'. This is Margaret Thatcher's society.

The rhetoric was crude, but heartfelt and effective.

In April 1989 a milestone was at last reached when the national executive accepted the principle of multilateralism on the basis of a report from Gerald Kaufman's Defence Review Group. Gorbachev's new policies and the effective ending of the Cold War had at long last permitted a fundamental rethinking of Labour's defence policy. This rejection of unilateralism was endorsed later in the year at the party Conference, together with the major recommendations of the other review groups. Many Labour Party shibboleths disappeared as a result: the old-style belief in nationalisation was rejected, and many of the Conservative trade union reforms (though not all) were impliedly accepted, such as the ban on secondary picketing, and on the closed shop. Proportional representation was decisively rejected. In any case, it had become of less practical importance with the decline and splitting up of the Alliance. At the end of the 1989 party Conference, Labour led the Conservatives in the opinion polls by a clear 10 points. In the spring of 1990, when the Conservative government was badly shaken by opposition to its policy of high interest rates, to its seeming indifference to the European Community and, above all, to the levying of the highly unpopular community charge (poll tax) in England and Wales, Labour's lead in the opinion polls increased to a remarkable 25 points. In March, the Conservatives lost the Mid-Staffordshire by-election, where they had had a very safe majority of over 14,000, as the result of a massive swing of 21 per cent to Labour – the biggest swing to Labour for over fifty years. At last there seemed to be a very real possibility that Labour might win the next general election.

It had been a long and hard haul for Kinnock, and there were times earlier on when it had seemed that the Alliance would supplant the Labour Party as the main opposition to the Conservatives. It had also involved the abandonment of one of Kinnock's most cherished ideals – unilateral disarmament. Yet it was argued that this was not mere expediency – the ending of the Cold War had made possible a change of direction in defence policy. As for the other changes in policy, it was a matter of facing the social realities of a new, property-owning society in which many of the old Labour war-cries were hopelessly out of date. The problem, of course, was to convince the electorate that the party had really changed in outlook. Its older image in the eyes of its opponents, however unfair, was that of a party which overspent when in office, was unsound on defence, and was too much under the influence of the trade unions, the loony left, and various fringe groups of gays, lesbians and feminists. This image remained to influence many voters for whom Thatcherite Conservatism was otherwise losing its glamour.

The Work Force, and Life at Work

During the 1970s and 1980s the labour force underwent substantial changes. To a minor extent, this was due to a decline in the growth of population which had characterised the previous decades: whereas the population had risen from 52.8 million in 1961 to 55.9 million in 1971, the figure for 1981 was only 56.4 million, and in 1987, 56.9 million. The projected figure for 1991, the next census year, was 57.5 million. A much more important influence than this, however, was the substantial rise in unemployment. Although the number of employees in 1988 was 22.1 million, an increase of a million on the low point of 1983, it had still not returned to the previous peak of 23.2 million in 1979. The average rate of unemployment was over three million in each of the four years 1983 to 1986 (see the next section of this chapter). As a consequence, the years of prosperity were replaced for many by sometimes long periods on the dole (the numbers of long-term unemployed claimants peaked at almost 1.4 million in January 1986, not falling to below a million till July 1988). Apart from changes in size, there were changes in the composition of the work force. Manufacturing industry shrank still further, while the service sector continued to grow. The employment figures for 1988 in the main branches of the economy are given in Table 6.4. It can be

Table 6.4   The Work Force, 1988 (000s)

Manufacturing industry	5,097
Services	15,212
Agriculture, forestry, fishing	313
Energy and water supply	459
Construction	1,022
Total employees	22,103

Source: *Social Trends*, No. 19 (1989).

seen that the numbers employed in services had increased to three times those in manufacture; deindustrialisation had progressed even further.

Meanwhile, as more men registered as unemployed, more women joined the labour force, so that the economic activity rates for women under sixty rose substantially between 1971 and 1987, with a further projected rise to 1995. The proportion of women at work changed from about a third in 1945 to about a half by the mid-1980s, while the proportion of married women at work more than doubled within the same period, reaching 60 per cent by 1987, though many of the married women were employed part-time. While more and more women went to work between 1971 and 1987, the proportion of males not at work increased from 9 to 12 per cent. This was due not only to unemployment, but also to early retirement, often due to a reduction in the numbers employed at the place of work, and referred to politely as 'voluntary redundancy'. Another significant change in the composition in the work force was the move to self-employment, in many cases with the support of government schemes designed to encourage the setting up of small-scale enterprises, sometimes based initially on the lump sums which came with voluntary redundancy. Although the self-employed numbers were fairly static in the 1970s, they rose by over a million in the decade 1979 to 1988.

Against this background, conditions at work may now be surveyed. Given the economic vicissitudes of the time, it would not be expected that there would be any marked reduction in working hours. Many firms were struggling to keep in business, and the trade unions were anxious to preserve jobs rather than make demands which would endanger them. Nevertheless, there was a minor reduction in weekly hours in the 1980s. The normal weekly figure in 1974 was 40.0 hours (with overtime, 43.4 hours). The figures for April 1987 are given in Table 6.5. Thus the normal basic

Table 6.5   Average Weekly Hours, 1987

	Manual males	Manual females	All employees
Normal basic	39.1	38.1	36.7
Overtime	5.5	1.6	0.8
Total	44.6	39.7	37.5

Source: *Social Trends*, No. 19 (1989).

week had been reduced slightly, though overtime had gone up. This last point is important, for the average male working week actually rose in the years 1984–6, mostly due to overtime. The majority of workers in 1987 fell into two main groups: those working thirty-six to forty hours a week (comprising 42.6 per cent of male manual workers, and 61.5 per cent of female manual workers), and those working forty to forty-four hours a week (16.2 per cent of male manual workers, and 11.0 per cent of female manual workers). Some, a sizeable minority, were working considerably longer – 14.7 per cent of male manual workers, and 2.3 per cent of female manual workers, were working over fifty-two hours a week.

What of working conditions? The trend to larger workplaces which characterised the previous period was not so marked after 1974. Indeed, in the early 1980s, large firms actually shed labour as an economy measure. Some employed sub-contractors, while others took on part-time labour, especially women. This permitted a more flexible use of labour, the numbers employed being varied to suit the demands of the market. At the same time, the number of smaller firms increased, many of them being unregistered for inspection, and making it even more difficult for the Factory Inspectorate to do its job. In fact, the task of safeguarding health and safety at work became more and more onerous following the passing of the Health and Safety at Work Act 1974, which required each firm to compile its own safety rules, so that (in theory, at least) safety was to become an integral part of efficient management. This Act brought an additional eight million workers within the protection of occupational health and safety legislation. As the Chief Inspector's Report put it in 1975: 'Inspectors rapidly became conversant with the hazards of safari parks and fun fairs, research laboratories and grave digging.'

The Inspectorate itself (part now of the Health and Safety

Executive) was reorganised into Areas and National Industries Groups in 1977, the latter being responsible for a very wide range of activities, including the National Health Service, the food industry and further education. In the same year, the Health and Safety (Enforcing Authority) Regulations 1977 allocated enforcement duties to local authority officers (usually Environmental Health Officers) under the 1974 Act. They already enforced the Offices, Shops and Railway Premises Act 1963, and now found themselves enforcing factory legislation in heel bars, key-cutting, engraving, and watch and jewellery repair workshops in departmental stores, together with the baking of bread in supermarkets. At the place of work, the Safety Representatives and Safety Committee Regulations also came into operation in 1977. The reporting of accidents was covered by new regulations in 1980, extending reporting to virtually all industries; these regulations were in turn replaced in 1985 by RIDDOR – Reporting of Injuries, Diseases and Dangerous Occurrences Regulations.

One would imagine from this plethora of rules and orders that the regulation of places of work was greatly improved in the 1980s, but this was not necessarily so. In the first place, the Inspectorate became responsible by 1985 for health and safety legislation affecting some sixteen million workpeople in 400,000 fixed establishments. It was obviously quite impossible for such a small body to police directly such a large workforce – nor was it the intention that it should do so. But even on the basis of self-regulation by the employers, the task of the Inspectorate was still immense, especially when their numbers (about 900 inspectors in 1978) were reduced to 552 by the end of 1985 (it was aimed to bring this number up again to 600). Secondly, the depression of the early 1980s meant that some firms, particularly the smaller concerns, were tempted to cut corners in order to reduce costs. As the Chief Inspector's Report put it in 1985:

> Economic pressures have adversely affected working
> conditions in many premises, and an increase in the numbers
> of small firms and sub-contracting businesses, some of which
> have standards of safety and health which fall well below
> what is acceptable, has added to the Inspectorate's problems
> of source deployment. The recession has led many employers
> to economise on safety. Some firms have made safety officers
> redundant and passed responsibility for safety to personnel

officers, line management or security officers with little or no experience in safety matters.

Thirdly, human nature being what it is, some accidents were inevitable due to errors of judgement, carelessness or sheer misfortune. A reading of the reports of the period will soon confirm this melancholy truth.

The result of all this is that although there was a reduction in the number of fatal accidents in manufacturing industry (which of course was in decline, and employed only 26 per cent of the total work force in 1985), the figures for all workplaces were still uncomfortably high in 1985. It is instructive to compare fatalities in 1975 with those in 1985, and Table 6.6 does this.

Table 6.6 Fatal Accidents at Work, 1975 and 1985

1975		1985	
Factory premises	231	Manufacturing	100
Construction processes	181	Construction	95
Docks and inland warehouses	15	Service industries	59
Total	427	Total	254

Source: *Health and Safety: Industries and Services*, 1975 and 1985.

At first sight, notable progress seems to have been made, and the figure for factory deaths shows a welcome reduction; but also in 1985 there were 27 deaths among the self-employed, and 133 deaths among the non-employed (including 57 deaths at the Bradford City Football Club fire), making 414 in all. Clearly this total is atypical, because of the Bradford fire, but it still leaves a formidable figure. There was also an upward trend in major injuries in manufacturing which had been noted over the previous three years, and a similar increase in the food industry, as well as in some sectors of metal goods and miscellaneous manufacturing. As for the total number of non-fatal accidents reported, this varied with the extent to which employers reported them. In the later 1970s, the annual figure was usually just under a quarter of a million, dropping to 184,824 in 1980 (a year of recession). Then in 1981 the new regulations for notification came into force, and the numbers jumped to 315,711, falling again in the following year to 297,221. Further changes in the notifying of accidents make generalisation difficult for the remaining years of the 1980s.

However, the Inspectorate did have its successes, sometimes of a very positive nature. For example, the dangers of power presses were well known in the 1960s, and were commented on in an earlier chapter. In 1965, when power-press regulations first came into effect, there were about 450 accidents a year at the tool and die. Thereafter, the total dropped steadily, until in 1979 there were only 48. No doubt there were fewer power presses in use by then, but the decrease in accidents is remarkable. Again, no amount of inspection would prevent some of the fatal accidents which occurred. For example, the 1975 reports remarks that 'One of the 231 fatalities occurred when a man fell backwards off a 22-inch wall, a mishap which might easily have had a far less serious result.' Another fatal accident occurred in the same year at the Appleby-Frodingham steelworks, when the eruption of ninety tonnes of molten metal from a torpedo ladle killed eleven men. A more common kind of fatal accident in 1985 was due to the lack of proper maintenance on a plastic injection-moulding machine:

> Failure to maintain the operator's guard and associated limit switches meant that when the guard was open, two switches which should have been held down by the guard's linear cam were signalling 'go' instead of 'stop'. When the operator reached into the machine, he leaned against a negative mode switch and pushed it into the 'go' position. The platens closed and crushed his head ...

Two industries in particular were potentially dangerous, the chemical industry and the construction industry. As for the former, its accident rate for the 1980s was not very different from the rest of industry, though the incidence rate for fatal and major injuries was somewhat higher than that of manufacturing industry as a whole. Many accidents in the industry were *not* process-related – traditionally, only 20 per cent were so related – but an enquiry in 1963 put the figure rather higher at 65 per cent. The construction industry, however, continued to present problems. In the mid-eighties, it still suffered a high proportion of fatal and serious accidents. The industry had a million employees, together with half a million self-employed. There were nearly 170,000 firms, and the number of small firms and of the self-employed was growing. The industry had a poor health and safety record, with at least two people killed on construction sites every week, and many more maimed. In 1985, there were 2,435 accidents reported, and the fatal accident rate was 10.8 per 100,000. Although deaths from excavation were no longer common, falls to lower levels were a major cause of injury or death; as the 1985 report remarks, 'People falling, or things falling on to people, still cause a majority of accidents.'

Some accidents could undoubtedly have been prevented if safety helmets had been worn; every year in the mid-eighties as many as a thousand head injuries resulted in at least three days off, one in five being serious, one in twenty fatal. No more than 30 per cent of construction workers wore helmets – self-regulation had proved a failure. There was so much concern in the Inspectorate at the dangers in the construction industry that in 1985 it was decided to increase the number of inspectors for the industry from 85 to 100. Meanwhile, workers continued to fall off or through roofs. A typical example was reported in 1985 as follows:

> A young roofing operator was killed when he fell through fragile asbestos cement sheeting while replacing some skylights. No crawling boards were provided. He was walking along the roof following the lines of the bolts when the sheeting gave way.

Accidents of this kind were depressingly common.

To sum up: the major extensions of legislative protection to many new workplaces, the appointment of safety officers and the further reduction of working hours all contributed to making life at work safer and more agreeable in the period 1975 to 1990. The reduction of fatalities is a clear indication of this. The legal position of the worker was also safeguarded further by the operation of industrial tribunals, which afforded protection against unfair dismissal or discrimination on account of colour or sex. On the other hand, some places of work were still inherently dangerous, such as iron foundries, steel works, coalmines, some chemical works and building sites. On the whole, workers in the expanding service industries were better off than workers in manufacturing. Office workers, in particular, obviously ran fewer risks of explosions, gassing or poisoning, all of which were routine hazards for some workers. As small businesses proliferated, it was commonly said that sweat shops sprang up here and there, especially in the clothing trade, often employing ethnic labour. In 1985, the Inspectorate reported under the heading 'Cottage Industry' that:

An inspector visited a 'factory' in an unconverted pigsty where five people were employed making up children's clothes. The weather was kept at bay by polythene sheets nailed to the walls, and heating was by portable gas heaters. The only toilet was a small chemical one behind a curtain in the corner of the store-room. Three months later, following advice, the firm had lined the walls, repaired the roof, and installed central heating and flush toilets.

Finally, a comment on job satisfaction: the *General Household Survey* of 1980 contains the results of surveys on attitudes to work carried out in 1979 and 1980. Degrees of satisfaction were recorded on a five-point scale, ranging from 'very satisfied' to 'very dissatisfied'. Rather remarkably, 41 per cent of males declared themselves 'very satisfied' with their work, with a further 43 per cent 'fairly satisfied'; the equivalent figures for women for these two categories were 48 per cent and 40 per cent. On the whole, job satisfaction was higher among women than among men, and also higher among part-timers than among full-timers; but further analysis shows that differences in job satisfaction varied most with age, for example, only 35 per cent of the 20–24-year-old age group were 'very satisfied', as compared with 73 per cent of those aged sixty-five and over. In fact, the main determinants of job satisfaction were age and sex, which were more important than marital status, or working full- or part-time. Other factors influencing attitudes were pay, organisation of the work, administration, colleagues and the kind of work. For men, pay was the most important; for women, the kind of work was more important than pay. It might be thought that hours of work would be an important consideration, but it seems that the five factors just mentioned were generally of more importance. Only those working the longest hours, such as foremen in manual occupations, agricultural workers and transport and communication workers, expressed any dissatisfaction with their working hours. Thus, of men working fifty-one hours a week or more, 25 per cent were dissatisfied with their hours, and 10 per cent were very dissatisfied with them.

The general picture presented in 1980 follows the pattern of similar surveys in the early years of the 1970s. Certainly it seems to show an impressive degree of job satisfaction. Among males, only 7 per cent considered themselves 'a little dissatisfied' and only 4 per cent 'very dissatisfied' (the comparable figures for women were

6 per cent and 2 per cent). Of course, surveys of this kind are not the most refined and sophisticated ways of assessing job satisfaction, and it is interesting to compare these results with the sociological surveys described in the last chapter. Nevertheless, on these results it does not appear that there was much serious discontent among the working classes with the work they performed. It might also be observed that in the years 1979 and 1980 those surveyed were of course in work, at a time when a million and a half workpeople were not, and this number was to increase substantially over the next few years.

Unemployment

Although unemployment was very limited in the quarter-century following the end of the Second World War, from the early 1970s it increased more and more, especially in the years 1979–81 when industry suffered a severe recession. During these years, output fell in the textile industry by 26 per cent, in metal manufacturing by the same amount, and in timber and furniture by 21 per cent. Unemployment rose by about 250 per cent overall at the time. It would be helpful if exact figures for unemployment nationally were available for the 1980s as a whole, but unfortunately a number of downward adjustments of the figures by the government makes it difficult to compare figures for 1982 onwards with those for the preceding years. For example, from October 1982 registration for benefit became voluntary (it had been estimated earlier that in mid-1979 there were as many as 300,000 unregistered unemployed), and those seeking part-time work were excluded from the registers. In 1983, men over sixty seeking employment were also specifically excluded (an estimated 161,800 men were affected). In September 1988 new regulations applied to those under eighteen, most of whom became ineligible for income support; this reduced the UK count by about 90,000. Given the fact that the figures were also adjusted to take account of seasonal variations in employment demand, it is not surprising that figures taken from different official sources are sometimes in apparent disagreement. It was reported in the *Guardian* on 14 August 1986 that while the official figure for total unemployment from the Department of Employment was 3.2 million (11.7 per cent), a calculation by the Unemployment Unit estimated that the correct figure was actually 3.8 million (15.4 per cent).

However, it is quite clear that the amendments to the official methods of calculation of the national figures were generally in a downward direction, and that in any case the overall trend is clear enough. After passing the million mark in the mid-seventies, the figures rose abruptly from 1980 onwards (1.79 million) to 2.25 million in 1981, and 2.92 million (12.1 per cent) in 1982. As we have seen, 1979–81 saw a serious decline in industry. Thereafter, industry recovered slowly, but the unemployment figures remained high – over three million in every year from 1983 to 1986, reaching their highest at 3.289 million in 1986. After this, unemployment fell in both 1987 and 1988, the number of claimants at last falling to below three million in May 1987. By October 1988 the decline was quite substantial, to just above 2.1 million. Subsequently, the trend has continued downwards, to about 1.75 million in the spring of 1990 (but still above the figure at the outbreak of war in 1939).

Who were the new unemployed? Between the wars, textile workers, miners and iron and steel workers were prominent among the ranks of the unemployed. In the 1980s, the continued decline of the old staple industries was less significant for the economy as a whole, but there were some similarities in that manufacturing was again hard-hit, and unemployment rates were again highest in the north-west, north-east and South Wales. One area suffering considerable unemployment for the first time was the West Midlands, prosperous enough in the 1930s, but in the 1980s badly affected by the reduction in demand for its skills in metal-shaping and engineering. The south-east, with its concentration of service industries, came off best, as usual. With 32 per cent of all employees, it had only 23 per cent of the unemployed in June 1982; whereas the West Midlands, with only 9 per cent of employees, had 11 per cent of the unemployed.

As for the constitution of the host of the unemployed, unemployment in the early 1980s was concentrated among elderly men and among the young. For example, men in the 20–24 age range were about 13 per cent of all male employees, but 18 per cent of all unemployed men. Among unemployed males, a fifth had been out of work for one to two years, and a further fifth for more than two years; but long-term unemployment was more marked among the old than the young – about half of all unemployed men aged fifty or over had been out of work over a year, but of men aged twenty to twenty-four, only a third. Unskilled workers were six times as likely to be out of work as professional men, naturally enough, and ethnic minorities twice as likely to be unemployed as white workers. Thus, in spring 1981, while the unemployed rate among whites was 10 per cent, among West Indians it was 21 per cent. Over half (54 per cent) of unemployed heads of household lived in a council property in 1982, while only 30 per cent were owner-occupiers. Curiously enough, where a married man was in work, he was increasingly likely to have a working wife, whereas an unemployed married man was much less likely to have a working wife (one would have expected the unemployed husband to be anxious for his wife to bring in some money, if only part-time; though this would reduce benefit, of course). This distinction has meant that an increasing gap has opened up between the gross income of households with the head in work, and that of households with an unemployed head.

What effect did unemployment have on the family? It is true that a variety of social security benefits were available to the unemployed married man – Supplementary Benefit was replaced by Income Support in April 1988, Family Credit replaced the Family Income Supplement, the Social Fund was introduced, and Housing Benefit was raised. But all depended on how liberally these benefits were administered, and there was a strong trend towards tightening up in order to reduce waste and discourage the scrounger. The Social Fund, for example, provided grants for essential household equipment, but by 1990 only in the form of loans repayable within the year. In addition, there was a great emphasis on the need for the claimant to show he was genuinely seeking work, and on the training for work of the unemployed school-leaver. The Youth Training Scheme, introduced in April 1983 to provide twelve months' training, was extended in April 1986 to give two years' training for sixteen-year-old leavers, and one year's training for seventeen-year-olds. The numbers of entrants fell between 1986/7 and 1987/8 from 420,000 to 397,000. In 1987/8 almost two-fifths of those trained under the scheme left for full-time work, while one-fifth were unemployed.

So far as family income is concerned, there could be cases where (as in the 1930s) an unemployed man was better off on benefit than on low-paid, unskilled work, but there is little evidence to show that benefit in itself caused a man to choose unemployment rather than paid work. In the vast majority of cases, the unemployed family was substantially worse off than the family with the householder in work. In 1982, the average household with an employed head had a weekly income of £160; if the head was unemployed, the income dropped on average to £109 – that is, suffered a reduction of about a third. In such households, money had to be spent cautiously – proportionately more would be spent on the basic necessities, of course, and according to the 1982 survey, twice as much on tobacco.

Curiously enough, the unemployment of the 1980s, though a damaging blow to the pride and morale of those affected, has not attracted the literary treatment which was so noticeable in the 1930s in the work of Orwell, Priestley and others. Perhaps the very fact that so much was written at that time about the plight of the unemployed has presented contemporary writers with a sense of déjà-vu; it has all been said before. However, a survey by the Economist Intelligence Unit in 1982 (reported in *Social Trends*, 1984) has provided some interesting information on attitudes to being unemployed. About a fifth of those interviewed (19 per cent) confessed to being miserable or unhappy since losing their jobs, 17 per cent to being restless and bad-tempered, 15 per cent to being less patient and tolerant, and 13 per cent to being easily upset or snappy. Interviewees often mentioned becoming more aggressive, emotional and ashamed. As for material disadvantage, 13 per cent said they had been affected very badly, and 24 per cent that they were affected 'fairly badly'; 32 per cent said they had not been affected at all (presumably they had been on low wages). Answers on this topic varied according to length of unemployment; of the long-term unemployed, 20 per cent said they had been badly affected, and 30 per cent affected 'fairly badly'.

When it comes to daily activities, there is a noticeable contrast with the 1930s. Before the war, the emphasis was often on keeping warm in winter, staying in bed, visiting public libraries (where there was free warmth) or going to the pictures. In the early 1980s, according to the Economist Intelligence Unit survey, in the mornings about half the women would spend the time doing jobs around the house, and a quarter went to the shops; but only a fifth of the men would do work in the house, and only a fifth go to the shops. In the afternoon, the men's favourite activity was watching TV, while women's activities were much more varied – in order of popularity; doing housework, cooking, visiting friends or relations, doing more shopping, job-hunting or (at the bottom of the list) watching TV. Generally speaking, men were more active than women in job-seeking and gardening (presumably in the mornings), while women were more likely to make social calls. The long-term unemployed spent less time than others in job-seeking and shopping. The younger slept late and went to town more. The 25–34 age range played sports, while those over forty-five simply went for walks. In her book *English Journey* (1984), Beryl Bainbridge reports a conversation with an older man at the Longbridge works of Austin-Rover in Birmingham in the autumn of 1983:

> I spoke to one who said that Birmingham's unemployment figures were higher than the national average. It was running at 18 per cent. He felt sorry for his lad who had left school and hadn't a chance of a job. Couldn't he use his influence, I said, and get him work here? What influence? he asked. His lad never got up till the late afternoon, as though he was an invalid, or on nights. Nothing to do but stay in bed all day and watch videos into the small hours ...

Bainbridge comments, 'Nothing then could surely match the degradation of being out of work and an inhabitant of Castlevale' (a local council estate, which in fact was among the worst of its kind).

Undoubtedly there were some who experienced a sense of shame and inadequacy because they were out of work, but it is difficult to say whether feelings of this kind were common to most of the unemployed, or only to certain age or occupational groups, such as the young, or the long-term unemployed, or the skilled. For the school-leavers, pressure was certainly exerted by the government to train under the Youth Opportunities Scheme (later renamed the Youth Training Scheme), though the training allowance was low, and the short-term jobs made available under the government Manpower Services Commission were low-paid and regarded by some as 'slave labour'. For the older man, and especially the unskilled, the outlook was bleak, and those approaching the retirement age were well advised to accept whatever redundancy pay was available and retire early. One problem was that some areas where unemployment was particularly high, such as the north of England, were at a considerable distance from the south-east, where jobs were still available; and when the leading Conservative right-winger, Norman Tebbit, cheerfully advised the unemployed to imitate his father in the thirties, who 'got on his bike' to look for work, this might be easier said than done. In fact, some in the north were prepared to get on to British Rail, rather than their bikes, and work in the building industry in the south-east, returning to their families only at weekends.

The effect of this long-distance commuting on family life is easily imagined, and indeed family life was inevitably affected when the father was out of work. The worst case was probably when there were young children and no other source of income (declared or undeclared) other than the fortnightly Giro cheque from Social Security. All then would depend on the careful housekeeping of the mother, just as it had in the 1930s. How far real depression was suffered is impossible to quantify, and would depend on individual circumstances. Probably there was more real suffering among single-parent families, the elderly and the sick than in families where the household head was out of work. It must be remembered, too, that the unemployed host was constantly changing in composition; younger people, in particular, moved on to and off the registers, while the older generation in time became officially retired and so reduced the numbers of unemployed. Other broader aspects of unemployment should be mentioned: unemployment in itself does not appear to have contributed much to sickness rates. The Economist Intelligence Unit 1972 survey found that the unemployed were no more likely than the employed to visit the doctor, though slightly more on average were liable to have a long-standing illness; and there were higher rates of chronic sickness among manual workers who (as we have seen) were more subject to unemployment than skilled workers. As for crime, there is no evidence that unemployment led to more crime. It might well be a contributory factor, but not necessarily a major factor. Lastly, gaining academic qualifications was one way out of unemployment for some, but only a minority. Among non-manual workers, according to the Economist Intelligence Unit, 18 per cent had considered this, and 10 per cent had obtained further qualifications such as A Levels, Higher National Certificates and the like. Among manual workers, only 10 per cent had thought about this, and only 2 per cent achieved qualifications.

Since the Industrial Revolution, unemployment has always been an important aspect of working-class life. Between the wars, it became a subject of great public concern. After 1945, economic prosperity and the welfare state combined for a time to make it appear simply a thing of the past, a painful reminder of the unacceptable face of unregulated capitalism. Since 1975, it has returned to its former ugly prominence in the social history of the working classes. Throughout the eighties, on average it was never less than two million, and in the mid-years of the 1980s it was over three million. In fact, the eighties constitute a longer period of mass unemployment than even the 1930s. Although the unemployment rate was falling at the end of the eighties, there was still the danger that a new sector of society had come into existence – a semi-permanent group of 'have-nots' living at a lower level than the rest of society, a kind of underclass with a different way of life, lived within severely restricted parameters. Whether the concept of Disraeli's 'Two Nations', the rich and the poor – or, in contemporary jargon, the privileged and underprivileged, the advantaged and disadvantaged – has really manifested itself again will be discussed in the last chapter of this book.

Trade Unions

It was suggested in an earlier chapter that trade union power had triumphed with the defeat of the Conservative government at the polls in 1974, and that this represents a peak of their political influence in the post-war years. For a time, and under the Labour administrations of Wilson and then Callaghan, this influence was continued. Heath's 1971 Industrial Relations Act was repealed, and the Trade Unions and Labour Relations (Amendment) Act 1976 strengthened the unions' power to enforce the closed shop. Two earlier Acts in 1975 improved the worker's position: the Employment Protection Act gave statutory recognition to the Advisory, Conciliation and Arbitration Service (ACAS) set up in the previous year, and also extended employees' rights regarding notices of dismissal and the right to compensation for unfair dismissal. In addition, women workers were given six weeks' maternity leave pay. By the Sex Discrimination Act 1975, the legal position of women in employment was strengthened further in that employers were required to offer most jobs to men and women alike, and an Equal Opportunities Commission was set up to deal with complaints. By 1979, trade union membership had climbed from 12.4 million in 1976 to 13.3 million – its highest ever. Trade unions now represented over half the entire work force. The average membership had grown from about 19,000 in 1969 to 30,000 in 1979, though this conceals the fact that about half the unions still had very small memberships, while at the other end of the scale were the largest unions, such as the biggest, the Transport and General Workers Union with over two million members, the Engineers, with almost a million, the General and Municipal Workers, with just under a million, and NALGO, with three-quarters of a million. The white-collar unions had been the fastest growing, while women's membership was also expanding, reaching 27 per cent of all members in 1974.

However, increasing trade union power was regarded with mixed feelings by non-unionists, business interests, many employers and middle-class critics generally, especially when it became evident that the Social Contract had not solved the problem of keeping wage settlements under control, nor had it prevented frequent industrial disputes. The figures for the latter, given in Table 6.7, tell their own story. Clearly, after the relatively peaceful year of 1976, things began to go awry, and 1979 was the worst year

Table 6.7   Industrial Disputes, 1974–9

Year	Stoppages	Workers (000s)	Days lost (000s)
1974	2,922	1,626	14,750
1975	2,282	809	6,012
1976	2,016	668	3,284
1977	2,703	1,166	10,142
1978	2,471	1,042	9,405
1979	2,080	4,608	29,474

Source: Halsey (ed.), *British Social Trends since 1900* (1988).

for days lost since the war. It will be recalled that the beginning of this year saw the so-called Winter of Discontent, with widespread strike action. It was not only the number of strikes which attracted criticism, but also the violent picketing which had become a feature of too many strikes. The most notorious example of this occurred earlier in 1977, at the Grunwick strike in north London, where a number of workers (mostly Asian) at a film-processing plant had been dismissed for attempting to join a union. There was a good deal of fighting on the picket lines which had been strengthened by secondary picketing, including Yorkshire miners, and even Labour MPs. It is not surprising that the Conservative election manifesto in 1979 included a lengthy section on industrial relations, promising the reform of the law on picketing, restrictions on the closed shop and government funding for postal ballots for union elections.

These promises were duly fulfilled by the Thatcher administrations of the 1980s. Briefly, the 1980 Employment Act sought to abolish secondary picketing by limiting it to the employees involved and to their place of work. It also increased exemptions from the closed shop and provided public funds for secret ballots both before strikes and for trade union elections. The 1982 Employment Act, piloted through by the hard-nosed Secretary for Employment, Norman Tebbit, prohibited the pre-entry closed shop altogether, and permitted a closed shop to operate only when 85 per cent of the work force agreed. A Green Paper, *Democracy in Trade Unions*, proposed compulsory balloting for trade union elections and before strikes, and the substitution of 'contracting in' for 'contracting out'. In 1984, a third Employment Act implemented the proposal for compulsory secret ballots, but after negotiation by the secretary of the TUC, Norman Willis, with the new Employment Secretary, Tom King, 'contracting out' was not banned but, instead, ballots were to be held every ten years by unions to ascertain whether the members still wished to retain political funds (subsequently all of the unions holding such ballots agreed to keep their political funds). By these three Acts, it was sought to remove what many regarded as the worst abuses which had developed in trade union practices – sympathetic strikes and secondary picketing, workshops closed to non-union entrants, and open (and sometimes rigged) elections and decisions to strike. To their opponents, trade unions had grown too big for their boots, and the time had come to restrain them.

Naturally, these enactments met with much opposition from the unions – there were protest marches, and so-called Days of Action – but in fact many individual trade unionists were not strongly opposed to legislation which was intended to strengthen their rights against their own organisations. Certainly the Acts had teeth: during the *Stockport Messenger* strike at its Warrington printing works in November 1983, the proprietor Mr Eddie Shah obtained an injunction to prevent the National Graphical Association from enforcing a closed shop by mass picketing. The union ignored the injunction and was fined heavily for contempt of court; its assets were also sequestrated. By January 1984 the NGA was forced to accept defeat. In a case of a different kind, that of the

Government Communications Headquarters (GCHQ) in Cheltenham, a government surveillance centre, the Foreign Office decided that on security grounds all trade unions should be banned. Existing union members were to resign their union membership, or be transferred elsewhere; government compensation was offered to those affected. In vain the unions concerned offered a non-strike agreement. The government were adamant, and were successful in the courts, on the grounds of national security. In the same year there began the greatest strike of the whole post-war period, the result of a major confrontation between the National Union of Mineworkers and the National Coal Board – the miners' strike, 1984–5.

This strike resulted from proposals made in March 1984 by Ian MacGregor, the new chairman of the NCB, to cut output by 4 million tons, and to get rid of 20,000 jobs, but without dismissals – the job losses would be achieved by natural wastage, or by voluntary and compensated redundancies. Strikes were immediately authorised by the NUM national executive, under its fiery president Arthur Scargill. On a previous occasion he had called for a national strike, but had failed to obtain the necessary majority in a postal ballot of members. This time there was no ballot before the strike was called – a fact much resented by some miners, particularly those on the Notts coalfield with the most modern and profitable pits, which were unlikely to be closed down in the near future at least. Many of the Notts pits continued working, though the strike was well supported in Yorkshire (Scargill's home territory – he had moved the NUM headquarters from London to Sheffield), in Scotland, in South Wales and in Kent. Picketing was reinforced by flying pickets from other coalfields, and soon became very violent as battles were fought between the police attempting to secure the free passage of men and supplies, and the pickets themselves. At the Orgreave coke store near Sheffield, 6,000 miners and 3,300 police were in confrontation, and on 19 June 1984 more than 100 arrests were made and more than 80 people injured. At Ollerton, in Nottinghamshire, a Yorkshire miner on picket duty was crushed to death in fighting at the pithead. The police were forced to set up an emergency headquarters in London from which they could be rushed into action wherever required. Sometimes they were able to forestall the movement of flying pickets by simply intercepting them and turning them back to their own territory – a fate which befell groups of miners setting forth from the Kent coalfield, well known for its militancy.

For the most part, the miners had to fight on their own. They found it difficult to organise sympathetic strikes, which were in any case illegal. Steel workers feared for their own jobs, and would not co-operate. Nor would the workers at the power stations, which had ample supplies of coal, so that at no time did power cuts become necessary. In July 1984 there was a national dock strike, but it was over within a fortnight, thereby providing little or no help for the miners' cause. For a short while in September there was a flicker of hope when NACODS – the colliery overseers union – fell out with the Coal Board. If they had gone on strike, virtually all pits would have had to close; but the dispute was soon patched up. Meanwhile, the South Wales miners were fined £50,000 for illegal picketing (that is, disregarding an injunction to stop such picketing), and, when this sum was not paid, a further £707,000 was seized from their funds. The NUM itself was fined £200,000 for conducting an illegal strike, and the High Court ordered that its assets be seized too, though Scargill had taken the precaution of sending funds abroad. He maintained his popularity among his own followers in Yorkshire, and also on the left of both the Labour Party and the TUC. Middle-class opinion was very hostile to him, of course, especially when towards the end of the year it was revealed that he had approached both the Libyans and the Russian trade unions for additional funds.

What were the basic issues in this strike? For the government's part, there was a determination to make the coal industry profitable by closing down uneconomic pits, and MacGregor was regarded as the right man for the job; he had already spent three years as chairman of British Steel, another nationalised industry, where he had similarly been entrusted to restore the industry to profitability. Moreover, the government was now ready to deal with any resistance by the NUM by implementing the recent trade union legislation, and if necessary by taking action through the courts. The police were on hand, of course, to deal with any problems arising from picketing, utilising their experience of crowd control gained in the recent urban riots. In other words, the government was ready to take on the miners. On the other hand, the miners were hardly ready to take on the government. It was a mistake to do so without securing united support throughout the industry; the failure to hold a strike ballot was a serious error (though admittedly it might have again failed to give Scargill the majority he required), and so was the calling of a strike in the spring, just when demand for coal was falling. The Notts miners were so aggrieved by Scargill's headlong action that not only did many of them continue working, but they set up a new union of their own, the Union of Democratic Mineworkers. Thus the miners were split, and great bitterness resulted, not only between families but even between working and striking members of the same family. Scabs were reviled, of course, and in some cases their houses had bricks through their windows, and worse. The sufferings of many families were intense. Efforts were made to reduce social security payments to the families of strikers, though soup kitchens were provided by sympathisers to ensure that they had a square meal from time to time. Nevertheless, the strikers were convinced they were in the right: they were fighting for their future livelihood, and held that it was morally wrong to shut any pit for economic reasons alone. As for the illegality of their actions, they refused to be bound by laws restricting their right to strike – as Mick McGahey, the dour Scottish vice-president of the NUM put it, 'We shall not be constitutionalised out of a defence of our jobs.'

By November, the government still stood firm, and some 15,000 miners went back to work in order to gain their Christmas bonuses. Meanwhile, violence continued on the picket lines. The miners continued to fight to prevent entry to the pits, while in scenes chillingly reminiscent of street clearing in police states, the police in riot gear, rhythmically beating their riot shields, advanced on the picket lines. It was the continued sight of violent struggles on their television screens, together with the defiant speeches of Arthur Scargill, usually couched in the most belligerent and class-conscious terms, which did much to alienate middle-class opinion. The Labour Party expressed sympathy for the miners, but could scarcely condone the violence or the breaking of the law. In South Wales, a concrete slab was dropped from a bridge on to a taxi taking a miner to work, and the driver was killed. The two striking miners responsible were charged with murder, and were sentenced to twenty years (they served only a few years of this sentence). By the spring of 1985, it was obvious that the strike had failed. In early March, the NUM decided to return to work, but without an agreement, after fifty-one weeks on strike (Scargill opposed this, yet afterwards claimed that the strike had been 'a victory'). So the miners went back, sometimes as in South Wales, with bands playing and banners flying; but it was more like a funeral wake than a victory procession. The miners had endured much and displayed great comradeship, as they had always done in the past. Yet the strike left a legacy of intense bitterness, against both the government and MacGregor (frequently reviled as an American, for much of his life had been spent in the States, though in fact he was Scottish by birth), and also against those regarded as scabs. At the end of it all, many miners had sold up and were heavily in debt. It has been estimated that each miner had lost about £9,000. As for the government, the strike had cost £3 billion, and 22.4 million working days were lost in 1984 as a consequence of the strike, representing 83 per cent of all days lost nationally. In 1985, days lost in mining fell to 4 million, this being 63 per cent of all days lost. As for the NUM, since the strike it has lost 70 per cent of its members, either to the UDM or through redundancy. In 1985, there were still 170 pits. Five years later there were 76.

The trade union movement had suffered a severe setback, as the government had intended, though the TUC itself played little part in organising the strike. Scargill dominated the scene, both metaphorically and literally – he was constantly to be seen on the TV screen. According to the *Employment Gazette*, days lost through industrial stoppages dropped sharply in 1986 and 1987–1,920,000 and 3,546,000 days respectively. Getting on for half of the latter figure was accounted for by a strike involving telecommunication workers. In 1986 there also began an extraordinary dispute at *The Times*. Eight years previously a similar stoppage had occurred in the printing section, and the newspaper closed down for a year. The owners could do little about this, since they were at the mercy of the print unions, who refused to adopt the latest methods of typesetting. There were revelations about the high earnings of the printers, about overmanning and about so-called Spanish practices, a polite name for fiddles which enhanced wages. Nevertheless, the management was forced to give in, and the printers triumphed. In 1986, it was different. The new proprietor, Rupert Murdoch, an Australian newspaper millionaire, built new premises in Wapping in the East End of London, equipped with the latest electronic machinery, and with a specially trained staff. When the Gray's Inn unions went on strike early in 1986, production started up promptly in Wapping, and 5,500 of the old staff were sacked. Distribution of the paper was ensured not by rail, but by a fleet of vans. Soon the Wapping site was engulfed by angry pickets and demonstrators, some from fringe political parties such as Militant and the anarchists. Pitched battles were fought with the police. There were by now familiar allegations of unnecessary violence on both sides – baton charges by the police, ball-bearings thrown down under police horses' hooves, and so on. The throwing of bricks, stones, even petrol bombs, and the overturning and burning of vehicles had become commonplace as features of urban violence. Undoubtedly the disorder reached dangerous heights, and it is remarkable that no one was killed. The worst violence occurred on 24 January 1987, the first anniversary of the move to Wapping. About 12,000 demonstrators were present, and 162 police officers were injured; 67 demonstrators were arrested and 65 convicted. Subsequently twenty-four police officers were charged with offences arising out of the disorders. However, the defences of the premises (nicknamed Fort Wapping) held firm – staff got in and out (often in coaches), and so did the vans and lorries. Murdoch's ruthlessly efficient organisation of the new-style newspaper production won the day, to the great satisfaction of his fellow newspaper proprietors; the printing unions' monopoly of power had at last been broken. Yet Murdoch's methods caused a good deal of unease among those who advocated co-operation in industrial relations rather than confrontation.

When the period 1975 to 1990 is surveyed as a whole, it is obvious that the trade union movement lost a good deal of ground in these years. To some extent, this was inevitable, owing to the recession, but Conservative legislation played a large part – and the attitude of the government, too, which was to keep the unions at a distance as far as possible. There were to be no more 'beer and sandwiches at No. 10' – the informal consultations favoured by Harold Wilson and other Labour leaders. The Conservatives' studied aloofness was very noticeable in the six months' national strike of ambulance drivers in 1989–90. Between 1976 and 1986 trade union membership fell by 15 per cent to 10.5 million, once more under half the total employees at work. Female membership was still growing, but the curious variation in the size of the unions persisted. Over half the unions had fewer than 1,000 members, while twenty-four unions with more than 100,000 each accounted for over 80 per cent of the entire membership. The eight largest unions alone, with over 350,000 each, represented 53.2 per cent of the total. The political power of these massive unions over the Labour Party was still in theory very great. Four unions alone had more than half the total trade union vote at the Labour Party Conference, and any of the three biggest unions could cancel out the entire constituency party votes. It is no wonder that by 1990 plans were on foot to reform the block-vote procedure. Lastly, it seems unlikely that the restrictions placed on the industrial power of the unions by the Conservatives will be changed to any large extent by any future Labour government, simply because they have been accepted for the most part by the Labour Party as a reasonable strengthening of the rights of the individual trade union member.

The Standard of Living

At this point it seems appropriate to consider what happened between 1975 and 1990 to the standard of living as indicated by the movement of real wages of the majority of the working classes who did stay in work. It will be recalled that, between the wars, real wages went up about 30 per cent, while after the war and up to the mid-seventies they did even better – approximately, they doubled. What happened thereafter is shown in Table 6.8, taken from the government publication, the *Employment Gazette*, for January/June 1988. The index figures are for average gross weekly real earnings of full-time men, based on 1986 prices.

These figures show that over the fourteen-year period, real earnings for *all* men increased by a fifth. During the years 1973–9, the overall earnings distribution narrowed, and many in the higher-paid occupations experienced a fall in real earnings; but after 1979

Table 6.8   Real Wages, 1973–86

	1973	1974	1975	1976	1977	1978	1979
All occupations	172.3	170.3	178.5	177.2	165.2	173.5	179.9
Manual workers	157.1	156.1	164.1	161.1	150.7	157.6	165.0
Non-manual workers	198.0	194.4	201.1	201.5	187.0	196.2	200.0

	1980	1981	1982	1983	1984	1985	1986
All occupations	180.9	185.6	183.1	190.9	197.0	198.3	207.5
Manual workers	162.7	158.5	159.0	164.1	168.2	168.6	174.7
Non-manual workers	205.4	211.6	212.2	222.3	230.3	231.9	249.9

Source: *Employment Gazette*, January/June 1988.

the distribution widened significantly. As for manual workers, their annual increases were all under 5 per cent, save for 1974–5, when it was 5.1 per cent. In each of the five years 1974, 1976, 1977, 1980 and 1981 they experienced a *fall* in real wages. Thus during the earlier part of the period, the overall increase was about 5 per cent; from 1979 to 1986 it was 5.7 per cent. Over the whole fourteen years, it was between 10 and 11 per cent. The figures for female workers show that their real earnings moved up by about two-fifths, thus doing much better than the men, perhaps because of equal pay for women.

As for individual occupations, up to 1979 the largest increases for men appear to have been in transport, where real wages moved up by 6.6 per cent, and in catering, cleaning and other personal services (an increase of 6.3 per cent). Construction and mining improved by just over 5 per cent. After 1979 and up to 1986, clerical work easily outstripped all other occupations with an increase of 16.25 per cent, followed by selling (13.3 per cent), and catering (8.3 per cent). Transport improved at only 5 per cent, and construction and mining at only 2.9 per cent. As for overtime, the proportion of workers receiving overtime fell by 8 per cent between 1976 and 1981, but from then to 1987 the average overtime hours increased to five and a half hours a week. Overtime earnings accounted for 15 per cent of average gross earnings for male manual workers by 1987.

It seems clear that between 1975 and 1986, improvement in real wages was very limited – much less than in the period up to the mid-seventies, and even less than in the 1930s. There do not seem to be any other social changes which could contribute significantly to changes in the standard of living. The conclusion must be that, although the marked improvements up to the mid-seventies were not lost, the increase in living standards from then on was certainly limited. In addition, it is worth repeating that a substantial proportion of the working classes could not participate even in that modest improvement, for the simple reason that they were on the dole. Their standard of living was kept at a deliberately low level, and as a rule changed for the better only with the annual increase in benefit in line with the official rise in the cost of living.

Concluding Remarks

In this chapter only a limited number of aspects of working-class life after 1974 have been considered, but already it is clear that a serious increase in unemployment overshadowed all else, and at the same time the trade union movement suffered severe setbacks. Although the standard of living improved for those remaining in work, the improvement was on only a limited scale. Obvious questions now arise: what increase was there in poverty? What happened to health, housing and state education? Did changes in the family continue? What about race relations, crime and leisure activities? These remaining aspects of working-class life will be addressed and considered in the next chapter, which continues the theme of 'Darkening Horizons'.

Chapter 7

Darkening Horizons 1974–1990: Part II

Poverty and the Welfare State

One of the major purposes of the welfare state was to ensure that poverty of the kind which existed between the wars would be banished entirely from this country; and that instead there would be 'security from the cradle to the grave'. Yet it was shown in Chapter Four that poverty was rediscovered by the social scientists in the 1960s, and that, however disputed its extent at that time, there was certainly a significant degree of poverty among (in particular) the elderly, among large families and among those on low wages. What then was the position after 1974?

In the first place, a new trend developed in welfare policy, even before the Conservatives returned to power in 1979. This was a move away from flat-rate benefit towards help directed to particular groups in need. This move was accelerated under Mrs Thatcher, whose general policy was to emphasise self-help, and to provide assistance only where positive need could be shown. In 1980 the basis of national insurance pension rates was changed from that of wages and prices to prices alone (which was a disadvantage to pensioners when wages were rising more rapidly than prices). Numerous cuts and adjustments to benefits were made. Employers, instead of the state, were required to pay sickness benefit for the first eight weeks of sickness (extended in 1986 to twenty-eight weeks). The administration of housing benefit was shifted back to local authorities. Benefit to strikers' families was reduced on the assumption that they were already receiving strike pay. By 1985 cuts amounted to £2.4 billion (though this was still only a small proportion of the total budget of over £40 billion). The underlying assumption in all this was that hitherto money had been wasted through inefficiency, and through fraudulent claims made by scroungers and layabouts. The new policy was to make payments only on the basis of selectivity – that is, only to means-tested applicants, who could prove their need. Admittedly it was necessary to make sure that money was not being wasted, but this was a considerable departure in spirit from the Beveridge principle of payment to those entitled to relief as a result of paying their national insurance contributions. Also in 1985, a White Paper was published on the reform of social security; legislation was proposed (to come into effect in April 1988) which would replace family income supplement by family credit, and supplementary benefit by income support.

Secondly, as we have already seen in the previous chapter, unemployment in the early 1980s rose to unprecedented heights. Given the fact that relief to the unemployed has never been intended to do more than provide a minimum standard of living, this fact alone suggests that poverty increased at this time. There was also an increase in the numbers of those in full-time employment but on low wages and forced to apply for supplementary benefit. Given, too, the sheer complexity of the Social Security system, and the increasing strictness of its administration, it is not surprising that by the early 1980s there were large numbers eligible for benefit but not claiming it. On *prima facie* grounds, therefore, the qualitative evidence is that poverty still existed, and on a formidable scale. What of the quantitative evidence?

If the numbers on supplementary benefit are taken as an indicator, these numbers doubled from 1975 to 1983, when they almost reached a record eight million; the rise from December 1979 alone to 1983 was about 60 per cent. At the same time, numbers increased of those in work but below 140 per cent of the supplementary benefit level, nearly doubling by 1983 since 1979. If all are taken into account, either in work on low pay, or for any other reason below the supplementary benefit level plus 40 per cent, then the total reached a remarkable 16.3 million in 1983, nearly one in three of the population. At the same time, it is worth noting that income was becoming more unevenly distributed: the share of income after tax of the bottom 10 per cent of earners fell from 2.9 per cent in 1978/9 to 2.4 per cent in 1981/2, while the share of the top 10 per cent increased from 23.4 per cent to 25.6 per cent. The share of the super-rich (the top 1 per cent) rose from 3.9 per cent to 4.6 per cent.

In 1984 a survey of the extent of poverty was made by Mack and Lansley, using the services of the MORI organisation, for the London Weekend TV programme *Breadline Britain*, the results being published subsequently as *Poor Britain* (1985). Their findings, based upon a definition of poverty as 'an enforced lack of socially perceived necessities' (a list of necessities for a minimum standard of life was contributed by respondents to the survey), have been summarised in Table 7.1. They also list a number of adjustments which could be made to these figures by way of fine-tuning, giving a possible range of about 6 million to 12 million people affected by poverty; taking all the adjustments together, the authors suggest that the true total might be about 8.5 million.

Table 7.1 Poverty in 1984

In poverty		In or on the margins of poverty		In intense poverty	
Adults	5.0m	Adults	7.9m	Adults	1.7m
Children	2.5m	Children	4.2m	Children	0.9m
Total	7.5m	Total	12.1m	Total	2.6m
(1 in every 7, or 13% of the population)		(1 in every 5, or 22% of the population)		(1 in every 20, or 4.8% of the population)	

Source: J.Mack and S.Lansley, *Poor Britain* (1985).

In terms of numbers, there was an almost equal three-fold division between those in work, those out of work but available for work, and those not working and not available for work. In terms of groups, there were five main groups: the unemployed, single parents, the sick and disabled, pensioners and the low paid. Surprisingly, the elderly constituted only about 0.65 million (about 13 per cent). The sick and disabled were about 1.5 million, while those on low pay were about a third of all households in poverty; 40 per cent of families in poverty had a head of household in full-time work. Low pay affected 1.75 million adults, and a million children, actually more than those made poor by unemployment (1.65 million adults, nearly one million children).

234

It must be said immediately that Mack and Lansley's findings did not go unchallenged at the time, since any definition of relative poverty based on a lack of at least three 'necessities' from a given list at once raises questions as to precisely what should go into the list as an essential and what should not. Further, since their survey is on a different basis from Townsend's 1968/9 survey (itself of a controversial nature), it is impossible to make direct comparisons. In any case, it is not entirely clear which is their preferred total for poverty – 7.5 million, 12.1 million or the suggested in-between figures of about 8.5 million. They themselves say that there is a danger that at the margins the argument becomes rather semantic; the important thing is that 'there are about 12 million people who are struggling by the standards of today'. Another difficulty is that of reconciling any of these totals with the figure of 16.3 million persons with incomes below 140 per cent of supplementary benefit level in 1983 (a similar calculation for 1981, two years previously, by Professor Townsend, has yielded a not too dissimilar figure of 15 million). The calculation of the extent of poverty in the mid-1980s therefore presents great difficulties.

Nevertheless, it is clear that in the 1980s there still existed a great mass of human misery which certainly had grown greater with the advent of large-scale unemployment. Two quotations from the many case histories available may suffice. First, a typical description of life on supplementary benefit made by a single mother with a nine-month-old baby:

> Sometimes in the middle of the week I've got no money and I've got to go and find some money in order to buy nappies for her. So I have to go and ask people. If I haven't got the money I have to borrow the money from friends and that. And I have to give that back when my next pay comes so that leaves me short again.

Next, the mother of three children whose husband is in a low-paid job:

> You are just living from day to day. We can't live from week to week, it's day to day. Because the money's so tight. We just can't manage on the wages Roy brings home.

For such young couples, life remained dreary, with a severely limited diet, little recreation, few toys for the children, and second-hand clothes from the charity shop. Fortunately, by the end of the eighties, public opinion was much less inclined than before to regard the poor as the authors of their own misfortunes, or to regard social security claimants as necessarily feckless or as scroungers. A number of poverty pressure groups have developed to provide support, such as Shelter, Age Concern, Help the Aged and the Child Poverty Action Group. Citizens' Advice Bureaux up and down the country provide invaluable advice to claimants unsure of their rights. Yet even when a benefit exists, it might be that there are not necessarily the funds available to pay it. Notoriously and admittedly somewhat exceptionally, in the spring of 1990 applications for social fund benefits (made in the form of loans for basic household equipment, such as beds and cookers) were being turned down as local Social Security offices ran out of the cash sums allocated to them. Meanwhile, the government which had previously claimed that the incomes of the poorest 10 per cent had increased nearly twice as fast between 1981 and 1985 as that of the population as a whole, had to retract its figures, which were statistically incorrect. The rate of growth was actually 2.6 per cent, less than half the 5.4 per cent growth rate of the whole population. It was also significantly worse than for the whole population for the period 1979 to 1987. Somehow, the welfare state was still failing to provide satisfactorily that life-long security for the working classes it was set up to achieve.

Housing and Homes

In the mid-seventies the post-war pattern of building both public and private housing continued for a time, and under the Labour governments of 1975–9, rather more council house building than private building was undertaken at first. From 1978 onwards, however, privately built houses increasingly outnumbered local authority building. During the years of Tory government in the eighties, this trend was accentuated, until in 1987 privately built houses outnumbered public housing by five to one. The figure for private house completions in that year was the highest since 1973. In 1988, the figure for public housing shrank still further to about 21,000. The annual figures for house building in Table 7.2 illustrate the trend very clearly.

The new council houses continued to provide the improvements made in the sixties, though by now high-rise building was quite out of fashion. Sales of council houses to sitting tenants became

Table 7.2   Houses Built, 1975–87 (in 000s)

	1975	1976	1977	1978	1979	1980	1981
Public	167	169	170	136	108	110	88
Private	155	155	143	152	142	130	119

	1982	1983	1984	1985	1986	1987
Public	54	55	55	44	38	34
Private	128	151	163	159	170	178

Source: *Social Trends*, No. 19 (1989) and No. 12 (1982).

increasingly popular. The Conservative government's Housing Act 1980 conferred the right to buy after three years, subsequently reduced to two years by the Housing and Building Control Act 1984. This Act also increased the maximum discount available from 50 to 60 per cent. Sales went up from about 93,000 in 1980 to a peak of 227,720 in 1982. They then fell back to 109,000 in 1986, rising again to over 142,000 in 1987. Total sales between 1980 and the end of 1987 reached over one million. One result has been that flats have become an increasing proportion (about a third) of all council housing.

The movement towards home ownership was certainly strong in the 1980s. In the past, some better-off workers had always owned their homes, but they had been a very small minority. By 1984, 13 per cent of the semi-skilled owned their houses outright, while a further 30 per cent owned them with a mortgage; of unskilled manual workers, 13 per cent owned their houses outright, and a further 23 per cent owned their houses subject to mortgage. By the end of the 1980s, the proportion of working-class households owning their house was approaching 50 per cent. The twentieth-century image of the urban working-class family as council house tenants was beginning to change. Over all classes, owner-occupancy increased from 43 per cent of all households in 1961 to 64 per cent in 1987. It is no wonder that one of the most striking changes in high-street shops in the 1980s was the apparently ever-increasing numbers of building society premises.

This emphasis on home ownership should not be allowed to obscure the fact that substantial numbers of working-class men and women still rented their accommodation in the 1980s. Of the economically inactive heads of household (a large group including the elderly, the unemployed and so on), 43 per cent still rented their homes from local authorities, and a further 12 per cent rented privately. Renting was particularly prominent among the young: in 1986, one in five households with heads aged twenty-four and under were renting furnished accommodation. Some accommodation, whether furnished or unfurnished, might be in a very poor condition. The House Condition Surveys of 1981 for England and Wales showed that of the total housing stock of 19.1 million dwellings, 1.2 million were unfit for habitation, one million of these being in actual occupation. Moreover, one million dwellings lacked basic amenities, and 1.1 million required repairs costing more than £7,000 at 1981 prices. A further survey in 1985 by local authorities of their building stock resulted in the authorities estimating that 84 per cent of their properties needed renovation, at an average cost of £4,900 per dwelling, that is, £1,884 billion in all. As for slum clearance, although by 1988 more than 1.5 million dwellings had been demolished since the war, the rate of demolition slowed noticeably in the 1980s. Whereas an average of 65,000 properties a year were demolished in the UK between 1961 and 1970, in 1987 only 12,000 were demolished. Perhaps the ambitious plans first announced by the government in 1988 for inner-city renewal, the Action for Cities Campaign, involving the spending of £4 billion on regeneration schemes, will help speed up slum clearance in the urban areas affected.

Two other working-class groups require consideration. Although overcrowding had been a feature of poor housing in the past, it was of much less consequence by the 1980s. Overcrowding, as defined by the numbers permitted per bedroom, declined overall from 7 per cent in 1971 to 4 per cent in 1984 (the most recent date for which figures are available). In more detail, 5 per cent of those renting from local authorities, and 9 per cent of those renting privately furnished premises, were overcrowded in 1984. The numbers of the homeless are rather more serious. Local authorities have a statutory duty to provide accommodation for homeless families considered to be in priority need (in practice, they also provide shelter for less urgent cases). The figures for homeless households accepted by local authorities for 1984 and 1985 (mainly for priority need) are set out in Table 7.3.

At the end of 1985, nearly 15,500 households known to local authorities were in temporary accommodation; of these, 4,500 were in bed-and-breakfast accommodation, 6,000 in short-life

Table 7.3   Homeless Households, 1984–5

	1984	1985
Priority needs category (in percentages)		
Households with dependent children	61	62
Household member pregnant	12	12
Household member vulnerable		
Old age	8	7
Physical handicap	3	3
Mental illness	2	2
Other reasons	4	4
Homeless in emergency	3	3
Not priority need	8	9
All households (000s)	97	109

Source: *Social Trends*, No. 17 (1987).

dwellings, and 5,000 in hostels (including women's refuges). These figures do not include the numbers sleeping rough in the big cities, such as the inhabitants of Cardboard City on the South Bank in London – a heterogeneous mass of the homeless consisting of youngsters from the provinces looking for work, alcoholics, drug addicts, the sick, the mentally handicapped (the result of being prematurely discharged into the community from mental hospitals), and drop-outs and weirdos of all descriptions. By the end of 1988, the number of households in temporary accommodation had risen to 32,000.

It remains to say something about amenities enjoyed by the large majority who did have homes. Generally speaking, homes became more comfortable in the seventies and eighties as they acquired more consumer durables, more central heating and more motor cars. Table 7.4 sets out the main changes. These figures show that the vast majority of homes had a television set (51 per cent had two or more), a washing machine, a telephone, a deep freezer and a refrigerator (refrigerators were dropped from the list once they reached 95 per cent; vacuum cleaners had been dropped earlier on). Ownership of video recorders and microwave ovens was increasing (the 1988 figure for videos was 53 per cent). Car ownership also rose by 1988 to 66 per cent of households. Though these figures as a whole give a clear indication of rising standards of comfort, they also show that a third of households were still without a car, and a quarter without central heating.

Table 7.4   Household Amenities, 1976–87

Percentages of households with	1976	1979	1981	1983	1985	1986	1987
Home computer					13	17	18
Television							
colour	49	66	74	81	86	88	90
black and white	47	31	23	17	11	10	8
Video recorder				18	31	38	46
Refrigerator	88	92	93	94	95	–	–
Deep freezer		40	49	57	66	72	74
Washing machine	71	74	78	80	81	82	83
Tumble dryer		19	23	28	33	36	39
Telephone	54	67	75	77	81	83	83
Microwave oven						23	30
Central heating	48	55	59	64	69	71	73
A car or van							
one	45	44	44	43	45	44	44
more than one	11	13	15	16	17	18	19

Source: *General Household Survey* (1987).

Perhaps the biggest change in the provision of working-class housing in the seventies and eighties was the increasing emphasis on home ownership. This had been a pronounced feature of Conservative policy, and the sale of council houses, at first opposed by Labour, proved very popular. It could be argued, of course, that this was only made possible by the rising standard of living of the working classes (though council houses were bought at a heavy discount on market prices). Apart from council houses, working-class purchasers were also in the market for smaller properties, sometimes built in the previous century and brought up to date, and sometimes purpose-built in the last few years as starter homes to attract first-time buyers. The wider ownership of a home well furnished with consumer durables (and some not so durable, being merely thrown away and replaced before their useful life had ended) may seem an admirable achievement, but the darker side of the picture is the continued existence of slum property on a considerable scale, and the problems of renovation of council property. Long ago Professor Galbraith warned of the dangers of private affluence existing side by side with public squalor. Such dangers had not ceased to exist in the 1990s.

Health

During the seventies and eighties the health of the nation as a whole continued to improve, to judge by the noticeable increase in the expectation of life at birth. Thus, for males born in 1971, the expected life span was 68.8 years. By 1985 it had increased to 71.5, and by 1988, to around 73 years. For females, the figures are: in 1971, 73.8 years; in 1985, 77.4 years; and in 1988, to about 78 years. At the same time, death rates in England and Wales remained steady in the 1970s at about 11.9; in 1985, the rate was 11.8. The infant mortality rate improved from 16 per thousand live births in 1975 to 9.4 in 1986 (though this rate was still higher than in some other states of the European Community). It should also be remembered that all these national figures conceal marked regional variations; mortality figures and the incidence of disease, for example, continue to be higher in the north-east than in London and the south-east.

As in the previous period, heart attacks, strokes and cancer took their toll of the elderly, but among the younger generation a new and mortal threat to health appeared – AIDS (Acquired Immune Deficiency Syndrome). This disease could be contracted through sexual contact, by a baby if the mother was infected, by contaminated blood transfusion, or by intravenous drug abusers using dirty needles. The disease first became known in the United States, especially in San Francisco, and spread swiftly to this country. By the end of October 1988, 1,862 cases had been reported here, of whom 1,002 had died. Of these fatalities, 97 per cent were men; 85 per cent of these men were homosexuals or bisexual, and 7 per cent were haemophiliacs. Only about 180 cases involved heterosexual conduct, but the proportion was expected to increase. In September 1988 the number with the HIV positive anti-body (Human Immunodeficiency Virus), who would probably develop AIDS within the next fifteen years, was 9,242. The government mounted a vigorous campaign with striking and unpleasant advertisements on TV and elsewhere to warn the public of the dangers, advocating the use of safe contraceptive methods, particularly the condom, which now became a familiar sight to young and old alike, at least on the television screen. The Working Party of the Public Health Laboratory Service predicted 1,300 new cases in 1990, and 750 deaths in England and Wales, an improvement on earlier predictions; but its report suggests that though the homosexual epidemic may not rise as rapidly as at first thought,

241

heterosexual and drug-abuser cases were rising faster than before.

Another more familiar threat to health – cigarette smoking – appears to be less of a danger to the working classes than in previous years. In 1976, 46 per cent of men, and 38 per cent of women, smoked cigarettes. Ten years later in 1986, the figures had dropped to 33 per cent overall of all persons aged sixteen or over (35 per cent of men, 31 per cent of women). The 1988 figures continued the downward trend to 33 per cent of men and 30 per cent of women. However, smoking still had an attraction for children: in 1986, among children aged eleven to fifteen, 7 per cent of boys and 12 per cent of girls were regular smokers. As for alcohol abuse, the heaviest consumption in 1987, as might be expected, was among 18- to 24-year olds. The average weekly consumption by those over eighteen was 9.5 units of alcohol. For women, there was a small rise in consumption to nearly 5 units per week. Customs records indicate a peak of consumption in 1979, followed by a fall until 1982, and then a small rise. There are no indications as yet that the new freedom of public houses in England to open all day has led to any marked increase in consumption.

Addiction to hard drugs continued to increase, though with some variations. Nearly eight times as many new drug addicts were notified in 1985 as in 1973 (6,409 compared with 806), though this was followed by a drop of nearly a third between 1985 and 1987 (6,409 down to 4,593), and then a further rise to 5,212 in 1988. What these figures of notified users really signify is hard to say. Using a multiplier of five, and taking into account previous and continuing users, the actual numbers in 1987 could have been in the region of 38,000. New addicts rose again to 5,639 in 1989, and the total of notified addicts reached 14,785. Fresh estimates, using this time a multiplier of ten, suggest a new overall drug population in 1990 of up to 150,000. Clearly there is a good deal of uncertainty and guesswork in all these figures. Heroin remains the greatest single narcotic drug of abuse. A new threat has been posed by a refined form of cocaine – 'crack' – originating in America, though solvent abuse (glue-sniffing), which was becoming popular among teenagers, seemed to be losing its attraction by 1990. Ninety-three deaths from this cause were notified in 1986.

Taking all things together, it seems that the general health of the nation had got better during the seventies and eighties, so that the working classes were healthier in 1990 than in 1975. The greatest threat to health of the younger generation – AIDS – appears to have been kept in check. On the other hand, there were still problems: as the population grows more elderly, the overall cost of medical treatment continues to rise. Further, the latest medical equipment in hospital is increasingly expensive. The result has been a marked increase in expenditure on the National Health Service. The Conservative governments of the 1980s sought to contain this by a combination of financial cuts and drastic reorganisation. There were severe cuts in 1987–8, and in October 1988 the number of hospital beds had fallen by 6 per cent during the previous twelve months, and by 21 per cent since 1977. Whole wards were closed, and smaller cottage hospitals were shut down. By March 1990 more than a million people were waiting for hospital treatment, and one in four had been waiting for more than a year (the longest waiting lists were in London; the shortest on Merseyside). Prescription charges went up again in 1990, while dental and eyesight examinations were no longer free of charge. Dental fees under the NHS sailed up, leading to fears that patients would stop going to see the dentist regularly. Of course, there were exemptions to charges for those on limited incomes – a large proportion of prescriptions were still provided free – but, for those on low incomes but still having to pay, the new charges were burdensome. Indeed, past and proposed changes in the NHS have so far shown no improvements in the services provided for the working classes, who form the overwhelming majority of its patients; very few of them can afford private treatment.

The future of the National Health Service, the cornerstone of the welfare state, remains to be seen. It seems fair to say that the health of working-class people is intimately bound up with that future. Mrs Thatcher claimed repeatedly in the 1980s that the NHS was safe with the Conservatives, but the reforms carried out then and planned for 1990 brought great protests from the medical profession itself, whether in hospitals or in general practice. It is to be hoped that the more efficient National Health Service which is promised will ultimately rival the services available in middle-class, private hospitals whose patients can afford the necessary medical insurance.

Education

Although the spread of comprehensive education was not without its critics, it was suggested in a previous chapter that it brought distinct gains for the working classes in the secondary schools. The advances in higher education before 1975 are perhaps more debatable, in that it can be argued that the middle classes took the lion's share of expansion; but in further education the widening of opportunities for working-class students seems undeniable. When Labour took office again in 1974, the main task appeared to be to continue the move to comprehensive education, bearing in mind that the school-leaving age had been put up to sixteen only two years previously. The Labour government had no great plans for further educational reform, though Wilson's successor, James Callaghan, did initiate a number of discussions in 1976 under the somewhat grand title, the Great Debate on Education. In the same year, the government discontinued the direct grant system whereby certain fee-paying schools received grants direct from the government in return for providing a number of free places. Most of these schools then became fully independent, privately financed institutions. The Labour government maintained its traditional hostility to the public school system, but did nothing to change it, and indeed the abolition of direct grant status actually added to the number of fee-paying schools.

It may be that economic problems and rising unemployment inhibited further educational reform under Labour, particularly when it was realised (somewhat belatedly) that the fall in the birth rate meant that school rolls would soon begin to decline. (This resulted in the virtual destruction of the system of colleges of education as they were then constituted. Many closed down, others merged with polytechnics, or combined together. Empty training places were filled up by starting new degree courses, usually in Arts subjects, in addition to the established BEd courses.) At all events, the economic climate did not stop the new Conservative government in 1979 from embarking on an extraordinary reform of the whole educational system. So far as the schools were concerned, the major ideas seem to have been to introduce more competition between schools, give more power to governors and parents so that the schools had greater freedom to manage their own affairs, and to reform the curriculum, with particular reference to the world of work. All these reforms were driven not so much by any new developments in educational philosophy as by the strong ideological beliefs of right-wing Conservatism (the so-called radical right). So many changes were set on foot in the schools (and also in further and higher education) that it seems best to survey these changes in chronological order, and then to supply comment as appropriate.

Starting as early as 1979, the Conservative government abolished the previous government's requirement that local educational authorities (LEAs) should produce reorganisation schemes for more comprehensive schools. Then, in 1980, parents were given the right to send their children to the state school of their choice, an assisted places scheme was introduced for fee-paying schools, and school examination results in state schools were henceforth to be published. In 1983, for the first time, Her Majesty's Inspectors of Schools were permitted to make public their reports on individual schools. Three years later, proposals for twenty city technology colleges were announced – schools equipped with the latest technology, and financed jointly by the LEAs and private enterprise. By this time plans were well in hand for a drastic revision of the long-established GCE examination, and both this certificate and the Certificate of Secondary Education (the CSE) were replaced in 1988 by the General Certificate of Secondary Education. Also in 1986 the Education Act (no. 2) reconstructed governing boards, providing for co-option from local business, for annual governors' reports to parents, and reducing the power of LEAs to appoint staff. The Act also laid down that political beliefs must be presented in school in a balanced way, while sex education must have 'due regard to moral considerations and the value of family life'.

The flood of educational innovations did not end there. Two years later, another wide-ranging Act was rushed through – the Education Act 1988 (also known as the Baker Act, after the then Secretary for Education, Kenneth Baker). Perhaps the most important part of the Act was that which set up a National Curriculum for state schools. There was to be a core of Maths, English and Science, together with History, Geography, Technology, Music, Art, Physical Education and, at secondary level, at least one foreign language. Religious education was to reflect the fact that the religious tradition in Britain was mainly Christian; as in the 1944 Butler Act, there was to be a daily act of worship. Four key stages were designated at which children were to be examined and assessed – at the ages of seven, eleven, fourteen and sixteen.

The governing and financial administration of schools also received further attention. The powers of appointment and dismissal of staff were to be transferred to the school governors – another attempt to give schools a greater degree of independence from the local authority. The most important provision in this direction, however, was the creation in the Act of a new category of school – the 'grant-maintained school', popularly known as the 'opted-out' school. These schools were in effect to be a new type of grant-aided school, since they were to be maintained directly by the Secretary of State, freed from the control of the local authority. The decision to opt out lay in the hands of the parents, and was to be decided by secret ballot. Lastly, quite apart from the National Curriculum, in 1983 pilot schemes were begun under the Technical and Vocational Education Initiative programme (TVEI). Fourteen LEAs were originally funded to the tune of £46 million by the Manpower Services Commission (MSC), the aim being to provide a greater experience of the world of work for the fourteen-to-eighteen age range. In 1986, the TVEI Extension Scheme was announced (now known simply as TVE), with further pilot schemes, while the White Paper *Working Together: Education and Training* (July 1986) proposed the extension of the scheme to *all* fourteen-to-eighteen-year-olds. As set out in a publicity state-ment of the time:

> TVEI's role is to help produce a more highly skilled, competent, effective and enterprising workforce for the 1990s. It is a bold, long-term strategy, unique among nations, for investing in the skills of ALL our young people 14–19 [*sic*] in full-time education, and equipping them for the demands of working life in a rapidly changing, highly technological society.

This statement, couched in the language of modern advertising, goes on to explain how this was to be done by improving skills and qualifications, providing work experience, enabling young people to be more effective at work through active and practical learning methods, and providing counselling, guidance and achievement records. The explanation concludes on a high note:

> The Vision
> The long-term goal is that all students leaving full-time initial education at whatever age should be equipped with the knowledge, skills and qualities needed in the workplaces of tomorrow.

All this was to be achieved not merely by some appropriate addi-tions to the curriculum, but by the inculcation of the necessary skills and outlook throughout the curriculum – TVE was to *permeate* the curriculum, not simply extend it. By the end of the 1980s, over a billion pounds was committed to TVE, not by the Department of Education and Science, but by the Manpower Services Commission (later renamed the Training Agency).

Before commenting on these remarkable developments, it should be noted that the late 1980s saw something of a crisis in the teaching profession. A dispute over pay led to a long-drawn-out struggle during which strikes took place up and down the country. Finally the long-established Burnham Committee representing teachers and LEAs was abolished as a body determining teachers' pay, being replaced by a government-appointed committee. Morale in the profession dropped with the failure of the strikes, while at the same time teachers' professionalism was constantly impugned by right-wing critics; it was openly suggested that too many teachers were simply lazy and incompetent. Tired of this denigration and of low pay, teachers began to leave the profession, and staffing problems intensified, particularly in London and the south-east, where the soaring prices of housing in 1987 and 1988 made it difficult for young teachers to find accommodation they could afford to buy. An attempt by the DES to make up the shortfall of teachers by licensing skilled men and women to learn on the job in the classroom (licensed teachers) was greeted with great hostility in the schools and by the unions. It is against this background of increasing demoralisation of the teaching profession that the educational reforms of the Thatcher era must be seen. Teachers certainly felt undervalued, yet at the same time the reforms made for more regimentation of the teaching profession, and much more bureaucracy, with teachers' hours closely defined, more in-service training (including the days in school nicknamed Baker Days), and greatly increased quantities of paper work.

How then did the working classes benefit from all the changes? Clearly, it is too early yet to reach firm conclusions, but some general observations might still be made. On the credit side, some of the earlier reforms would certainly be regarded as beneficial by most people, for example those inherited from the earlier period such as the raising of the school-leaving age and the continued development of co-education. Again, one reform not hitherto mentioned was a positive advance – the phasing out of the three-year Teachers Certificate course, and its replacement by the four-year BEd course, so that the teaching profession at last became an all-graduate profession. Then again, the drop in the school population allowed an improvement in the staff–pupil ratio in the UK from 23.2 to 1 in 1971 to 18.3 to 1 in 1987. The average size of classes in England and Wales was accordingly reduced:

	1971	1981
Primary	27.5	25.5
Secondary	22.4	21.5

The movement to comprehensive secondary schooling continued, while a smaller school population allowed a reduction in the size of the comprehensive school. In 1979/80, 32 per cent of secondary schools had over 1,000 pupils; in 1986/7, the proportion was down to 24 per cent.

Among other advances, many would place the publication of examination results, and the annual reports made by governors, since both should permit parents to have a better understanding of what goes on in school. Similarly, the management by schools of their own finances (known as LMS, or local management of schools) is arguably another gain, though clearly it added to the administrative burden of head teachers and their assistants; one head teacher of a primary school with 200 pupils in the Midlands found herself responsible for paying the wages of fifty-six members of staff and ancillary workers. As for the National Curriculum, this certainly forced teachers into a valuable rethinking of what should be taught. One practical difficulty, however, is that of covering all the ground set out in the approved syllabuses, while many teachers remain hostile to the testing and assessment of children at seven, eleven, fourteen and sixteen. There is the further major problem of integrating National Curriculum syllabuses with TVE, which itself contitutes a massive readjustment of the teaching of older children. How far this can be done so as to provide a coherent, acceptable new approach not only in subject matter but in teaching method remains to be seen.

All the same, once the possible benefits of all these changes have been reviewed, certain doubts about the whole thrust of Thatcherite reforms in schools should be registered. Many critics found it odd that the MSC or Training Agency (which is a branch of the Department of Employment) should be playing such a major role in what at first sight is none of its business. Why should

technical education suddenly figure so largely in the school curriculum, and reappear in the form of city technical colleges, not in
answer to any new educational philosophy, but simply because of
the needs of industry? Then again, LMS appeared democratic
enough, but it placed great strains on schools; and it did involve a
drastic reduction in the powers of the LEAs, who had built up a
wealth of experience and expertise in the running of schools over
the past century. Perhaps the LEAs are an inevitable casualty of
the Thatcherite emphasis on the enterprise culture, if not also the
result of central government's dislike of local government, especially when in the hands of an opposing political party. Only the
passage of time will supply the longer perspectives which permit a
fair assessment of all these changes.

Fortunately, further education will not require so lengthy a
treatment as the schools. During the period 1975 to 1980, the
number of enrolments in the further education colleges dropped
noticeably, by 182,000, as unemployment grew. Enrolments then
rose again to the year 1986–7 by 174,000. Table 7.5 provides more
detail of these changes.

Table 7.5 Further Education, 1975–87 (000s)

	1975–6	1980–1	1985–6	1986–7
Full-time and sandwich				
Males	144	154	166	174
Females	156	196	208	210
Day release				
Males	477	453	373	378
Females	257	225	316	332
Evenings only				
Males	309	244	274	287
Females	511	399	433	466
Total	1,854	1,671	1,770	1,847
Evening institutes	2,197	1,798	1,925	1,565
Other courses, e.g. WEA	434	398	468	–

Source: *Social Trends*, No. 19 (1989).

Nearly three-quarters of the increase from 1980–1 onwards was
due to additional numbers of female part-time and day-release
students, and of female evening students. Overall, as can be seen,

the numbers do not vary greatly over the whole period, though the various youth employment training schemes financed by the MSC became a feature of the further education colleges from 1983 onwards. In some industries, these schemes have replaced apprenticeship, and though they have been regarded by teenagers with a certain amount of suspicion they have led to jobs for a considerable number. For example, in 1987–8, nearly three-fifths of all YTS leavers secured full-time work; only one-fifth remained unemployed. Meanwhile, the courses provided for office and technical skills continued as before, though the Ordinary National Certificate and the Higher National Certificate work now came under a new body, the Business and Technicians Educational Council (BTech.). All in all, the further education colleges have escaped the kind of buffeting experienced by the schools, though they had to struggle with financial cuts in the early eighties. Perhaps the most striking change in the last decade was the introduction of youth training. From the working-class point of view, on the whole this has been a welcome development.

The picture presented by higher education (that is, education beyond A Levels) is somewhat different. Although the numbers of higher education students rose by 19 per cent between 1975–6 and 1986–7, this expansion was confined almost entirely to the polytechnics and colleges, which provided a cheaper form of education to degree level. University numbers stayed relatively static, though from 1981 they were subject to severe financial economies, reductions in staff and investigations of academic standards. On the one hand, opportunities for taking degrees were widened by the provision of subject degree courses in the colleges of higher education, many of them formerly colleges of education, so that the student wishing to take a degree course could choose between applying to university, polytechnic, or college (or institute) of higher education. Mature students could also consider a part-time degree with the Open University, which accounted for 22 per cent of part-time higher education students by 1986–7, and over 70,000 students in all. On the other hand, no new universities were founded in the 1980s, and the social composition of university students remained very much as before. Working-class students constituted only a fifth of the university intake in the late 1980s, as Table 7.6 illustrates. It is clear from this that the proportion of working-class entrants to university was not increasing, and was actually less than in the mid-seventies (see Chapter Four). It

Table 7.6   Home Candidates and Acceptances by Social Class (percentages), 1986–8

		Percentages of acceptances		
	Social class	1986	1987	1988
I	Professional	20.4	20.3	21.0
II	Intermediate occupations	48.2	48.0	48.1
IIIN	Skilled – non-manual	10.7	11.1	11.0
IIIM	Skilled – manual	12.5	12.9	12.5
IV	Partly skilled	6.9	6.6	6.3
V	Unskilled	1.2	1.1	1.1

Source: Statistical Supplement to the UCCA 26th Report, 1987–8.

remains to be seen whether the introduction of student loans in 1990 will exacerbate this situation. Economic factors still weigh heavily with working-class families when education beyond the school-leaving age is under consideration.

All in all, the 1980s in particular proved to be a tumultuous period for the educational system in England and Wales. In theory, the many changes should have resulted in a leaner, tauter system in the schools, more in tune with the social realities of the time, a system much more responsive to parental choice and control, and with an added element of competition. If these changes were good for the schools, it is logical to assume that they were of advantage to the working classes, whose children provided the bulk of the state school population (the better-off middle classes and upper classes still had their own system of private and privileged schooling). Again, since state education has always been an important agency for social mobility for working-class children, an improved state system (it can be argued) must be of benefit to working people. In practice, it remains to be seen how far such sweeping changes prove ultimately to be beneficial. Some critics would certainly argue that too much has been attempted in too short a time. It may well be that the first requirement if the reforms are to show their worth is for the teaching profession, battered and demoralised, to regain its self-confidence and self-respect as it shoulders the many new burdens imposed by the legislation of the 1980s.

The Family

The changes which affected the family in the earlier post-war period continued in the years after 1974, but with some interesting

251

variations. The size of the typical family with dependent children was reduced slightly from 2.0 children in 1971 to 1.8 children in 1981. Thereafter there was no further change up to and including 1987. At the same time, the number of one-person households increased from about an eighth of all households in 1961 to a quarter in 1987. The increasing number of elderly persons living alone played a part here. The number of one-person households was expected to increase from 5.3 million in 1987 to 7.1 million by the year 2001. Lone-parent families continued to grow more common as divorce rates accelerated, but more especially in the 1970s than in the 1980s. The proportion of such families went up from 8 per cent of all families to 12 per cent in 1979, then stayed fairly constant at about 13 or 14 per cent in the 1980s. It was 14 per cent in 1987. The familiar picture of the typical household consisting of a man, wife and children must be put into perspective in view of all this; such a household was really in a minority in 1987. The figures are set out in Table 7.7.

Table 7.7 Household Composition, 1987

	Percentage of households
Married couple with dependent children	28
Married, no children, or with older non-dependent children	36
Living alone	25
Lone parent	8
Two or more unrelated adults, or two or more families	4

Source: *General Household Survey* (1987).

Numbers were kept down by contraception, of course. In 1986, almost three-quarters of all women were using contraceptive methods, and as many as 81 per cent of married or cohabiting women in the age-range sixteen to forty-nine. Overall, the pill was still the most commonly used method, but its use declined with the age of the women: 55 per cent of the 20–24 age-range used it, but only 1 per cent of the 45–49-year-olds. Conversely, the condom was used increasingly with age; only 6 per cent of teenage women used it, but 15 per cent of those aged thirty and over. Among older women, sterilisation was quite common. Thus, in the 35–39 age-range, more than two-fifths had been sterilised (or their partners), and nearly half of those aged 40–44. Legal abortions continued to increase. In 1971 the number was 101,000; in 1981, 139,000; and in 1987, 166,000.

As for the institution of marriage itself, its popularity continued, though with some diminution. The figures for *first* marriages for both parties are (in thousands):

1971	1976	1981	1984	1987
369	282	263	259	260

Of *all* marriages, by the 1980s remarriages formed about a third. Divorces continued to increase in number:

	1971	1976	1981	1985	1986	1987
Petitions filed (000s)	111	145	170	191	180	183

The divorce rate actually went up more than five times between 1961 and 1985. Cohabitation became more prevalent. In 1979, about 3 per cent of women between eighteen and forty-nine were cohabiting. By 1987, the figure had increased to 6 per cent. Divorced women were more likely than others to be cohabiting, and the peak age of cohabitation for women was twenty to twenty-four, of whom 13 per cent in 1987 were cohabiting. Births outside marriage were also increasing, from 6 per cent in 1961 to 12 per cent in 1981, and then (a remarkable increase) to 25.6 per cent in 1988. Thus about a quarter of all children born at the end of the eighties were born out of wedlock.

So much for the bare statistics: at a first glance it would appear that the conventional marriage with its traditional restraints was increasingly rejected in the seventies and eighties, when there were more divorce, more single-parent families, more cohabitation, more abortion, more illegitimacy and more sexual activity among teenagers: in 1986, more than a quarter of 16–17-year-old girls were using contraceptives, and a half of 18–19-year-old girls. Yet in the 1980s there were, if anything, more censorious views expressed on sexual relationships than before, even though in 1986 the UK had both the highest marriage rate and the highest divorce rate in the European Community. A survey printed in *Social Trends*, 1989, showed that in spite of the fact that a certain degree of premarital sex might be tolerated, extramarital sex was condemned by a large majority, and so were homosexual practices. The figures are provided in Table 7.8.

Table 7.8   Attitudes to Sexual Relationships

	1983	1985	1987
Percentage thinking *premarital sex*			
Always/mostly wrong	28	23	25
Sometimes wrong	17	19	21
Rarely/not wrong at all	50	52	50
Percentage thinking *extramarital sex*			
Always/mostly wrong	83	82	88
Sometimes wrong	11	11	9
Rarely wrong/not wrong at all	3	3	1
Percentage thinking *homosexual relations*			
Always/mostly wrong	62	69	74
Sometimes wrong	8	7	8
Rarely wrong/not wrong at all	21	16	13

Source: *Social Trends*, No. 19 (1989).

So much for the parade of virtuous attitudes: one wonders, in particular, whether the attitudes expressed to extramarital sex were always maintained in practice. Attitudes to homosexual practices are interesting, considering that adult homosexual relations have been legal since 1967. In all probability, attitudes of distaste have grown stronger with the advent of AIDS. Another survey in 1987 showed a remarkable amount of hostility (probably dictated by fear) towards AIDS sufferers. As many as 38 per cent thought that employers should definitely or probably have a legal right to dismiss employees with AIDS: 31 per cent thought doctors and nurses should definitely or probably have a right to refuse treatment; while 24 per cent thought schools should definitely or probably have the right to expel AIDS children.

To return to the working-class family: life in the working-class family continued to evolve between 1975 and 1990 in the direction of a looser and more impermanent institution. As we have seen, more marriages broke up than before, more children were brought up mainly by a single parent, or found themselves with a new step-parent, more children were born illegitimate. As for the working-class mother, she continued to have more control over her own life as a result of better contraception, but she could be affected adversely by two major developments. One was the severe rise in unemployment, which presented new challenges in managing the family budget if her spouse should fall out of work. The other was the increase in employment among married women (though often part-time in nature). In 1990 for the first time married women were assessed for income tax purposes separately from their husbands. As noted earlier, when a married woman went out to work, there resulted a welcome increase in family income. On the other hand, in spite of equal pay, women still earned on average only two-thirds of men's pay. Frequently, only part-time work was available because this gave employers a more flexible work force. Lastly, taking a job, whether full-time or part-time, usually brought the married woman little relief from household chores. She was still expected to take the major responsibility for them.

A fascinating analysis of the household division of labour published in 1985 makes it clear that men played little part in household work, nearly three-quarters of the married women surveyed claiming that they did all or most of the housework. The details are provided in Table 7.9.

Table 7.9   Domestic Duties, 1985

Household tasks	Allocation of tasks (percentages)		
	Mainly men	Mainly women	Shared equally
Washing and ironing	1	89	10
Preparing evening meal	5	77	17
Household cleaning	3	72	24
Household shopping	5	51	44
Evening dishes	17	40	40
Organising household money and bills	29	39	32
Repairs of household equipment	82	8	10

Source: *Social Trends*, No. 15 (1985).

A further survey in 1987 published in *Social Trends*, 1989, confirmed the earlier findings, but with reference to how far domestic duties were shared when the woman worked full-time or part-time (see Table 7.10). It is clear that the age-old tradition that women do

Table 7.10 Domestic Duties, 1987

	Respondents in households where		
	Man works, woman works full-time (%)	Man works, woman works part-time (%)	Man works, woman does not work (%)
Mainly women	72	88	91
Shared equally	22	7	5

Source: *Social Trends*, No. 19 (1989).

the work in the home still persists, even when the woman works full-time outside the home, and markedly so when working part-time. As *Social Trends* remarks somewhat tersely, women with part-time jobs may have the worst of both worlds; and the number of such women was increasing in 1990. Andy Capp, it appears, was still alive and well.

It would be wrong to end this section on too negative a note: the position of women at work had certainly improved. Though this was probably seen at best among professional or entrepreneurial middle-class women, equal pay, maternity leave, the outlawing of sexual discrimination and sexual harassment, the increasing numbers of women in trade unions, all made for better conditions at work in the 1980s. Nevertheless, many women, especially of the older generation, still worked part-time in unskilled jobs at low wage rates, and were still regarded by many men as naturally inferior in the workplace; at home their place was still in the kitchen, while the men put their feet up and watched TV.

Race Relations

What was said earlier about the family relates very largely, of course, to the indigenous white population. They formed the vast majority of the working people of this country. Yet an important minority of workers had different ethnic origins. Since the 1950s and 1960s, immigration had been severely restricted, but by the mid-eighties about one and a half million of the population of working age (4.6 per cent) were in ethnic minority groups. Of these, 484,000 were of Indian origin, 278,000 Pakistani or Bangladeshi, 378,000 West Indian or Guyanese, and the rest of mixed Chinese, African or Arab origins. West Indian women were prominent among the employed – overall, 73 per cent of them were employed; Indian or Pakistani women less so – overall, only 18 per cent, mostly under twenty-four. As for the nature of their employment, 27 per cent of the males worked in hotels and catering – the proportion of Pakistani and Bangladeshi was especially high in this sector – while 20 per cent of Indian men worked in retail distribution. Males were also represented in transport and communications, the health service and some manufacturing industries. Females were more likely than their white counterparts to be in the health service and manufacturing (a quarter of West Indian women were in health), while Asian women were found more in distribution, hotels and catering. Over half of all racial communities lived in the south-east region, including two-thirds of West Indians, just over half of Indians and over a third of all Pakistanis and Bangladeshi. About 14 per cent of the labour force in Greater London and 10 per cent in the West Midlands came from ethnic minorities. During the years of greatest unemployment in the first half of the eighties, their rate of unemployment was twice that of white workers. It was still 19 per cent compared with 11 per cent over the years 1985 to 1987.

This raises once more the vexed question of racial prejudice. A survey in 1985 produced remarkably unanimous answers on this subject; 90 per cent of those questioned said there *was* prejudice against Asians and blacks, the majority affirming there was 'a lot of prejudice'. Nearly two-thirds said that coloured workers were denied jobs because of their race. Over a third described themselves as more or less prejudiced (4 per cent 'very', 31 per cent 'a little'). Those admitting prejudice were more likely to be under fifty-five, to be male, to be non-manual workers, and to be English, rather than Welsh or Scottish. Given this degree of prejudice, it is surprising that more race riots did not occur in the 1970s; but in 1980 a severe riot took place in the St Paul's district of Bristol, the result of a police attempt to arrest some coloured suspects in a café. In 1981 there were serious riots in Brixton, Toxteth (Liverpool), Handsworth (Birmingham), Southall in west London, and Preston. Although these disturbances took place in areas where there was a heavy local concentration of ethnic minorities, large numbers of white youths joined in the attacks on the police, on motor cars and on shops, which were looted. In three nights of rioting in Brixton, 149 police were taken to hospital, and 224 rioters were arrested. In 1985, a violent riot erupted on the Broadwater Farm estate in Tottenham, north

London. There was some evidence of firearms being used by the rioters, who were again a mixture of coloured and white youths employing the more customary bricks, stones, paving slabs, bottles, sticks and petrol bombs. A policeman, PC Keith Blakelock, was murdered by the crowd, and it appeared that attempts were made to behead him. In all, 243 policemen were injured.

It hardly needs to be said that the vast majority of the coloured population were entirely law-abiding, and opposed to violence of any kind. However, it is true that over the years hostility towards the police among the young of ethnic minorities probably increased, and for a number of reasons, principally suspicion of racial discrimination and a dislike of the police as a symbol of white authority. Rising unemployment, a poor standard of living and a bleak urban environment also made their contribution; but these factors affected white city dwellers, too, and once racial conflict gives rise to violence, anyone can join in. Fortunately the racial riots of 1981 and 1985 were not repeated during the rest of the eighties, and great efforts were made to prevent their repetition through the improvement of community relations and the adoption of more sensitive policing. Nevertheless, although relations in the workplace remained reasonably tolerant, an important element of the work force in 1990 lived in their own communities; in particular, the Asiatics have their own distinctive culture, many of them being Muslims. By 1990 there was a growing demand for separate, local authority Muslim schools, just as there were separate Church of England and Roman Catholic schools. The publication of a novel, *The Satanic Verses*, by Salman Rushdie in 1989 caused great offence among Muslims, who claimed it was a blasphemous attack on their religion, and called for the assassination of the author, who had to go into hiding. Clearly there were still problems in maintaining peaceful coexistence at the end of the eighties between communities of different ethnic origins in Britain. Racial antagonism still existed, encouraged by extreme right-wing political groups, but it was seldom openly expressed in public, save in the form of racial abuse by spectators at football matches, along with routine obscenities.

Crime and the Working Classes

During the period 1975 to 1990, the trends in crime noted in the earlier chapter continued as before. In the 1980s the police were supported strongly by the Conservative governments of the time, who emphasised their commitment to law and order. Police forces were expanded and pay increased. At the same time, the duties of the police became more onerous, both in the keeping of public order and in seeking to prevent crime and catch villains. While keeping public order, not only had they to deal with the race riots mentioned in the previous section, but they also had to control unruly football crowds, supervise pop concerts, maintain order on picket lines and occasionally disperse urban disorders which developed suddenly for no very apparent reason, such as the poll-tax riot in central London on 31 March 1990 in which 431 were arrested and over 400 injured. As for the incidence of crime, new methods of counting were introduced in the 1980s, so that quite apart from the uncertainties previously mentioned in the reporting of crimes by the public, it is impossible to make specific comparisons throughout the period. Generally speaking, however, recorded crime continued to rise by about 5 per cent per year in the 1980s. Towards the end of the decade, there was some variation in this figure: in 1988, the total actually dropped by 4 per cent, the first big drop since the 1950s, but in 1989 the total rose disappointingly again by another 4 per cent. The Home Office claimed that an important part of this increase was due to the improved reporting of crime, especially of rape, child abuse and domestic violence.

In fact, there was a clear statistical increase in some crimes in 1989. Violent offences against the person rose by 12 per cent, rapes by 16 per cent, and vehicle thefts by 7 per cent; but burglaries dropped by 1 per cent and muggings by 14 per cent. Once more, the figures may be interpreted in different ways. For example, as noted above, according to the Home Office the apparent steep rise in sexual crime is explainable by the fact that victims had become more willing to report the crime. Further, to put the 1989 figures into perspective, it should be pointed out that the total number of crimes recorded was still less than the total for 1986, that violent crime acounted for only 4.3 per cent of the total, and that a woman in London ran only a million to 1.5 million chance of becoming a rape victim. There was accordingly a certain amount of unnecessary fear of being attacked in the streets.

As in the previous chapter, it must be said that the majority of the working classes had little contact with the police in the seventies and eighties, except perhaps for motoring offences, drink and disorderly charges, and domestic offences. Their knowledge of the police was limited to what they saw in the news on television, to the numerous TV cops and robbers series, and to *Crime Watch* programmes, which invited the viewers to help solve actual crimes. They might or might not join Neighbourhood Watch schemes, though these seem to have gained most support in middle-class residential areas. As for that proportion of the working classes who were themselves members of the criminal classes, they lived in a world apart, with values not generally shared by the rest of the working-class community. Fortunately it is not the business of this book to discuss the roots, genetic, environmental or otherwise, of criminal behaviour.

Leisure

Earlier patterns of leisure activities were continued after 1974, though for some the leisure was involuntary, and the result of unemployment. For those in work, the holiday entitlement was further increased. In 1961, the vast majority of manual workers had only two weeks' annual holiday. By 1987, this had doubled to more than four weeks, and those taking two or more holidays away from home increased from one in seven in 1971 to one in five in 1987; but there were still about four in ten adults in 1987 who stayed at home during their holidays. Of those going abroad, about a third went to Spain. The total of holidays taken abroad trebled between 1976 and 1987, reaching twenty million.

At home, watching TV was still the favourite activity. In 1987 the average time spent weekly watching television was 25.5 hours – a noticeable increase over the 1973 figure; people over sixty-five watched 37.5 hours, while those under fifteen viewed for about nineteen hours. By 1990, there was a fourth channel (Channel 4), and satellite TV provided by Sky Television. Radio was still more popular than TV before 1 p.m.; between 8 a.m. and 8.30 a.m., about 14 per cent in the UK listened to radio in the first quarter of 1988. In the evening, of course, it was different. Between 9 p.m. and 9.30 p.m., 41.7 per cent watched TV. Other indoor activities now included listening to tapes or records (69 per cent of men, 65 per cent of women), carrying out house repairs or DIY jobs, reading books, and gardening. Women were more likely to read books than men. The *Sun* was the most popular newspaper in 1987 with a readership of 11.3 million. Its circulation rose by 33 per cent between 1971 and 1987, aided no doubt by its policy of presenting large pictures of bare-breasted beauties on Page Three. The circulation of the *Daily Mirror* fell by 34 per cent in the same period. On Sundays, the *News of the World* continued to be the most popular paper with a readership of 12.8 million. The *Sunday Mirror* was also popular, with a circulation of 9.1 million. Of the general magazines, the *TV Times* had the top circulation in 1988 of 9.1 million, with the *Radio Times* close behind at 9.0 million. The two most popular women's magazines in 1987 were *Woman's Own* (4.8 million readers) and *Woman* (3.6 million readers).

Outside the home, going out for a drink was still a favourite activity with men (men, 65 per cent; women, 47 per cent), while cinema-going experienced something of a revival, in spite of an overall fall in cinema admissions from 1,181 million in 1955 to 75 million in 1987. This last figure represented a 29 per cent increase on the lowest figure recorded of 58 million in 1984. Going out for a meal also continued to be popular, second only in popularity to going for a drink (47 per cent of men, 47 per cent of women). The number of public houses opening their own restaurants and also providing bar meals increased further, while Chinese and Indian restaurants continued to flourish, as did the American chain of hamburger joints, McDonalds. Visiting out-of-town eating places usually required personal transport, as did trips to historic buildings and sites, which were becoming more popular. Car ownership still increased, but as mentioned earlier in this chapter the rate of increase slowed down in the eighties: 66 per cent of households had cars in 1988. Among households with the lowest incomes, in 1985–6 only 25 per cent had cars. Of households of unskilled, manual workers, the figure was 38 per cent with cars. As for participation in sports, walking (including rambling and hiking) was the most popular activity, followed by swimming and snooker (including billiards and pool). Next in popularity was darts, then keep-fit and golf. Other activities (and of equal popularity) were fishing, football, squash, cycling and tennis.

Spectator sports continued to attract the crowds, but sometimes on a reduced level. Attendance at football league matches fell by over 36 per cent between 1971 and 1987 (nearly all between 1971 and 1982). Spectators with young families tended to be put off by the increase in football crowds of hooliganism, drunkenness, fighting, swearing and the abuse of players. Unemployment may also have reduced the numbers attending. Attendance figures for the main spectator sports are set out in Table 7.11. The increased

Table 7.11   Attendance at Sporting Events (000s)

	1971	1982	1987
Football League (England and Wales)	28,704	18,766	18,273
Greyhound racing	8,800	5,300	4,800
Horse racing	4,200	3,700	4,349
Motorcycle sports			
(excluding speedway)		3,000	3,750
Motor sports		4,000	4,050
Rugby football			
League	1,170	1,668	1,380
Union	700	750	2,500
Test and country cricket	984	782	713

Source: *Social Trends*, No. 19 (1989).

attendance at Rugby Union football is striking, due possibly to the greater popularity of rugby on TV, the decline in attendance at association football matches, and the organising of clubs into leagues.

One specialised form of leisure activity different from all the rest was membership of a church or other religious denomination. Membership of trinitarian churches, both Protestant and Roman Catholic, in 1987 amounted to 6.9 million (15 per cent of the adult population), but fell by over a million between 1975 and 1987. Membership of non-trinitarian churches, on the other hand – Mormons, Jehovah's Witnesses, Spiritualists and others – amounted to 418,000, and had gone up by 26 per cent since 1975. Other religions, including Muslims, Sikhs, Hindus, Jews and others, showed the greatest increase, nearly doubling their membership from 814,000 in 1975 to 1.57 million in 1987. By 1988, church attenders were roughly one in eight, or 12 per cent. All in all, the long-term decline in membership of the leading Christian churches continued, though the smaller, non-trinitarian churches were more than holding their own. Adult conversion, popular in the United States in the form of the born-again Christian, had some effect here; and virtually all churches, in addition to their Sunday services, provided weekday social meetings as before. On the whole, the urban working classes continued to be attracted as previously to the nonconformist and Roman Catholic churches rather than to the predominantly middle-class Church of England, sometimes described somewhat unfairly as the Conservative Party at prayer, since in the 1980s its social comments in such publications as *Faith in the Inner City* (1984) drew sharp criticism from some members of the Conservative government.

Something must be said of the remaining leisure activities. For the young, pop music continued its fascination, and it could now be heard not only on large stereo radios ('ghetto-blasters') but also on earphones combined with small, portable tape or disc players ('the Walkman') at home, on trains or merely when walking the streets. Discotheques were still well attended. For children and teenagers, skate-boards had a brief popularity, and for older youths roller skates returned to fashion for a while. Greater attention to health needs brought a rash of health centres, an increase in keep-fit, aerobics and yoga classes, and, even among the middle-aged, a craze for jogging round suburban streets. Mass marathon runs also became popular, with the runners often sponsored for charity, and so did national charity fund-raising stunts (such as Comic Relief) for aid to Third World countries. It should be noted, too, that the revival of interest in the cinema mentioned earlier found a particular response among the young: a survey in 1986 showed that about a quarter of the sixteen-to-nineteen age-range went to the pictures in the four weeks before interview (28 per cent of the women, 24 per cent of the men).

Clearly, working-class leisure activities in the seventies and eighties were shaped very largely by the patterns established in the previous, post-war decades. They did not exhibit any marked divergences from earlier activities – the pub and working man's club were still important, and so were weekend sport, the TV at home, trips in the family car and the holiday abroad. For the great majority in work, leisure pursuits continued as before. For the out-of-work, especially the long-term unemployed, there was obviously too much leisure and little money available to spend on it.

Darkening Horizons

How far has the rather sombre title of this and the preceding chapter been justified? A fuller description of the significance of the period 1974–90 in the social history of the English working classes awaits the reader in the next chapter; but it seems fitting to close this survey of these years by emphasising some of their more prominent features. The most important of these was probably the downswing in the economy and its consequences, for both the employed and the unemployed. For the former, the standard of living showed only minor improvements; in some years, it actually declined. For the latter, unemployment reappeared in its former guise as a social blight affecting millions; and to the unemployed seeking to make ends meet on social security benefit, there were added millions of the new poor on low wages, or as single-parent families, the elderly, sick and disabled. Since work was no longer so readily available as in the sixties, the trade unions lost their predominance in industrial relations, and the legislation of the eighties further reduced union influence and power. There were no very striking advances in health, public housing or higher education for the working classes.

Of course, it is necessary to keep a sense of perspective: for those who stayed in work throughout, life could still be tolerable enough. For them, there was no long-term fall in living standards, many owned their homes for the first time, leisure-time increased, and, as already pointed out, the customary visits to the pub, the occasional meal out and holidays abroad continued as before. Nevertheless, for a sizeable minority it was otherwise. If the labels 'The Affluent Society' and 'The Permissive Society' are still acceptable as useful descriptions of aspects of society in the fifties and sixties, then undoubtedly something more downbeat must be applied to the kind of society which emerged in the eighties. Moreover, as social attitudes and values changed, so did public perceptions of the working classes change, as will be seen in the next and concluding chapter. For the present, it is enough to suggest that the late seventies and eighties saw the dawn of a distinctly post-Beveridge era, when indeed it appeared at times that it was back to the thirties and worse, and that there would never be glad confident morning again. If this is so, there is some justification from the working-class point of view, at least, to speak of 'darkening horizons'.

Chapter 8

Rise and Decline: An Interpretation

The Rise

In this chapter it is proposed to reconsider the evidence set out in the preceding chapters as it relates, firstly, to the *rise* of the working classes in England between 1918 and the mid-1970s, and then, secondly, to their *decline* from then on until 1990. There is no abrupt dividing line, of course, in the mid-1970s, and factors relating to both 'rise' and 'decline' are to be found in both the earlier and the later periods. But it will be argued that on the whole, there was a rise up to the seventies, and a decline thereafter. So far as the 'rise' is concerned, surely there can be little dispute. In 1918 the working classes consisted of a great mass of mostly manual workers employed very largely in the manufacturing industries on which England's greatness as an industrial nation in Victorian times had rested. Their working conditions were still harsh, and working hours were still relatively long, though somewhat reduced in 1919 and 1920. They were certainly not well housed, and the worst slum areas in both London and the industrial towns were notorious. Compulsory education for all up to the age of fourteen had only recently been established, and there was really no state system of secondary education for other than a small minority of the working classes. Welfare services were very limited: most (but not all) working men were compulsorily insured against ill-health (but not their families), and only a small number in a limited range of trades were insured against unemployment. Women had gained a temporary measure of increased economic freedom during the Great War, only to return to domestic life *en masse* when the men came back from the trenches. Divorce was beyond the reach of the vast majority of working-class women, abortion was illegal and contraceptive methods were primitive and unreliable. Politically, no woman had a vote for Parliament before 1918, and even then, the 1918 Act gave the vote only to certain women of twenty-eight and over (the same Act at last gave the franchise to the one-third of adult men still without votes). The trade unions were increasing in power, but the Labour Party was of only recent origin, and had yet to form a government. Working people in public were usually easily recognisable by their dress, even when in their Sunday best. Working-class manners in public could also be somewhat unrefined: there was a good deal of hawking and spitting on pavements, and elsewhere (Child's question: 'What is the ship canal for, Dad?' Answer: 'To spit in').

Is there any doubt that there was a very great improvement in the material condition of the English working classes between 1918 and the 1970s? Of course, many suffered from unemployment between the wars, but its extent and persistence did result in a great extension of the previous meagre provision for assistance to the unemployed; and, for the majority who stayed in work, the standard of living went up, and the entertainment industry boomed with the growth of the cinema and the new home entertainment, the wireless. There was a great improvement in the public provision of housing. The Second World War brought hardship in many forms, especially for those in the armed forces, and to civilians subjected to air raids, but at the same time it brought the forming of plans for the welfare state, with its aim of social security for all. If the people of England did indeed rise during the Second World War, as A. J. P. Taylor has so memorably observed, then new heights were reached during the post-war Labour governments, 1945–51, when the welfare state came into being. Curiously enough, it was a time of shortages and considerable economic difficulties; yet it was also a time of hope, of belief in a new future for a more united nation, and a lessening of the gap between the haves and have-nots which had been so painfully apparent between the wars. Naturally enough, there were mistakes and shortcomings, but it could still be argued that the immediate post-war period was indeed Labour's finest hour, a triumph based on an unprecedented degree of class co-operation, forged during six years of total war. A dictatorship of the proletariat it certainly was not (attention has already been drawn to the middle-class nature of Attlee's administrations); and the welfare legislation of the Labour governments was not without blemish or lacking in critics. Yet the reforms of Conservative policy carried out by Butler and his supporters are themselves a testimony to the example set by the Labour Party.

The result was that during the fifties and the sixties there was continued all-party agreement on the need for the welfare state, and a good deal of national pride in its achievements. In fact, this is the period of consensus (only later to become a dirty word under Thatcher), though there was some concern even then at the increasing cost of the social services. The continuance of full employment set the tone of these two decades of affluence. At the root of it all was a confidence bred of everyone's having a job to go to. Young persons especially of the middle classes could decide to take a year off, travel round the world and still find employment when they returned; jobs were plentiful. If by any chance there was no work immediately available, then social security would help out until a job appeared. The one jarring element was the occasional warning by social investigators that real poverty and social distress still existed, a fact brought home from time to time to the general public not so much by sociological surveys as by such heartrending television programmes as *Cathy Come Home* (1967) on the plight of young unmarried mothers.

The emphasis so far has been very much on the improvement in economic conditions, together with the safety net provided by welfare services for the unemployed. The result of the improved economic scene was an unprecedented doubling of the standard of living of the working classes, manifesting itself in increased real wages, and in better housing, better health, more education, more consumer durables and better furnishing generally, more cars and longer holidays, especially abroad. Much of this is highly materialistic in nature, and it is right to emphasise it; for masses of ordinary men and women hitherto used to rubbing along at not much more than subsistence level, an increased standard of comfort was a real advance in the quality of life. Yet there was more to it than this: there was also a significant increase in individual liberty. Partly this was the result of security of employment, and of being able to change one job for another; but partly, too, it was a consequence of the permissiveness of the sixties. Generalisations about

267

the 'spirit of the age' are always dangerous for the historian; but the permissive society was a reality, and the greater sexual freedom, the mini-skirt, the political satire on TV, the new emphasis on consultation and discussion, the demos, the sit-ins, the teach-ins, all contributed to a unique social atmosphere. Women, in particular, benefited from equal pay, more jobs, better contraception and legal abortion (all of twenty-one and over had gained the vote in 1928, and the voting age was lowered to eighteen in 1969). Some aspects of permissiveness, of course, were merely trivial, and some of it, as we have seen, was of more interest to the earnest, *Guardian*-reading middle classes than the working classes, but it all contributed to a heady mixture which suggested that society was developing in new directions. The old gods were dead; new gods were arising.

Unfortunately, this was not entirely true. Old demons were to reappear later, in particular the demon of unemployment. However, before the oil crisis and economic dislocation of the mid-1970s, the combination of job security and welfare services, allied with the confident and cheerfully irreverent outlook of the permissive society, seemed to indicate the dawning of a new age for the working classes. Plainly, life was getting better, in both the material and non-material senses. Perhaps only the unreconstructed Marxist would quibble with the notion of the 'rise' of the working classes interpreted in this way. He might be inclined to claim that the improvement in material standards had seduced too many working men and women into bourgeois ways, to the neglect of participation in the class struggle and the overthrow of the bourgeoisie. In his view, they had become corrupted by the false values of the middle classes, and by the hegemonic control by the middle classes of the cultural agencies of capitalist society. Yet even he would have to admit that in the political sphere the Labour Party, in spite of its unfortunate class-collaborationist nature, had become a national party, which had formed six governments between 1918 and 1974. Further, the trade union movement had manifestly increased greatly in size and influence, being strong enough in effect to topple the Conservative government in 1974. So that even in the narrower sphere of political influence the working classes again appear to have risen, and to have played a greater part in the direction of national affairs.

Finally, a simple comparison of the appearance of working people in 1918 and fifty years later points up the changes which took place over the half-century. In the early twenties, malnutrition was still to be encountered among the working classes, tuberculosis was still rife, and rickets common enough among the children. The improvement in vital statistics of the time tells its own story, and so do the photographs of young and old alike. By the 1970s they are noticeably heavier and better fed, as well as better dressed. Teeth, which nationally had always been badly neglected, were much improved; between the wars, it was common enough for people in their forties (or even earlier) to have all their teeth extracted and be fitted with false teeth – a practice virtually abandoned since the Second World War. By the seventies, people washed a good deal more; more hot water was available in the home, and, in addition to the provision of a bathroom, showers become a popular home-fitting. Women showed the way with personal deodorants, to be followed by the use of similar aids to personal freshness by men, sometimes including pungent after-shave lotions. The use of such toiletries by men had earlier been regarded as showing signs of effeminacy. The result of all this was a considerable gain in personal cleanliness. People simply smelt less, at least of perspiration (or of Body Odour, BO, as the pioneering advertisements for Lifebuoy Soap put it). There do not seem to be any statistics illustrating the improvements in personal cleanliness since 1918, though in 1990 the Archbishop of Canterbury, Dr Runcie, commenting unfavourably on the unsatisfactory conditions in English prisons, remarked on the fact that convicts had to go a whole week without changing their underwear, and were limited to only one shower a week. In 1918 this would have been regarded as entirely normal among working-class people. Clearly the conventions in these matters had changed since the First World War.

The Decline: Some Basic Considerations

The decline is rather more difficult to define and assess. It hardly needs to be said that it is not simply a matter of numbers, although admittedly there was a marked decrease in the numbers in manufacturing industry, while many of those in the expanding service sector were not so readily identifiable as working class. In this elementary sense, there was certainly a numerical decline in the industrial working classes as they were constituted in 1918. Indeed, manual workers, skilled or otherwise, declined as a percentage of all occupational classes from 78.3 per cent in 1921 to 56.6 per cent in 1981. However, in 1990 a large section of the nation was still there, of course, recognisable as working class in nature, whether skilled, semi-skilled or unskilled manual workers; but this is not really the point at issue. The question is, how far had the characteristics of this section of the population undergone significant change by 1990, and change of a kind which merits the word 'decline', with its implications of change for the worse. In fact, certain indicators of change can be detected even before the mid-1970s, and indeed attracted comment by social scientists at the time. These will be given preliminary consideration before proceeding to the central issues.

The first is the very obvious change in lifestyle adopted by the more prosperous working classes. In many cases their income had become comparable with lower-middle-class incomes, such as those of clerical workers, and in some cases exceeded them. The result was the apparent adoption of a more middle-class way of life – a household well stocked with consumer durables, owner-occupancy of the house, and a car on the drive outside. Sociologists have referred here to the *homogenisation* of incomes and living standards of skilled workers and white-collar workers. Further, it has been argued that there was even an adoption of middle-class cultural outlooks and practices in modes of speech, dress, eating habits, entertainment and so on (though this part of the argument is rather more doubtful). Again, in those workplaces where there had been technological advances, work had become less labour-intensive and more technical, requiring more team work and co-operation, so that class differences became less marked as between manager or supervisor and the shop-floor worker. Away from work, the movement of workers away from the old central urban areas into new suburbs has meant the weakening and indeed break-up of the old solidly working-class communities.

All this, of course, amounts to the by no means novel idea of the *embourgeoisement* of the working classes – the idea that some of the most highly paid have really become middle class in their way of life. However, while it may readily be conceded that in the 1960s some skilled workers gained a much better standard of living, fully comparable with that of many white-collar workers, there are obviously a number of weaknesses in the embourgeoisement argument as a whole. From both the common-sense and the more theoretical Marxist standpoint, the basic relationship at work remained unchanged – the worker still had only his labour to sell, had no ownership of the means of production and, put simply, was still obviously in a subordinate position. Moreover, white-collar workers and manual workers were still treated very differently at the workplace. So far as lifestyle is concerned, although it is a matter of observation that some working-class housing, furnishing, and general way of life were very similar to those of the lower middle class, there is little evidence of aspiring workers adopting middle-class social habits such as regular dinner parties, or an active participation in club and society activities. It might also be observed that there is no evidence at all for the sixties and seventies of any new mass membership by the working classes of what had hitherto been middle-class tennis clubs, bridge clubs, golf clubs and the like. Plainly, the idea is absurd. Of course, this is not to say that individual workers could not achieve a degree of social mobility as they had always done in the past. A survey in 1972 showed that 16 per cent of the middle-class men interviewed admitted to working-class origins. This is by no means surprising. There has always been movement from the working classes into the middle classes, and even in Victorian times there might be little difference in appearance between representatives of the skilled working classes and of the lower middle classes. John Burns' famous description of skilled workers at the TUC in 1890, already quoted in the Prologue, again comes to mind. The older unionists, according to Burns, looked like respectable city gentlemen, with their very good coats, large watch chains and top hats, being (as he put it) of aldermanic, not to say magisterial form and dignity. Burns himself, who went to work at ten and became an engineering apprentice at fourteen, was to become President of the Local Government Board, then President of the Board of Trade just before the Great War. Thus there was nothing new about upward social mobility among the working classes after the Second World War. It might even have increased. In a survey made in 1983, 23.6 per cent of men questioned gave their social origins as working class (compare the 16 per cent in 1972 mentioned above), while in 1984 29 per cent of a national sample thought themselves in a higher social class than their parents.

Nevertheless, although by the mid-seventies the working classes were less of the homogeneous mass they had been earlier, there is really not much of a case to be made for embourgeoisement. True, the old cloth cap and muffler (and shawl and clogs) image had gone, and also the proportion of unskilled manual workers engaged in manufacturing of the old type had greatly diminished. What had happened was that the public image of the working classes had become much less monolithic, much less set in stone by the workings of the class system; but much still remained of the old class-separateness. Working-class men and women on the whole were sufficiently aware of their class identity, though perhaps it was of less importance to them than before. They continued to regard middle-class ways with some suspicion – middle-class people were often thought snobbish and too concerned with keeping up appearances, altogether too la-di-dah and toffee-nosed. Trade unionism was still strong, and still grounded largely in 'them and us' attitudes. Perhaps the most that can be allowed to bourgeoisification theories relating to affluent workers is that they reveal what Goldthorpe *et al.* have called *convergence* – a weakening of the traditional collectivism of manual workers, together with an increase of 'family-centredness' (though one might remark that this has always been strong in working-class families); and at the same time there has been a weakening of the traditional individualism among non-manual employees and a stronger move among them towards trade union collective action. So the divisions between the upper working classes and the lower middle classes were weakened further during the prosperity of the sixties and seventies, but without any merging of identity.

To move on: after the mid-seventies, more important changes began to appear which had more serious repercussions for the working classes. The most important, of course, was mass unemployment. If full employment had implications for the welfare and self-esteem of the working classes, the large-scale unemployment had consequences no less profound. Not only did it result in the reappearance of long-term unemployment, to the creation of far more part-time jobs, to a drastic slowing up in the improvement in the standard of living, but it meant also a division between those who remained in work and those who were either out of work or in low-paid jobs requiring income support or family credit. This division was deepened by the large number of married women going out to work. As noted previously, married women earners were more likely to be found in families where their spouses were working than where the husband was unemployed. So a wider income gap has opened up between those families in work and those dependent on benefit. This in turn brings the prospect of a deepening fissure in working-class society: on the one hand, those still earning and reasonably prosperous, and on the other hand, a depressed minority, consisting of the unemployed, the low-paid, the sick, the old, one-parent families and the unemployed ethnic minorities (whose prospects of obtaining work, it will be recalled, are less favourable than for the white unemployed). Professor Halsey has described this division in terms of a new version of Disraeli's two nations (the rich and the poor), a kind of social polarisation. Others have described it as the development of a new underclass, comprising all those unfortunates mostly on benefit and not in receipt of a regular and sufficient income from employment.

A further dimension has been added perhaps to this division in the working classes by the efforts of the Conservative Prime Minister, Mrs Thatcher, to spread the new Conservatism with its emphasis on the so-called enterprise culture. Home ownership has been greatly encouraged – hence the sale of council houses at discount prices in the 1980s. Hence also the encouragement of the ownership of shares, especially in the newly privatised industries of gas, water and electricity; the first issues of shares in these industries were very heavily publicised. In 1987, 25 per cent of all men owned shares: among skilled manual workers, the figure was 17 per cent, among the semi-skilled 13 per cent, and among the unskilled, 9 per cent. In the second half of the eighties, a new figure emerged in the business world, the YUPPIE – the young, upwardly mobile professional person, a thrusting commercial figure, intent on profit-making, life in the fast lane and (appropriately) the ownership of a Porsche sports car. Financial deals in the City, the reorganised Stock Exchange in London, wheeling and dealing conducted with the aid of visual display units and personal telephones (sometimes in-car), all became familiar sights on the domestic TV screen. The more conservative and older generations were surprised to hear that in these financial circles, at least, 'greed is good'. A member of the Glasgow University Business School wrote to *The Times* in early 1990, assuring its readers that telling lies in business (short of actually breaking the law) was quite normal, and indeed right and proper:

> Competitive commerce is not a game of cricket. An entrepreneur who baulks at misleading some jack in office, with no legal comeback, is clearly derelict in his duty ... If

the Fayeds [proprietors of Harrods] lied to the Department of Trade and Industry, breaking no law, this must be judged as the normal and proper behaviour of competent and responsible entrepreneurs. The wrath which has been directed at them would be better targeted at the officials who were so incompetent as to be duped.

This was the spirit of the New Age of Thatcherism, very different from the flower-power and the 'let it all hang out' philosophies of the permissive society.

All this made the aims of traditional socialist thinking seem to some to be increasingly naive, unrealistic and remote from the real world. The trade union movement had already lost authority as a result of the persistence of unemployment and the anti-trade union legislation of the Thatcher governments. The unions had also suffered damaging defeats at the hands of the employers in the miners' strike and in *The Times* dispute at Wapping. Some unions sought to adjust to changing circumstances by developing a kind of market-based trade unionism – in other words, a willingness to bargain with employers for the best deal they could make, offering no-strike agreements, an acceptance of arbitration and the single-union shop. A leader in this respect was the Electrical, Electronic, Telecommunication and Plumbing Union (EETPU), its secretary being the sober-suited and business-like Eric Hammond. Such policies caused great offence to more conservative trade unionists, and at one time EETPU was expelled from the TUC. Nevertheless, this new-look trade unionism was at least an attempt to face up to the new conditions in industry, and to move away from confrontational tactics which had far less hope of success by the nineties than in the balmy days of the sixties and seventies.

What of the Labour Party in these changed circumstances? We have already seen how it sought to adjust to a world which had changed greatly since it was last in power, eleven years before. Its new policies in 1990 are one of the best illustrations of the way the working classes themselves have changed, or rather, of the ways in which their outlook and values are thought to have changed. For the Labour Party, the class struggle and the injustice of the exploitation of the working classes have not been central issues for some time now, and Clause Four apparently has at last been laid to rest. Old and traditional interpretations of the political struggle have been discarded; Nye Bevan's speeches of the 1930s now appear extraordinarily dated. The future, it appears, lies with an accept-ance of modern capitalism, with an economy which is basically market-orientated, but with a strong element of state welfarism, a kind of up-dated welfare state. A recent Labour Party slogan sums it up: 'Meet the Challenge, Make the Change'. The working classes are not what they were, so that new political aims and objectives are required to meet the needs of a new situation. *Tempora mutantur, nos et mutamur in illis.*

Lastly in this section, something must be said about the changing social role of women. Can this in any way be said to contribute to the 'decline' of the working classes? At first sight, the various emancipating events of the pre-seventies decades cannot be regarded as otherwise than beneficial, and hence contributing to the 'rise' rather than to the 'decline' – equal pay, greater sexual freedom and so on. These changes for the better certainly con-tinued to take effect into the 1980s. The figure of the working mother drawn by Richard Hoggart in his *Uses of Literacy* (1957) is hardly to be encountered among the trim matrons collecting their children from primary school today; and corsets and stays, quite common between the wars, have long been abandoned. According to Hoggart, in the mid-fifties:

> It is evident that a working-class mother will age early, that at thirty, after having two or three children, she will have lost most of her sexual attraction; and that between thirty-five and forty she rapidly becomes the shapeless figure the family know as 'Our Mam' ... By forty-five or fifty, ailments begin: you hear during the poorer periods that she is 'nobbut middling' just now. There may be rheumatism, or a regular backache from a twenty-year-old prolapse. The big fear, the one which recurs constantly in conversation, is of a growth ...

Modern screening for breast cancer and the use of cervical smears have at least lessened fears today of cancerous growths. But there is another side to the coin. The increasing numbers of mar-ried women at work, the proliferation of part-time and of temporary jobs for women, the increase in divorce and consequent increase in the numbers of single-parent families, the continued burden of housework and child-rearing for women in both part-time and full-time work – all these changes have taken effect not only upon the nature of the work force and upon the family, but necessarily upon the individual woman herself. In many cases, the married woman finds herself working just as hard as her predecessor before the war, and without the leisure hours previously enjoyed at home once the children had gone to school. The stability of the working-class family and indeed of the marriage which formerly had been entered into for life, appears to have diminished greatly. Probably it is impossible to assess these fundamental changes in the lifestyle of working-class women in terms of 'rise' or 'decline', but it is evident that they are significant changes in themselves which actively contribute to the new image of working-class people in the early 1990s.

Decline: Real or Apparent?

Obviously, all depends on how 'decline' is defined. In one sense, it is undeniable that there has been an important change in image, and not merely since the seventies. We have already referred to the 1918 worker in cap and muffler, his whippet by his side, dart- and domino-playing, football-match-attending, deferential to his superiors when not blind-drunk on a Saturday night – that image rapidly went out after the Second World War. It was by no means wholly a caricature, especially in the Midlands and the north. Priestley, for example, refers in 1933 to 'these Geordies, stocky toothless fellows in caps and mufflers'. But do the changes discussed in the previous section really constitute a 'decline'? If attention is concentrated on the political and economic power exercised by working-class agencies since 1979, then undoubtedly by this criterion there has been a decline, for after 1979 the Labour Party was out of office, and many former Labour supporters voted not so much for the Conservative Party as for the centre parties of the time, the Liberals and Social Democrats. The very existence of the Social Democratic Party demonstrates the loss of Labour Party authority in the early 1980s. In the economic sphere, the trade union movement certainly declined in influence and power, and it remains to be seen how far the adoption of new conciliatory policies will revive both membership and authority in industrial affairs. Meanwhile, one of the greatest of the trade unions, the National Union of Mineworkers, renowned for its fighting qualities and deep fraternal feeling, has become a shadow of its former self, its membership greatly reduced and in part lost to the Union of Democratic Mineworkers. In the broad field of social change, for those in work since 1974 the standard of living has been maintained and even improved; but for the millions who have experienced unemployment, and for the low-waged, the single-parent families, and all the others who have had to live in or on the margins of poverty, life has been hard, and it is difficult to avoid the word 'decline' here. In this connection, it must be observed that although the welfare state has survived, and spending on social services has actually increased in real terms under Conservative governments (not really surprising, given the increase in unemployment and in the numbers of the aged), the repeated complaints of doctors and nurses at financial cuts and the re-organisation in the National Health Service make it difficult to assess the quality of the service provided in 1990.

One last influence must be considered. Between 1979 and 1990 the working-class electorate was subjected to a constant bombardment of right-wing propaganda in favour of individual enterprise, the supremacy of market forces, the need for cost-effectiveness and the wickedness of the dependency culture. Members of the Conservative government who took a more radical view of the obligations of government were labelled 'wets' and soon found themselves on the back benches; once it had become apparent that they were not 'one of us' (a Thatcherite phrase), they did not last long. What effect all this had on the average working-class man or woman is hard to say, but perhaps it is not too fanciful to suppose that it became easier for those in work to forget the plight of the unemployed and others on social security. As long as the rent or mortgage repayments could be paid, the family fed, the car serviced and the holiday booked in Spain, all appeared to be well. Working-class solidarity seemed increasingly to be a thing of the past. It became easy to suppose that unemployment was due, at least in part, to a failure to get on one's bike; or to the workings of the economic system, which had to be left to work out its own salvation. Such beliefs tend to be divisive among the working classes, widening the gap between those in work and those who are not. The very phrase 'working class' acquired an old-fashioned ring, seemingly a kind of survival from the past, inappropriate in an age when everyone (apparently) had fitted carpets, a TV, re-frigerator, deep-freeze, microwave, car and so on. In fact, by no means everyone did possess all these requisites, but by 1990 the life of the unemployed received little publicity, even though the numbers out of work were as great as in 1939. More and more it seemed that life on the dole as a great social evil was best ignored and forgotten. No new Orwell appeared in the 1980s to appeal to the conscience of the nation. Meanwhile, sociologists writing about the employed and more affluent sections of the working classes drew attention to their self-centredness, at the same time referring to 'sectionalism', 'privatism', 'instrumentalism' and even to 'consumption cleavages' with reference to different social outlooks based on different consumption levels.

On at least four major counts then – the reduction in working-class political and industrial authority, the changed patterns of employment and economic status, the new instability of family life, and the change of image – it can be argued that distinct changes have occurred in the nature of the English working classes since the mid-seventies of this century. How far these changes deserve the simple epithet 'decline' is really for the reader to decide for himself or herself, though it is presumably clear by now that the author finds the word appropriate, or it would not be in the title of this book. Certainly the changes described can be distinguished sharply from all those influences which made it far easier to label the earlier period as one of the 'rise' of the English working classes. Of course, this is not to ignore the fact that even in the later period there was a material improvement for the many working-class men and women who remained employed, and they constituted the large majority. The essence of the argument presented here is that, in spite of this, there was a decline in the corporate strength and identity of the working classes as a whole, due partly to economic circumstances and partly to the onset of an aggressive Conservatism which rejected consensus policies, stressed market forces and individual advancement and had severe repercussions on the welfare services.

Lastly, it may be as well to state the obvious: proximity to the events described always makes it more difficult for the historian, especially so perhaps for the social historian, who is often concerned with longer sweeps of time and sequences of events than his political counterpart. So inevitably there are problems in particular in attempting to see the developments of the Thatcherite decade of the 1980s in due perspective, for they happened only yesterday. There comes to mind the splendid warning of the perils of writing contemporary history unearthed by Bernard Levin from Sir Walter Raleigh's *History of the World*, and quoted by Levin on the title page of his book, *The Pendulum Years*: 'Who-so-ever, in writing a modern history, shall follow truth too near the heels, it may haply strike out his teeth.' Raleigh continues with the further admonition regarding the nature of the writing of history: 'There is no Mistresse or Guide, that hath led her followers and servants into greater miseries.'

In another ten years it should be somewhat easier to pick out the truly significant characteristics of the period surveyed in this book. In the meantime, the reader has been supplied with enough basic information, it is hoped, on which to form his own conclusions. Only time will tell whether the changes of the 1980s have been presented here in anything like their true proportions, and whether there has been a real loss of working-class identity and class-consciousness with the growth of individualism, affluence among the employed and apathy among the unemployed – the triumph of the enterprise culture over the dependency culture, as Thatcherites would have it. Fortunately, the historian's task is limited to trying to make sense of the past, and does not include predicting the future.

Select Bibliography

This is necessarily a select bibliography – publications relevant to the principal themes of this book cover an enormous field. I have listed only those which I have found helpful on particular aspects. There are lengthy bibliographies in the general surveys by Arthur Marwick, John Stevenson, Edward Royle and François Bédarida noted below. For statistics for the more recent years, the government publications are invaluable. The place of publication is London unless otherwise stated.

Government Publications (HMSO)

The Ministry of Labour Gazette (to 1967)
The Employment and Productivity Gazette (1968–70)
The Employment Gazette (from 1971)
The Annual Reports of the Chief Inspector of Factories (to 1974) (these reports are continued from 1975 in *Health and Safety: Industries and Services*)
Social Trends (from 1970)
General Household Survey (from 1973)
Abstract of Regional Statistics (1965–74)
Regional Statistics (1975–80)
Regional Trends (from 1981)
Decennial Census Returns

General Social Histories

Bédarida, François, *A Social History of England 1851–1975* (1979)
Hopkins, Eric, *A Social History of the English Working Classes 1815–1945* (1979)
Marwick, Arthur, *British Society since 1945* (Harmondsworth, 2nd edn, 1990)
Royle, Edward, *Modern Britain: A Social History 1750–1985* (1987)
Ryder, Judith, and Silver, Harold, *Modern English Society* (3rd edn, 1985)
Stevenson, John, *British Society 1914–45* (Harmondsworth, 1984)

Select Bibliography

Other Books

Abel-Smith, Brian, and Townsend, Peter, *The Poor and the Poorest* (1965)

Addison, Paul, *The Road to 1945: British Politics and the Second World War* (1975)

Adeney, Martin, and Lloyd, John, *The Miners' Strike 1984–5: Loss without Limit* (1986)

Alcock, Pete, *Poverty and State Support* (1987)

Aldcroft, Derek, *The Inter-War Economy 1919–39* (1970)

Alford, B.W.E., *Depression and Recovery in the British Economy 1918–39* (1972)

Ashworth, William, *An Economic History of England 1870 to 1939* (1960)

Ball, Michael, Gray, Fred, and McDowell, Linda, *The Transformation of Britain: Contemporary Social and Economic Change* (1989)

Barnard, H.C., *A History of English Education from 1760* (1961)

Bartlett, C.J., *A History of Postwar Britain 1945–1974* (1977)

Bogdanor, Vernon, and Skidelsky, Robert, *The Age of Affluence* (1970)

Bruce, Maurice, *The Coming of the Welfare State* (2nd edn, 1965)

Burnett, John, *Plenty and Want* (2nd edn, 1968)

Burnett, John, *A Social History of Housing 1815–1985* (2nd edn, 1986)

Butterworth, Eric, and Weir, David (eds), *Social Problems of Modern Britain* (1972)

Calder, Angus, *The People's War* (1969)

Castle, Barbara, *The Castle Diaries 1964–70* (1984)

Causer, Gordon A. (ed.), *Inside British Society: Continuity, Challenge, and Change* (Brighton, 1987)

Coates, Ken, and Silburn, Richard, *Poverty: the Forgotten Englishman* (Harmondsworth, 1970)

Constantine, S., *Unemployment in Britain between the Wars* (1980)

Cook, Chris, and Ramsden, John (eds), *Trends in British Politics since 1945* (1978)

Crossman, Richard, *The Diaries of a Cabinet Minister* (2 vols, 1975–6)

Curtis, S.J., *History of Education in Great Britain* (7th edn, 1967)

Davies, Christie, *Permissive Britain: Social Change in the 60s and 70s* (1975)

Davies, Hunter, *The Beatles* (1968)

Eatwell, Roger, *The 1945–51 Labour Governments* (1979)

Fiegehen, G.C., Lansley, P.S., and Smith, A.D., *Poverty and Progress in Britain 1953–73* (Cambridge, 1977)

Floud, Roderick, and McCloskey, Donald, *The Economic History of Britain since 1700*, vol. 2: *1860 to the 1970s* (Cambridge, 1981)

Fraser, Derek, *The Evolution of the British Welfare State* (2nd edn, 1984)

Fraser, Ronald (ed.), *Work*, vols 1 and 2 (Harmondsworth, 1969)

Gilbert, B.R., *British Social Policy 1914–1939* (1970)

Goldthorpe, John H., Lockwood, David, Bechofer, Frank, and Platt,

281

Jennifer, *The Affluent Worker: Industrial Attitudes and Behaviour* (Cambridge, 1968)

Goldthorpe, John H., Lockwood, David, Bechofer, Frank, and Platt, Jennifer, *The Affluent Worker in the Class Structure* (Cambridge, 1969)

Gorer, Geoffrey, *Sex and Marriage in England Today* (1971)

Gosden, P.H.J.H., *Education in the Second World War* (1976)

Greer, Germaine, *The Female Eunuch* (1970)

Halsey, A.H. (ed.), *British Social Trends since 1900* (2nd edn, 1988)

Halsey, A.H., Heath, A.F., and Ridge, J.M., *Origins and Destinations: Family, Class, and Education in Modern Britain* (Oxford, 1980)

Healey, Denis, *The Time of My Life* (1989)

Hoggart, Richard, *The Uses of Literacy* (1957)

Hughes, Colin, and Wintour, Patrick, *Labour Rebuilt: The New Model Party* (1990)

Kavanagh, Dennis, and Seldon, Anthony (eds), *The Thatcher Effect* (Oxford, 1989)

Lawson, J., and Silver, H., *A Social History of Education in England* (1973)

Levin, Bernard, *The Pendulum Years* (1970)

Lowe, Roy (ed.), *The Changing Secondary School* (1989)

Mack, Joanna, and Lansley, Stewart, *Poor Britain* (1985)

Marshall, G., Newby, H., Rose, D., and Vogler, C., *Social Class in Modern Britain* (1988)

Marwick, Arthur, *Britain in the Century of Total War* (Harmondsworth, 1970)

McClintock, F.H., and Avison, Howard N., *Crime in England and Wales* (1968)

McKibbin, Ross, *The Evolution of the Labour Party 1910–1924* (1974)

McKie, David, and Cook, Chris, *The Decade of Disillusion: British Politics in the 60s* (1972)

Morgan, K.O., *Labour in Power 1945–51* (Oxford, 1989)

Morris, Terence, *Crime and Criminal Justice since 1945* (Oxford, 1989)

Mowat, C.L., *Britain between the Wars 1918–1940* (1955)

Noble, Trevor, *Modern Britain: Structure and Change* (1975)

Orwell, George, *The Road to Wigan Pier* (1937)

Pelling, Henry, *A History of British Trade Unionism* (4th edn, 1987)

Pelling, Henry, *The Labour Governments 1945–51* (1984)

Phelps Brown, Henry, *The Origins of Trade Union Power* (Oxford, 1983)

Pollard, Sydney, *The Development of the British Economy 1914–1980* (3rd edn, 1983)

Prest, A.R., and Coppock, D.J. (eds), *The United Kingdom Economy* (8th edn, 1980)

Roberts, Kenneth, *The Working Class* (1978)

Rowntree, B. Seebohm, *Poverty and Progress: A Second Social Survey of York* (1941)

Rowntree, B. Seebohm, and Lavers, G.R., *Poverty and the Welfare State* (1951)

Seabrook, Jeremy, *Landscapes of Poverty* (Oxford, 1985)

Sissons, M., and French, P. (eds), *The Age of Austerity 1945–1951* (1963)

Sked, Alan, and Cook, Chris, *Post-War Britain: A Political History* (2nd edn, 1984)

Sked, Alan, *Britain's Decline: Problems and Perspectives* (1987)

Skidelsky, Robert (ed.), *Thatcherism* (1988)

Smith, Keith, *The British Economic Crisis* (Harmondsworth, 3rd edn, 1989)

Stevenson, J., and Cook, C., *The Slump: Society and Politics during the Depression* (1977)

Taylor, A.J.P., *English History 1914–1945* (Oxford, 1965)

Thane, Pat, *The Foundations of the Welfare State* (1982)

Townsend, Peter, *Poverty in the United Kingdom* (Harmondsworth, 1979)

Townsend, Peter, *Why are the many poor?* (1984)

Wedderburn, Dorothy, and Crompton, Rosemary, *Workers' Attitudes and Technology* (Cambridge, 1972)

Young, M., and Willmott, P., *Family and Kinship in East London* (1957)

Index

Index

Index